Encouraging Words Regarding Paddy's Book and Ministry

"If any individuals or churches are considering whether to participate in any way in the ministry of Paddy Cook, I am more than happy to add my enthusiastic endorsement. I have known Paddy for more than 55 years, first when he attended the L'Abri in Switzerland (1971) under Dr. Francis Schaeffer and later in many different places and ministries.

He is a man of deep faith, strong integrity, and great faithfulness who combines an old-fashioned passion for the gospel with an unforced freshness and originality of style that is both appealing and effective. Paddy reaches people for Christ whom few others today could even approach. To work with or support Paddy Cook will be a fruitful investment in the growth of the Kingdom of God."

Os Guinness D.Phil. (Oxon.)
Executive Director
The Trinity Forum

"Paddy Cook's travels have stretched to nearly 70 countries. You'll love his story, lived in different corners of the world, including his formative time at L'Abri. I don't know of any missionary that depends as much on prayer and God's providence. Wherever he goes, he meets strangers, shares the gospel, and passes on a rich treasury of Reformed literature. *Paddy the Englishman* lets you travel the world with an earnest and winsome ambassador of Jesus Christ."

Roger Schultz, Ph.D.
Dean, College of Arts and Sciences
Liberty University

"In this delightful read, *Paddy the Englishman: Memoir of a Presbyterian Evangelist,* you'll follow along in the footsteps of his adventures, as this REF evangelist and friend to countless pastors and students, treks across the Old Continent. Under his ministry banner, "Every Country in Europe," he hand-delivered thousands of gospel books to them, to build libraries of the Reformed faith, books of teaching, history, church heritage, and yes, books of doctrine too. From the frozen landscapes of the Nordic realms to the warm, subtropical climates of the Canary Islands, from the steppes of Russia to the Crusader castles of Malta, this book never stops impressing upon its reader that God *uses the ordinary to accomplish the extraordinary.*

This book is a must-read for the evangelist, and anyone in full-time ministry. Paddy's complete, surrendering dependence upon the Holy Spirit, as the central driver in his life, should cause each of us to ponder: what could God use me to do, if I truly gave my life to Him?"

Dr. Rick Light
CEO
Reformed Evangelistic Fellowship

"It is with great delight that I have the honor of endorsing this wonderful, insightful, and illuminating work by my dear brother, the Reverend Patrick "Paddy" Cook, whom I have known since 1986—thirty-nine years of faithful friendship and ministry. I was privileged to review his very first draft!

Over these decades, I have watched Paddy traverse the world, bringing the gospel into sixty-eight countries. I have seen him interact with people of remarkable diversity, always with the conviction that the Gospel should be freely offered to all. His ministry has been one of energy and mobility, extending the invitation of Noah's Ark to every nation, tribe, and people.

I have traveled with him to various countries and witnessed him handle the most difficult situations with poise, resilience, and grace. Paddy is truly a man of God. I have urged him to produce a second book—a manual for personal evangelism—and to consider mentoring through seminaries, so that his wealth of experience from eighty-one years of life and ministry can be passed on to future generations.

May God bless this work to posterity.
In Jesus's name, ..."

Rev. Dr. George J. Gatgounis, Esq.

"*Paddy the Englishman* is an extraordinary journey through God-given faith, holy direction, adventure, and old-fashioned English creativity and perseverance. Throw in stories that amuse, and this book is easy to recommend. It offers an amazing account of how God has used Paddy in evangelistic missions in 68 countries (and counting). His gripping stories bring alive encounters with cultures and striking providences that shape his calling. *Christ in Paddy* is the real story as we are treated and inspired by Paddy's God-given confidence in His sovereignty. No wonder Paddy has such a passion to witness and proclaim the gospel. He knows he cannot fail with Christ in him and the Bible in hand. And that is data that helps inspire us. The life of one Christian disciple ripples across the nations. Beware, Paddy's holy zeal is contagious. I highly recommend this book to anyone in need of encouragement, a spiritual reboot, or simply a good read to relax and reflect."

Rev. Dr. William Allen Church
President
National Clergy Council
Washington, DC

"Global trekking by an intrepid adventurer; a pastorate on an exotic Caribbean isle; bold declaration of the gospel by a fearless evangelist; a visionary with a goal of influencing all of the nations of Europe through distribution of books to national ministers; meetings with strangers and political leaders that only Providence could orchestrate; even a college prank that made it into the newspaper. These stories and many more are found in *Paddy the Englishman*. What more could you want from an autobiography?"

Frank J. Smith, Ph.D., D.D.
Chancellor
Tyndale International Theological Seminary
Pastor
Atlanta Reformed Presbyterian Church (RPCNA)

PADDY the ENGLISHMAN

Memoir of a Presbyterian Evangelist

PATRICK A. COOK

STONE TOWER PRESS

Stone Tower Press
7 Ellen Rd.
Middletown, RI 02842
stonetowerpress.com

ISBN: 979-8-9992313-6-9

Formatting and cover design by Amy Cole and Emily Olson, JPL Design Solutions

Drawings by Matthew Cook

Printed in the United States of America

TABLE OF CONTENTS

PART TWO: PROCLAMATION

"If anyone is going to boast, let him boast
in what the Lord has done and not about himself."

2 Corinthians. 10:17

INTRODUCTION

I once asked an Iraqi who was unloading his bags at the airport in Irbil, Iraq. "Why are you here on this earth?" He replied, "I am here to eat!"

He was a successful chemical engineer from Portland, Oregon and had come back to Iraq after some 22 years to visit and enjoy his family. I re-phrased my question. "Do you have any idea why you are on this earth?" Eventually, I was able to explain to him, that the reason why any of us are put on this earth is to worship the God who created us and who sustains the universe.

After a lengthy time passing through Iraqi customs, I was the last person on the bus that was to take us through the layers of armed security. The only empty space was right next to him. He looked at me and asked, "Where are you going to sit?" I replied, "Right next to you."

"And then what are you going to do?" I think that he was afraid that I was going to preach to him. So, I said, "I might hug you."

We parted good friends, and he gave me permission to take a head and shoulders photo of him. "What are you going to do with my picture?" I had promised him that I was not going to steal his soul. He replied, something to the effect, "Good luck if you try, you won't get much for it."

I told him that I was planning to pray for him, and his picture would help me remember to do that.

So many folks I have talked with simply choose not to believe that there is an afterlife. They do not have any reason to believe that this life is preparation for the next life. This life could be compared to a bucket of water sitting beside the shore of the Atlantic Ocean. This life is so short compared to eternity. Seventy years plus a few extra years compared to an eternal life that never ends.

I want at least to tell those I know that there is another life after this one and that there is a way for them to know about it and prepare for it. I say that, as there are only two addresses to go to when we die. Just like on your street, different things happen at different addresses.

It has been my privilege for more than 60 years to proclaim the gospel (the "good news") of Jesus Christ around the globe to thousands of people in 68 countries. I suspect that many of us remember looking at maps in the back of a Bible or in Sunday School that charted the missionary journeys of St. Paul. Though in no way comparable in significance, what follows in the coming pages is my attempt to highlight through words, rather than maps, some of my journeys bearing witness to the love of God, the virgin birth and sacrificial death of Jesus Christ as the eternal Son of God on the cross for our sins, and His bodily resurrection and return to heaven. Because He lives, we too may do so—eternally. This is a memoir of one pilgrim's progress to the Celestial City.

PART ONE

PREPARATION

Beginnings: 1944–1988

1

CHILDHOOD

Earliest Years

I was unique, just like everybody else. "I was born, and I remember, every day of my life, except the first one."

I remember hearing someone say that, and it made me smile. However, my earliest memory, although I cannot verify it, was falling off a wooden draining board, aged four in the scullery on to a concrete floor, in the vicarage at Holy Trinity Church, Aldershot, in Hampshire, England. I was born in Cambridge, England in 1944 but my family soon moved to a new parish ministry for my minister father.

A few years after World War II, I remember being in the breakfast room in the vicarage of Holy Trinity Aldershot. Aldershot was the home of the British army. My Dad, the Rev. Alan J.N. Cook M.A. was the vicar at Holy Trinity Church, Aldershot, in Hampshire. We must have had a lot of toast and marmalade, as I recall having that for breakfast. I do not remember ever doing anything else in the breakfast room except having breakfast. I remember also that we had enough lawn in the back garden for my parents to have evenings when people came to play croquet.

My worldly possessions included clothes and the school uniform of my elementary school, West End Elementary School. I also had a cricket bat and ball, a simple repainted light blue bicycle with only one gear, and of course a football and big leather soccer boots that somehow, I managed to persuade my mother, that I had to wear to church on Christmas morning the first day they became mine. We lived across the road then from the Evangelical Anglican Church, Bishop Hannington Memorial Church, Hove, Sussex in England. So, there was minimal pain for me, breaking my new boots in, on the way to church!

During my early school years, instead of reading books like I ought to have done, I spent endless hours throwing my tennis ball up onto the sloping tiled roof of our house, 82 Holmes Avenue, Hove, Sussex. When it rolled down, I would practice kicking it first time onto the garage door 90 degrees in front of me. I was preoccupied with sports rather than studies.

When I was about 16 years old people in the church assumed that I would apply to go to university. Church folks started to ask me what I was going to do when I grew up and what university was I applying to for my studies. I am embarrassed to recall that in all honesty I knew myself and all that I was sure that I could do was to ride a bike and deliver meat. Of course, I never told anybody, but that is what I thought. When I consider then and look at the blessings that God has showered upon me over the years and how He has brought me to where I am now. I have so much to be amazed about and for which to thank God. I can say with David (that is King David) in 2 Samuel 7:18b. "O Lord, God why have you showered your blessing on such an insignificant person as I am?"

One of the reasons that I never rebelled against Christianity, growing up, was that the people I met because of Dad being a faithful evangelical Anglican minister were far more interesting than folks out in the world. I recall sitting down to one of mother's fine Sunday lunches with the Bishop of the Arctic sitting at the head of our table. He had preached at the morning worship service.

Dad had been delayed after the worship service and had told us to start lunch without him. For some reason, known only to God Himself, I let out one of the loudest and most impolite belches that ever passed my lips. It was an almighty belch. I do not recall even being embarrassed because at that moment the bishop, took charge of the moment. "Let us pray together for this fine lunch God has provided." I dread to think what would have happened if father had not been delayed for lunch.

I remember one of Dad's friends from Cambridge going to Russia in the 1950s with a British Government Scientific group (Peter Trier) and one of the first things that they did was to make a schedule for one in the group, to read Scripture 24/7, into the microphone for whoever would be trying to monitor everything that was being said! I have wondered about that faithful and creative witness to the unknown and probably "unreached people group" listening in, as they "meditated" on what they were hearing and then trying to make sense of it all.

Godly Parents

I was blessed with godly faithful and hardworking parents. Dad was a faithful evangelical Anglican pastor for some 40 years and a creative evangelist. I am told during the changing of the reels at the local movie cinema, Dad was given permission to preach the gospel while the reels were being changed.

I remember how he argued with the local school education authorities in Hove because they wanted to close a church school. The school authorities claimed that it was because of the outside toilets. Dad turned the tables on them and discovered that it was not their only revealed reason for closing the church school. He argued that it was not a valid reason for closing the church school.

He showed that the school attendance records demonstrated that the church school with its clean outside toilets must have produced hardier and healthier children and he used the school attendance records of the school against the public-school attendance statistics to prove it.

Another story was one in which Dad's bishop wanted to close a certain evangelical church because it was not being used enough. Dad took it upon himself to take a communion service for the requisite number of Sundays so that he could argue his case at a synod meeting. He argued passionately and won the argument on the basis that there was a regular worshipping community who were being served the sacraments and should not be closed based on inactivity.

My mother, Elizabeth (Betty) Ferguson Cook, died early. She died in 1971 at age 50 of a cerebral hemorrhage. I was in Australia at the time, and it was a long way from home and a grieving family. I remember calling home and saying "Mum was always out in front, encouraging and inspiring us, even in getting to heaven. Trust Mum—to get there first!"

When the Second World War broke out, Mum trained as a nurse at Addenbrookes Hospital, in Cambridge, under the famous Matron Alexander. It was there in Cambridge that she had met Dad. She was an assistant leader of the King's Own Bible class at Holy Trinity Church, Cambridge and Dad was a guest speaker.

After their marriage, Mum's leadership of the Women's Fellowship, Young Wives, and the Younger Wives Group filled her time, after organizing the vicarage and the family life. But her greatest pleasure was "to beautify the house of God" at Festival times. She was a natural at floral decorations, and for her it was an act of worship. Her faith was simple, practical, and wholehearted—very much like the good news of salvation through Jesus Christ. Spared a long and painful illness, her last conscious thoughts were of some old spirituals she enjoyed, and especially, the words "Open up them Pearly Gates for me, you hear the trumpet call, and your maker bids you come, then sing 'Open up them Pearly Gates for me.'"

Sundays—"Tea and Church."

Sundays, as I recall, were very structured and ordered. We had breakfast then off to morning church. Usually, we either had folks for lunch or for afternoon tea. When mum invited folks to tea they were always invited to "tea and church."

When we were growing up the only shops that were open were the newsagents (newspaper shops) and the pub at lunchtime. Of course, it being England, it was often raining on Sunday, so without an invitation to someone's home Sunday could be a lonely day. After lunch we had "King's Own" a young people's worship service and Bible class. After tea, we always went to evening worship service, and then after it, the young people would have an after-church gathering. We enjoyed that each week and looked forward to it. We always had great musical talent in the form of lively and enthusiastic piano players to lead the singing.

Because of loving parents who both had a profound knowledge of and commitment to the Word of God and proclaiming it good news whenever and wherever possible, I was blessed during my formative years with a foundation for my later years and ministry even though I had no inkling of it at the time!

Holiday Trips to Northern Ireland

Britons are known for their love of "holidays," by which Americans mean "vacations." For the Cook family, holiday trips were often to Northern Ireland to visit mother's family in Belfast and near Cookstown at "Doons" in County Tyrone. "Doons" was the name of mother's 10-acre family farm. It was there and elsewhere in Northern Ireland that we spent time with Mum's many siblings, my cousins, and my Grandmother MacFarlane.

One of my aunts, Auntie Rita, had a small country store-like shop. Outside the front of the shop, by the side of the country road, there was a courtyard where people used to congregate in the evening. You couldn't see any houses in any direction as you looked out of Auntie Rita's house. However, you could enjoy the unique Ulster countryside.

Others of Mum's family, Uncle John & Auntie Vi had a beautiful homestead in Belfast on a hill overlooking Stormont and the parliament buildings. I probably shouldn't say but Auntie Vi was my favorite Auntie. The fact that we had 5 hearty meals a day was just like being at Auntie Rita's shop in Doons. Auntie Rita never married but Andy, a single farm hand working for Uncle Davey, was living in the family farmhouse up the lane. Andy had no teeth, and it was hard to understand him as a child. He kept a notebook in his back pocket of the dates when everybody he knew died. It was said Andy never traveled more than 20 miles from the family farm on his bike.

As small children we would sit on the steps and watch the cars go by. Often, we took a break from bagging up the sugar or cutting up the tobacco. That was a huge responsibility for children our age, is what I thought. My Uncle Gordon and Auntie Jean had a corner shop in Moneymore (County Londonderry). Uncle Gordon was the oldest of Mum's 11 siblings. He and Auntie Jean had a general store on the right hand, side of Moneymore, going out of town on the way to "Doons." Uncle Gordon McFarlane also had a trucking business as well as gasoline pumps outside the general store on the corner. Auntie Jean would allow my brother and me or even just one of us to "mind the store." If we needed to ask her a question, we would just use the phone, and she would come up from the house across the cobbled courtyard and through the large opening on the property that the trucks emerged through. Emerging from that she would turn right passed the petrol pumps on the sidewalk and into her corner shop.

One day, it was raining, and a man came into the store smoking his pipe upside-down. The fact it was raining did not register with me. I was afraid of this man smoking his pipe upside down. I hurriedly called Auntie Jean. Auntie Jean come up to rescue me from this man with such odd behavior. When Auntie arrived, she burst out laughing and said the man was a good friend and a regular customer and that there was nothing for me to be afraid of. The reason he smoked his pipe upside-down was because he did not want the rain to put his pipe out!

Usually, we arrived by boat in Belfast Harbor. For some holidays in N. Ireland, Uncle Eddie who lived in Belfast would come and meet us as we came off the boat. I was often trying to recover from my seasickness on the voyage across the Irish Sea. (The propensity to seasickness is something that has continued to plague me throughout my ministry travels. Fortunately, I have suffered only that—what the ancients called *mal de mer*—and not a shipwreck like St. Paul off the coast of Malta as recorded in Acts 28.) Uncle Eddie McFarlane had a fine furniture shop with used but nicely preserved household furniture. Directly opposite his shop was his home, a modest two-story terraced house on Castlereagh Road.

Each day started with the ritual of Uncle Eddie unpacking his furniture from the shop and displaying fine pieces of furniture on the sidewalk. Each day started this way and each evening the sidewalk was cleared, and the furniture neatly stacked back inside the shop. The story goes that it was cheaper to pay the street fines than to rent a larger shop floor space!

When all the family were together, one of us would suddenly say, "Whose house are we all going to eat at tonight?" There were 35 of us when we were altogether. Once, when we told my Uncle Rowley that we had never eaten in his house he said, "If you come to my house tonight all I can offer you is 'Horseshoe broth!'" Being interpreted, that was a horseshoe submerged in boiling water and any flavor that could be pried off the horseshoe was what gave the water the flavor, so in his eyes that qualified as soup.

One morning at 4.00 a.m., Dad and I and my brother Peter were sitting outside Auntie Rita's shop waiting for Uncle Rowley to come from Belfast to take us grouse shooting on the first day of the season. I saw a big black car approaching in the distance and with the binoculars I thought it was uncle's car. So, my dad got a deck chair and sat in the middle of the road pointing his shotgun at the approaching car. I had made a horrible mistake. It was a police car speeding along to check on early Grouse shooters to see if they all had their hunting licenses on the first day of the season. They did not stop but they did call Auntie Rita to ask who that man was sitting in the middle of the road pointing his shotgun at us as they sped by!

Why do I recount these family holidays? I do so because God's providence never ceases to work in our lives. Childhood holidays to Northern Ireland were fun and good times of family reunion. However, unknown at the time, they were more than a jaunt across the Irish Sea. They were the first of many journeys that would take me far from home and the certainties and safety of close family. Even then, God was preparing me for proclaiming the gospel and being a "witness unto the uttermost part of the earth."

2

EARLY TEENAGE YEARS

School Days

I do not remember much of any significance about my schooldays except that if you had asked me then what folks often ask children now, I probably would have answered the question as they often do. "What is your favorite class at school?" "Recess."

I only remember two school masters who I respected. One was my maths teacher, Mr. Jack Mutton. Looking back, he could have been a film personality. He was a manly, tanned, rugged, outdoor-weathered face type of person. He always took pride in his appearance and wore three-piece Harris tweed suits, which to teach students such as myself I often thought was more than we expected or deserved. There was one other teacher, Mr. Spain who always took an interest in me. He took me for soccer and was always spinning a ball on his finger when he had the opportunity. What is important about these two teachers is that they cared about students as individuals and they were role models for us.

This was an early lesson for me to experience and learn and one that has served me well throughout my decades of ministry—remember the power of one-to-one relationships and respect for individuals regardless of their age or station in life. Every person is uniquely and individually created in the image of God and therefore has infinite value and worth.

Around the age of 11 years old I was picked to play for the Brighton & Hove Boys soccer team. I suspect that Mr. Spain arranged for me to try out. I had delusions of playing professional soccer as I was not very good at anything else I had tried. Although I recall that I reached the heady position of being Head Choirboy in the choir at Bishop Hannington Memorial Church, Hove, Sussex. Dad was the Vicar. I wore a wide ribbon with a medal attached to it around my neck that was a clear contrast over the white surplice, I wore and always sat on the end of the front row in the choir stalls. I still love to sing. If I ever run out of things to do, I think I would like to travel and sing in a barbershop quartet. At my age now, listeners might question whether or not I am still able to "make a joyful noise unto the Lord." I don't know, but it would be fun!

I should have paid more attention in my science classes as it took me far too long to figure out why the teacher was always able to catch me talking in class. Our classrooms were divided by wooden partitions with glass panels. All my teacher had to do was watch the reflection of me in the glass panels and spin round and catch me every time! I finally learnt that scientific fact outside of my science class, the hard way. It is not hard to figure out that I was not a good student. When I discovered later in life that there are seven tools/styles for learning I wish that my teachers had offered me the choice to choose one of the other six!

One time I heard a visiting evangelist who came to Bishop Hannington Memorial Church, Hove say that "if you are having trouble at school, you can ask God for help, and for wisdom." I was at least smart enough to know that I was having trouble at school. I must have prayed to God asking for wisdom. After that, things went better at school. Not that much, but better enough to be encouraged to pray occasionally and be strengthened in learning to trust God.

Saturday Sports and Sunday Services

When I was a boy, the not-so-well-known Brighton & Hove Albion Football Club often helped us hope for better things. I was about 11 years old when my older brother Peter and I were first able to leave behind the box that we had to carry so that we could stand on it with the grown-up supporters in the stand to see the game. We often had enough money to buy a bag of peanuts at half-time.

Most Saturdays I had a school soccer game in the morning, Dad would drive me to wherever the game was, along with any of my friends who showed up needing a ride. In the afternoon, I often had a game for the cub or scout team. I ran around all morning, so I volunteered to play as the goalkeeper in the afternoon.

I also loved cricket a game many Americans claim to be incomprehensible! I liked to play wicket keeper as I could wear a big pair of wicket keeper's gloves to protect myself from the fast-hard ball. To score a "4," the batsman had to hit the ball over the boundary. If you scored a boundary in this way, you did not have to run 4 times between the wickets. To score a "6," the batsman had to hit the ball from his bat over the boundary line without bouncing. On one occasion a "6" was scored and it bounced once in front of me and hit me in the mouth. It did not damage my teeth, but it did split my lip so that when I was rushed home to see my mother my white shirt was all red and even as a nurse, Mother was shocked to see me like that on our front doorstep!

Sunday always was a busy day for Dad for many years of his life. He would have a Holy Communion service before breakfast, then a service at the police convalescent home then back for morning worship service. Often, we would have folks for Sunday lunch.

Sundays began with breakfast and then morning church. At Bishop Hannington, we literally lived across the road. You could not afford to be late because if you were late, there was no time to make it up.

Sunday lunch was always the best meal of the week with juicy roast potatoes, roast meat, either beef or lamb along with Yorkshire pudding, gravy and vegetables. Often instead of just water to drink we had lemonade in some form or another. We also usually had desert on Sunday. Most of the family developed the habit of going to the bathroom after dinner so as not to be the first one at the sink to do Sunday dishes!

After lunch there was Sunday afternoon Bible Class which was called King's Own. I always enjoyed that as there was always great singing and an enthusiastic pianist to carry us all along. King's Own had a cricket team which played in the local leagues and a soccer team also.

Camps and Holidays on the Norfolk Broads

The Norfolk Broads is a special part of England for many of us. During the summer, Christian camps were often held under canvas tents to provide a context of fun and adventure along with the opportunity to get away from "the world" for biblical discipleship. At Eastertime, we slept on board larger yachts, enjoying lively winds or the sun, all producing lifelong memories.

There are 250 miles of navigable waterways on the Norfolk Broads. There were rivers of varying widths which opened into little lakes or broads. Each year Dad would unite two or three Anglican youth groups together. We always looked forward to the church summer camp which had around 120 teenagers under canvas in Bell tents, provided by the British Army.

Part of the fun of summer camp was to be chosen to be part of the advance party. That meant that after the furniture moving van was loaded with all the camp equipment all the mattresses that were stored at our church hall were then stacked in the back of the moving van. It was on top of all of them that we sat and rode in the back of the van, as the advance party, all the way to camp.

We rode in the back of the van from Brighton to Cambridge via London waving to the motorists that would often wave back. The tents were collected in Cambridge so that was a time to stretch and eat a meal out, which was such a treat in those days.

I have vivid memories of walks around Frensham Pond. Part of the attraction was to watch the young sailors from a private school learning their skills to race around the pond without capsizing their small sail boats. I recall at least one time that Dad & Mum and Peter and I had a special treat. Dad took us to the Frensham Pond Hotel. It was a grand old English hotel. Dad ordered a pot of tea for four and 4 rounds of hot buttered toast. We sat in a beautifully furnished hotel lounge. That was a real treat in those days!

Usually, we would arrive at our familiar field in time to go to bed ready to set up camp the next day. Camp would be a sailing camp on the Norfolk Broads. We always enjoyed that. Everybody learned to sail during the week. Many new friendships were established. Camp was for 10 days and in the central week we often had a dozen "half-decker" open sailing yachts.

Each day a girl's tent and a boy's tent would stay behind to peel potatoes for the evening meal and make the picnic lunch that was delivered by throwing packages from the camp's only motor launch into the sail of each boat to be caught by one of the campers in the boat. It always dropped from the sail into eager hands to feed the campers in the boat. Regattas were organized, and places of interest were sailed to during the day.

One vivid memory I had was the year a troop of sea scouts camping in an adjoining field were flooded out and were forced to break camp and go home. We on the other hand, followed Dad's plan and lined up all the campers in a row armed with metal food trays from our army chef's kitchen and on command we "walked the water" across the field a few times and into the natural dikes beside the field. Eventually the surface water was removed so we continued with the camp. The local baker suspended his baking for the morning and dried our bedding.

The days were always full. After mooring the yachts for the night, games were organized, field hockey or soccer or touch rugby before dinner.

It was during a day of sailing with a family friend that I was asked directly about salvation. I was about 13 years old when I spent the day with the Rev. Tony Danes. He was an Anglican missionary home from Africa. He had rented a small sailing dingy while he was at camp with us on the Norfolk Broads. He decided to sail it back to the boat yard from our camp site instead of towing it behind his car. The day was spent sailing the dingy to the boat yard in the small village of Potter Heigham.

We set off from the friendly farmer's field in which we always camped. Along one side of the field was a small dike where the rented yachts were moored. From that dike, we could enter the river and head down to Horsey Mere. I spent the day in this small dingy being astounded that we were even moving since there did not appear to be any wind at all to propel us. Tony was watching the reeds bend and watching the birds fly and whatever else he considered as we continued to make our way down the rivers and into the Broads (open areas—like little lakes) until we found the entrance to the next river we needed to sail down. Finally, around 5 p.m. we arrived at the boat yard. During the day Tony asked me, "Paddy, how long have you been a Christian?"

That was a direct and gentle question bearing in mind that I had grown up in a visibly Christian home. I blushed, even though I thought I was one. I did not know what to say!

An annual tradition at the end of the camp was for the whole camp to spend a day gathering sheaves in a field of wheat for the local farmer whose field we were camping in. Each stack would have 8 sheaves. I think of that at times when I hear the old gospel song "Bringing in the Sheaves."

After the war, it was a treat for our family to eat out. Postwar rationing remained in effect in the UK until 1954. Eating out then and eating out now is in stark contrast. Dad loved to walk in the forest. I remembered that we used to walk with him through parts of Ashdown Forest, collecting pinecones. He spoke to us of his love for the New Forrest. A few times we would go as a family to Frensham Pond in Churt, Hampshire. Frensham Great Pond and the surrounding area with smaller ponds is a wildlife sanctuary that was originally created in the 13th century to supply fish to the Bishop of Winchester while he was visiting Farnham Castle.

We would go into the grand old Frensham Pond Hotel after our walk to get warm and have a treat. I am thankful to be able to say that at the time we all knew it was a treat and we enjoyed it.

Later in Life we would have dinner treats at The Beach Hotel in Worthing, Sussex, 10 miles west of Brighton on the edge of the seashore of the English Channel. That meal was a grand 5-course meal beautifully served as a silver service with linen table clothes and serviettes/napkins. Food and fun! What better memories might a young boy desire?

3

LATER TEENAGE YEARS AND EXPANDING HORIZONS

First Trip to Europe: (1960)

In 1960, I was 16 and my older brother Peter, and I decided to go camping in Europe and drive a car that I bought for 10 English pounds. I knew, with the wisdom of 16-year-old that it must be a good car as it belonged to the neighbor of my best friend David Beate, who rode his bicycle to school with me.

We loaded the car with everything that we could think of including toilet paper as we, in our youthful naïveté, did not know if the French had any! Once in Europe, we spent a day-and-a-half driving up the French Alps in reverse as the car had a gravity feed system that expected the petrol to find its own way to the engine. Finally, we even made it into Italy so we could say that we had been to two countries! We left England with three gears and arrived home with only two. A couple of weeks later the engine died, so we took the car and rolled it over the tip or landfill as we would call it now.

On that first European journey, Peter, 18, and I, 16, drove to Nice, France to visit a friend named Jacques, one of the many international students who lived in our home while they studied English in Brighton for 3 months.

In the picturesque south of France, all we could afford to do was buy French bread and cheese to live on and take pictures of beautiful boats in the harbor when we arrived in Monaco. Later we discovered that a murder was committed near our tent campsite!

It is interesting to me looking back on my teenage years, that even then I had a desire to go to America. That desire would be fulfilled, but not for a few years.

Second Trip to Europe: (1961)

The following summer I arranged with Eberhard, a German student who stayed in our home, to take my 1953 MG TD to Europe for the summer. (A 1953 MG TD in mint condition today can sell for around $50,000. I should have kept it!)

I was to provide the car, and Eberhard was to provide the contacts and places to stay. We were to visit his co-ed classmates and their families at their summer houses where they were vacationing. They were dotted around France and even into Spain.

When I first saw the 1953 MG TD sports car for sale in Brighton, I did not have 200 English pounds to buy it. At my bank, Barclays Bank, in Western Road, Hove, I asked the teller, "What do I have to do to get a car loan?" I told him I needed a loan for 200 pounds. When I told him that it was for the MG for sale a few blocks from the bank he confessed that he had considered buying it himself but that he was committed to getting engaged instead of buying the car. I recall that I thought that he had made a wise choice and was thankful I was not competing for the same car!

Getting a car loan was so different than it would be today! This was the process that enabled me to get my first car loan and buy the car that was not in the range of 10 or 15 English pounds. The teller called out to the Bank Manager, who I had never met but had seen many times. "Is it O.K. for us to give Paddy a 200-pound bank loan?" The Bank Manager put his head around his door and looked me in the eye and asked, "Are you planning on paying it back?" "Yes, sir!" I replied. That was it!

Back to the trip with Eberhard. It was a great trip! We arranged to meet up at café Renault on the Champs-Élysées, in Paris at an arranged time on an arranged day. That went off as planned and we took off that night on our adventure. But before meeting Eb in Paris, I had to find a place to park the car and get some sleep. I arrived in Paris extremely late the night before our rendezvous and I could not find anywhere to camp or even park. I still wonder where I got the nerve to do what I did next. I think I was 17. Around 1:00 am, I finally pulled up on a traffic roundabout in a suburb of Paris. I was very tired, and I decided to pitch my little tent on the traffic island.

In the morning after a decent nights' sleep, I must have grown comfortable in my situation as people were already going about their business dashing around the traffic island and waiting to cross the roads within sight. Some folks even waved and of course I waved back. Since I was hungry, I got out my little camping stove and cooked my breakfast.

I made some tea and cooked a couple of fried eggs and whatever else I decided to have probably a couple of sausages or bacon and some of the delicious French bread with some cheese. It seemed so natural at the time. I think I even wondered if that is what French people did when they found themselves in the situation that I found myself in. I have never been able to verify that.

A Detour and Youthful Lesson in Love

I packed up camp the next morning and like a good boy scout tried to leave my campsite cleaner than when I arrived. That was not difficult to accomplish, but I do not recall that part of it. However, on the way to Paris to meet up with Eberhard, I decided first to go and visit Miki, a beautiful young lady I had met in London and with whom I was somewhat smitten, who was in Belgium, near Brussels. When I got close to her given address, I went into a tavern to ask if anyone could help me locate the address in my hand. A man spoke up and said that he knew the house and would be pleased to lead me to it. We agreed that we would go to his house first so that he could change his clothes. Sounded reasonable, although I was not sure at the time, why that was necessary.

When we arrived at the house, I understood why he thought he ought to change clothes. Miki's house was an enormous château-like property replete with huge closed wrought iron gates. The proverbial oval gravel drive and a palatial looking house set in as grand a situation as could be. Out of politeness, I left my MG outside and made my way up the gravel drive crunching my way up to the front door.

Whoever opened the door called out to Miki and she appeared, in the distance, at the top of the stairs. I had surprised her, and she appeared pleased to see me. A room was prepared for me, and I enjoyed staying overnight. She showed me around the house, but I do not remember what I saw. After breakfast the next morning, she took me into the center of Brussels to see the sights. I had suggested we have a picnic, but then I remembered that she surprised me by saying that she had just got engaged the day before and did not think that was a good idea. I agreed and yet her fiancé still managed to pass us in the MG on the highway with a puzzled look on his face.

Well, the fact that she had just become engaged the day before closed any thoughts of developing a future relationship! She was beautiful to look at for sure on the outside, but when she indicated that she had no intention of picking something up that had floated out onto the front lawn, with "Oh, that's why we have servants to do that sort of thing." I knew then that we would never be on the same page!

It also helped soften the news that she was now engaged and confirmed to me that I was way out of my league. My assessment of her was that she was pretty, and lazy. With my translation skills, that translated, as "pretty lazy." We parted friends and I said goodbye to her and the group of folks that were in the house at the time and set off for Paris to meet Eb. True love entails more that attraction and beauty!

Travels with Eb

Eb seemed quite popular with his classmates, and they were pleased to see him when we arrived to visit. One family we visited was vacationing on the iconic island of Mont-Saint-Michel, off the north coast of France. You could only get to it at certain times each day as the road to it from the mainland floods when the tide comes in cutting off access twice a day.

In the 8th century, a monk named Aubert (later the sainted bishop of Avranches) had a vision in which the Archangel Michael told him to build a monastery on a rock cut off by tides twice a day. Although Aubert hesitated, after a third vision and visitation by the Archangel Michael, he obeyed and started building. Over many centuries, his vision became a reality, and Mont-Saint-Michel is now the second-most-visited site in France, after the Eiffel Tower.

Our impromptu tour visiting Eb's classmates on their French summer wanderings even took us as far as Spain. We arrived in Spain at the ocean front after I had enjoyed a spectacular drive down the French and Spanish mountain roads which was about as much fun as I have ever had in my MG! We pulled into a tropical island-type Spanish sea-side beach resort. It was just beautiful.

Unfortunately, the couple that we had come to see were nowhere to be found. Eventually, we were told that they had been there, and they had left a note for Eb. They had gone to meet some friends but told us to eat all their meals which were paid for at the hotel. Welcomed hospitality!

Hardly believing our good fortune, we slept in the woods and went in for breakfast to a luxury hotel with linen tablecloths and fine cutlery before heading off to the beach to sunbathe. We spent the day at the beach interrupted only by a walk to the hotel for a fine lunch, and later for dinner.

That week, as the Brits would say, we lived the life of Riley. Enjoying the sun and the ocean and meeting folks along the way. Not to mention the double life we were living of having to sleep in the woods as we had no money and then eating three fine meals a day.

Towards the end of our time there Eb and I discovered that we liked the same girl, a German girl from Manheim. I do not remember the details but on his last day Eb stormed off. I decided to stay. I soon felt badly as we had agreed to split all the expenses on our adventure.

So early the next morning, I set off thinking I could find him along the way. It was not long before I saw Eb hitch-hiking on the side of the road. We did the right thing by reuniting again and he started to set me up telling me that everything had worked out well for him since he had left. He even told me that he managed breakfast in bed. "How in the world did that happen?" I asked. His answer betrayed him and his time since he had left. It had not gone very well at all for him."Oh, I slept under a bunch of grapes!" That said it all. We made up and continued our way. When it came time to part company, for me to set off for England and for Eb to make his way home to Germany, we calculated that in splitting the money we had left, there was not enough for his train ticket and my gas for the two hundred miles I had to drive home.

I do not recall specifically praying to God to ask Him what we should do. The idea came to us for me to buy Eb's train ticket and even though I would be a little short on gas money, I made it to the cross-channel ferry that would take me back to England by driving following an awkward pattern. My MG was a stick shift, so I gradually accelerated up to 50 M.P.H. and coasted or free wheeled back down to 30 m.p.h. That way I used less petrol/gas and made it back in time to catch the ferry to cross the English Channel. Ever since then, I have tried to keep a full tank of gas if possible!

A Friend Named Korky— God's Good Providence in My Life

If it were not for the fact that a family friend named Korky had a soft spot for our family, this book probably would never have been written. Mother was a nurse in Cambridge, from N. Ireland, where she met Dad during the Second World War. I remember Korky talking to my mother and mother said, "Korky, what kind of soap do you use?" With the full force of his fascinating personality Korky said, "Oh, I always use Lifebuoy soap." Mother replied, "Well, why don't you try using something else?" Korky had tried many treatments to clear up some facial skin problems that folks often get growing up. Mother's advice soon took care of the problem. I have always thought that a special family bond developed in part because of mother's counsel!

Korky was, and still is, an interesting Englishman. He was a successful child actor and God opened his heart and God's Holy Spirit entered Korky and Korky's life took a dramatic turn in the direction that God had purposed for him. I recall standing in our driveway of 82, Holmes Avenue, Hove, watching enviously as my brother Peter and Korky got ready to set off on Korky's 650 cc. Norton motorcycle for their trip from Brighton to Jerusalem in the Holy Land. Korky noticed how envious I was watching them get ready. He resolved then that we would go on another trip by car. He kept his promise!

Third Trip to Europe—and beyond! (1963)

It was the "trip of a lifetime"—30,000 miles in three months in the summer of 1963, with Korky and three others. The five of us set off in a new 1963 Ford Cortina that Korky bought. A 3-month road trip from Brighton through Europe to North Africa, down the Nile to see the temples in Abu Simbel, then back to Cyprus and on to the Holy Land, Syria Afghanistan, ending up in Iran.

I was to be the accountant on the trip and take care of the different currencies. Korky had already chosen Mike, an officer in the Merchant Navy and clearly a colorful character to come on the trip. Mike's folks lived next door to the field where Korky's horse pastured. Korky kept his horse in the delightful English village of Rottingdean, Sussex. It was arranged that the five of us going on the trip would all meet up in Korky's club in London.

The club was just as I expected it to be as I had seen in the movies. That was when we met Mark who was an English major and a graduate from Sandhurst, the British Army's training school for officers. We also met the 5th member of the team, Peter. Peter, as I recall, had been orphaned and was successfully making his way in life in London— no small accomplishment! At the time we met Peter, he was a "petrol pump attendant." He was also a motor mechanic and Korky made a smart choice inviting Peter to be a part of the 5-man team. Remember, a 1963 Ford Cortina was a five-seater saloon car. We were allowed one change of clothes each for the 3-month trip that turned out to be a trip of around 30,000 miles. My wardrobe was two soccer shirts, two pairs of soccer shorts and I guess, two pairs of shoes, but I can only picture one pair of sandals.

Leaving England, the countries visited were France—Germany—Switzerland—Austria—Italy and Sicily—Tunisia—Libya—Egypt—Greece—Cyprus—Syria—Lebanon—Jordan (Holy Land)—Iraq—Afghanistan—Iraq—Syria—Turkey—Bulgaria—Yugoslavia (Serbia, Croatia, Slovenia)—Austria—Germany—Belgium—and home to England. It probably couldn't be done today!

Korky, is what the 'Brits' would call, a "one off." He is unique, just like the rest of us! He is thoroughly English, from an aristocratic family, yet in part, thoroughly un-English. My brother had a good trip to the Holy Land with him although I do not recall hearing anything about the trip on his return. I do remember that he sent a post card home from Jerusalem saying, "bike is doing fine, but I have 'big end' trouble!" Another thing that was unique about Korky was that in addition to the Norton motorcycle, he had a red E-type Jaguar sports car, a Cessna airplane, and a horse. He also married the girl I thought one day I would like to marry. One day, when I had paid off my car! Later in life he added a family sized wooden crafted sailboat that he kept in his driveway. His presence and influence in my life has been enormous and, I have always believed, providential. I have often thought that without that 30,000-mile trip when I was 19, I probably would not have been prepared for the travel I am privileged to do to today.

One might reasonably ask "why recount these youthful wanderings?" I do so, in part, because I believe that God directs our steps even when we are unaware that He is doing so. He uses our strengths and weaknesses, our likes and dislikes, our successes and failures, for His glory and His plan—for us and for others. We are reminded of this many times in Scripture. Proverbs 16:9 states, "A man's heart plans his way, But the LORD directs his steps." Likewise, the psalmist has written, "The LORD says, 'I will guide you along the best pathway for your life. I will advise you and watch over you.'" In these early travels I thought I was simply having fun and enjoying my youth. God knew otherwise.

4

COLLEGE YEARS (1961–1964)

My three college years were spent at Brighton College of Technology. (In England, college is three years rather than four as in the United States.) Somehow, I walked away from college with a degree in Building Construction. For three years, our class had a close-knit group of 10 students. Five of us were English and five were men from Uganda, Africa. The Ugandan government sent them to study Building Construction in England. It was a great class, and we enjoyed being together as a class.

One of those students in our group was also a "Paddy" Paddy Leney. He was a great friend who, picked me up each day and drove me to college. It was from Paddy, who had limited parking space in the street outside his father's house and Building company that I was able to buy an English Daimler with leather seats and a walnut dashboard. It even had a pre-selector gear box. Unfortunately, it did not have all it needed to stop the wind and rain from entering between the windscreen and the passenger window! I was so pleased to be able to afford the 15 English pounds for the car. I do not think I ever asked about why it was like that. I think my mum must have paid for my petrol. I do not remember having any money for "gas" as I would say now.

My friend Paddy was always buying cars and when the police needed him to move his new purchase out of the 4th space outside in the street, I would be asked if I wanted to buy the car, so he did not get a parking ticket. I bought a French Renaud, for 10 pounds. I also bought a car for one pound, which did not have any brakes. Because I lived uphill from Paddy, I arranged to drive my great bargain home and arranged to have someone ready to place chocks under the wheels when I arrived!

One of the highlights of my time at college no, it was *the* highlight of my time at college, was my last three-month summer vacation between my 2nd and final year. Looking back, one might suggest that Geography would have been a better course of study for me rather than Building Construction!

As discussed in Chapter 3, our small group traveled 30,000 miles in three months. I took off a week at the end of my second year and arrived back a week late after classes had started beginning in my third year. Physically, I didn't realize how run-down I was from the trip.

We went from Brighton to Europe, Africa, the Middle East, Asia Minor and Teheran, Persia. We drove 30,000 miles in three months, in the summer of 1963. It was the trip of a lifetime!

Often, we would sleep by the side of the road, put up our 5-person tent and set up our camp beds for a good night's sleep. That is something you would never do today!

We all had a dare to do on the trip. No surprise that our friend Mike instigated the first one. One evening we were talking to a small group of American girls standing on the side of the Grand Canal in Venice, Italy. During the conversation Mike was heard to say that "for 'ten bob' each I'd swim out into the middle of the Grand Canal and conduct the music coming from the two Gondolas, moored in the cool of the evening."

I called his bluff and collected the money. A few minutes later there was an audible splash. It was the kind of splash that only someone like Mike in his silk Hong Kong suit would make. I think even though we did not know anybody on site and were heading off to drive all night. We were a little taken aback! When Mike got out of the Grand Canal we did not hang around. I recall that we had to drive much of the night with the front window open.

My dare was to sleep in the General Walker Hotel in Berchtesgaden, Germany without being discovered. My payment was a free breakfast in the village at the bottom of the hill in the morning. Korky drove me up to the hotel and if challenged I was to ask if a certain British officer (a friend of Korky's) had arrived yet. He never arrived but I did not need his help. I wrapped my sleeping bag around my waste under my anorak, and Korky dropped me off in my quarters! All was fine, and I was thinking that I would be getting my free breakfast in the morning until folks started returning to the hotel from dinner.

Of course, I could not know if the banging on the door was a new person or a returning hopeful. I developed a routine in response to the banging. First, I would cough. Then I would turn on the water in the hand basin. After that I would run the shower and then run the bath and then sit on the pot and grunt. Finally, the air conditioning went off, so I began a series of fake pukes, trying to be sick.

Finally, I thought it was time to change bathrooms, which a few moments later sounded like an incredibly wise plan as a man, probably a repeat hopeful returned and was banging on the door down the hall with his fists in frustration. I finally went to sleep and walked out through the front lobby exceedingly early in the morning before folks got up. The only two people I saw were two ladies on their hands and knees washing the floor in the Lobby. They looked up and asked if I had a pleasant stay. I answered positively and went down the hill to collect my free breakfast.

The first restaurant meal I remembered Korky ordered for us in Europe was blue trout in a beautiful Austrian restaurant in Grindelwald in full view of the Swiss Mt. Eiger. Mt. Eiger is a 13,015 ft. mountain in the Bernese Alps, overlooking Grindelwald. Grindelwald was one of Korky's favorite ski resorts. As the accountant on the trip, I did speak up and say we needed to come down a notch if we are going to make the money last!

One of the reasons that we went on this trip was to visit the temples in Abu Simbel in Egypt, Africa, before they were submerged by the Nile River, IS THAT EVEN POSSIBLE? I was given a Rotary scholarship to help study buildings on the trip so there was some legitimate study along with the grand adventure!

The other object was to drive to Teheran in Persia now Iran to visit a Persian student, Hamid Mosaddegh. He was the grandson of President Mohammad Mossadegh who was President after the Shah of Persia. His grandfather was the 35th prime minister of Iran, holding office from 1951 until 1953, when his government was overthrown in a coup d'état orchestrated by the United States' Central Intelligence Agency and the United Kingdom's MI6.

That may explain why we had so much trouble finding his house when we arrived by car in Tehran! We would show the address to someone, and we would be directed in one direction. A little later we would be directed in the opposite direction. The house had a front gate that as I recall was at least 4 inches thick steel. A week before we arrived, apparently there was a full-size tank parked outside the front gate. I remember Mark had saved half a cigarette behind his ear and asked one of Hamid's servants for a light.

Almost instantly a 3-tiered silver trolley was wheeled out with a world selection of cigarettes and cigars. After that we were each given 5 golden cushions to make our beds with. We all slept well that night!

I have always had a great affinity for people from countries and cultures that are not my own. Biblical hospitality and a desire to spread the gospel to as many people and nations as I can, have been a hallmark of my ministry. That burden was formed early in my life even though at the time, I did not know that God was shaping my life and my ministry.

While growing up in Hove my parents hosted many international students in our home along with European secretaries who were studying for three months learning English in England, French or Italian in country and German in Germany. While they came and went, we also had an international student who stayed for a two-year period. We had a wonderful student from Singapore, a John Tan whose father owned a large rubber plantation in Singapore. Sadly, we lost touch with John Tan many years ago. (John, if you ever read this, we would love to hear from you again!)

While we were in Egypt, we travelled down the Nile River by boat. The roads to Abu Simbel which were close to the border of Sudan, were so bad (corrugated), that we chose to leave our Ford Cortina in Cairo. We invested in catching a boat down the Nile. There were 5 boats, all tied together. Apparently, only one of the engines was in working order!

We had queued up in the blistering sun for 3 or 4 hours. Finally, Korky collected our 5 passports and marched up to the front of the queue which seemed frozen in time. He shook hands with all the Egyptian officials at the table and, formally introduced himself as "Korky Davey" and helped himself to an official rubber stamp. He then expertly stamped all our passports, as if he knew what he was doing. The consequence was that we got on the boat early with enough time to be able to lie down, full length on an open deck with a space for our shoes as pillows!

One boat had an engine that started and continued to run, i.e., it worked. The other four boats were tied together, because their engines did not work. The 5-boat flotilla was able to transport animals, cattle, household goods and people. We were told that we could be dropped off at the Temples and stay overnight at the temples and we would be picked up on the way back from Sudan by our friendly flotilla. If I recall correctly, we were there for three days with no food and Mark's flask of water to drink!

Well, the Egyptian did have some lemons to sell. We called him Lemon man. The reason we were silly enough to jump into the Nile and hang onto the docking pontoon was because it was so hot, and we hung on to avoid being swept away. (I suspect we all have memories of youthful experiences that now, being older and wiser, we would not replicate. We have probably all kept some angels working extra hard on our behalf!)

The current was so fierce, and we were so hot and had not been able to take shelter from the burning sun buy sleeping or resting in the sacred temples. The only relief available was to lie down on the cool granite tombstone of a British Officer from the Heavy Camel Corps, who was buried there. His granite tomb was by the temple, and it was sheltered from the sun and at the right time of day it was cool to the touch.

While there, one person we met was a "Brit" from Manchester, England. He just appeared with a rucksack. I do not know where he came from. He could have appeared out of the desert, or maybe he was on our boat, and we did not know it. His rucksack was half full, with tinned corn beef and tins of sardines along with an unbelievable budget of 10 English pounds in his pocket to get back to Manchester. He probably made it back to the UK—eventually!

Our community flask that Mark brought was working and contained all the water that we had, for all five of us, as it turned out, for three days. Soon we were trying to drink water from the Nile, in all its "brownness." Why we thought that pouring the brown liquid through eight layers of Mark's army handkerchief before it trickled its way through a tin of Egyptian sand only to be "purified" by lemon juice squeezed in, I will never know. We had no other option, and it cost us all, because all five of us took sick with severe diarrhea. I also had a huge poisonous carbuncle on my leg, which thankfully was lanced when we returned to Cairo.

The temple guard would not allow us shelter in the sacred temple. It was unmercifully hot outside and so cool inside. "Lemon Man" selling lemons and guarding the Temple was there for his own comfort.

Thankfully, eventually, when we made it back to Cairo, we put ourselves up for the week, care of the Insurance Co., in Winston's Churchill's favorite Hotel in Cairo, the "Mena House Hotel." It quickly became our favorite hotel too!

Paddy and Mike took a sail on the Nile in an Arab Dow. How we enjoyed dangling our hands and feet in the cool water! I vividly recall what a delight it was to be on the water of the Nile after so many miles in the car over 'roads' with sand all around us. It was so refreshing to dangle our hands in the water and so peaceful to have the wind carry us silently along the Nile. The Arab Dhow, otherwise known as an Arab Market boat, is the sailing boat of choice on the Nile. No experience is ever wasted in life. If I had not been taught to sail on the Norfolk Broads at a church sailing camp, I would never have been able to enjoy the refreshment of quietly sailing down the Nile in Egypt.

At various periods during the week, we all thought that we might have been getting better. We rose from our beds to walk out of the room and a little way up the hall. On my return, the usual question put to all was, "How far did you get?" Answer, "Just outside the bedroom door!"

When we returned to Cairo, we were amazed to find our car alive and well. We still had a steering wheel, and all four wheels were still on our car. All through the trip the Cortina performed well for us. Peter proved himself to be a worthy mechanic in a Wadi in Jordon by stripping the engine down, to clean out the sand that found its way into places that it had no business to be in. It was impressive, and nobody doubted that he would fix the problem and put it all back together again. Thankfully, that is what he did!

We had one day in the Mena House Hotel where we were all well enough to have a 'slap up meal' and of course, quench our thirst, in glorious luxury. That was so enjoyable and much needed to revive our spirits.

Early in our travels driving west along the N. African coast we stopped for lunch at a local restaurant with a view. During lunch, a man got into a fight right near our parked car and was knifed, in his arm pit. Before we knew what was happening, Korky went down to the car and opened a bottle of TCP, an antiseptic liquid that we Brits used, and poured it into the man's arm pit. The incident occurred in the town of Sousse in Libya, Egypt. The hometown of Dr. Anees, a dear and godly friend who is the founder and director of "Church Without Walls." A ministry to Muslims. We finished our lunch without incident and continued driving west. A little shaken if I recall and not having enjoyed our lunch. Because we were in the car most of the time, we had no further problems with it or with folks who might have been tempted to think that it was in better condition than their own car and decide to "liberate" it from us!

Ur of the Chaldees

In Genesis 15:7, we read: "And he said to him, (that is Abraham) "I am the Lord who brought you out from Ur of the Chaldeans to give you this land to possess." I never imagined that I would ever get to the old train station at Ur Junction in Iraq, but here I was taking a picture of Korky, Mike, Peter, and Mark in front of me walking out to a ziggurat. At Ur Junction, there was a railway line and a shed—and not too much else! But it was a biblical site.

You might remember the words of Acts 7:2–4: "The Glorious God appeared to our ancestor Abraham in Iraq before he moved to Syria. And told him to leave his native land, to say goodbye to his relatives and to start out for a country that God would direct him to. So, he left the land of the Chaldeans and lived in Hama Syria until his father died. Then God brought him here to the land of Israel."

The Dead Sea

There were many other biblical sites we visited during our journey. One was the sight where the Dead Sea Scrolls where found. When we saw the cave in 1963 where the Dead Sea scrolls were found, it was open and not the tourist attraction that it is presently. Now it is fenced off. We did spend time "swimming" in the Dead Sea and that was just as amazing as we expected it to be. We did not read a newspaper as we sat in the water, but we could have if we had found a newspaper that we wanted to read. There was a group of young men splashing and annoying a group of girls and we told them that if they did not stop that we would dowse them with salty water and that would stop their antics until they had rinsed their eyes. That is what we eventually had to do!

Syria

Visiting Syria was amazing and nothing like it is presently. Acts 15:40,41 tells us

"But Paul chose Silas and departed, having been commended by the brothers to the grace of the Lord. And he went through Syria and Cilicia, strengthening the churches." I wonder sometimes if our experience of Syria was closer to that of St. Paul or current tourists!

On one occasion when we drove through a Syrian village one of the children threw a sizable rock at us. I stopped the vehicle in disbelief and took off after him. In those days I was able to keep up with him. The chase took us through a series of houses and gardens until we arrived in the living room, in what I supposed was the boy's home or the home of his grandfather.

Not speaking Syriac, I pointed to the child in the house and made signs for the child to be disciplined by the occupant for throwing a stone at us. I made sure that it was understood that I had not and could not do it myself, but I made it clear that the occupant should discipline the child. I left a little breathless after my chase through the village with the reasonable belief that the adult got the message. But who knows?

After our 30,000-mile trip, we were safely home in a restaurant near Brighton Station, we all ordered our favorite meal. I chose steak, and kidney pie and chips. There was no music gently playing in the background, but we were treated to a bubbly English lady praising her dear hubby for changing a wheel on the side of the road on their vacation to Paris, France. We thanked God that everybody eventually returned home safely.

What Became of the Five Summer Vagabonds?

All good things eventually come to an end, as did our summer sojourn. Though decades and miles separated us, memories of our time together and the friendship and experiences we shared have not faded.

- Korky became Director of Open-Air Campaigners in Bristol, England.
- Mike married a Russian lady and went from Rottingdean, to live in Russia.

- Mark was left behind in Jerusalem and turned up two years later having been in Saudi Arabia teaching English.
- Peter went into business running trips to India and Nepal.
- Paddy eventually became a Reformed Presbyterian Minister of the gospel and now lives in Greeneville, Tennessee as a Presbyterian evangelist.

With 30,000 miles, many countries, and many experiences behind me, it was time to trek a few more miles—back to Brighton and a final year of college.

5

MY SENIOR YEAR (1964)

Studies and Student Stunts

I do not have academic accomplishments that I boast about from my college days, although I do have a degree in Building Construction. However, I was asked by the President of the College, Dr. Watts if I would captain the college "Tiddlywinks" team. That was an honor that came my way because of a successful impersonation of King Saud of Arabia's 4th son, Prince Emir Khalid Aziz ibn Aziz ibn Saud at the Royal Pavilion Estate in Brighton as a 19-year-old Building student in my senior year at Brighton College of Technology.

Each year Brighton College of Technology had a student "Rag Week." Students created stunts to get local press coverage so that they could remind the public that the following week students would be going "door to door" collecting for the 3 officially chosen college charities.

One year a Civil Engineering student, John Rowe, attempted to cross the English Channel in a motorized bathtub. He was within a few miles from shore when had to abandon his crossing. That was a student stunt that caught the imagination of the public and made it into the newspaper. We had the privilege of getting our stunt in the local press and all the national press except *The Times* of London.

In the *Life in Brighton* written by Clifford Musgrave, you will find a chapter relaying how Queen Elizabeth II and Princess Margaret had donated Regency furniture to the Royal Pavilion. Then followed these words, "One thing that the Pavilion had never had, was a Royal Hoax, but that was put right by Paddy Cook a 19-yr. old Building student."

There was a photograph of me being formally greeted by Clifford Musgrave, the Director of The Royal Pavilion Estate that made its way into the local paper as we had hoped and brought attention to the upcoming "Rag week." That was all that we expected, a picture in the local paper to bring attention to next week's Rag week.

A letter had been sent to the mayor of Brighton from a hotel in London by Korky's wife. It was announcing that the "Prince" was coming the following day to Brighton and would like to visit the Royal Pavilion and "take tea" with a couple of his staff members.

The mayor of Brighton was unable to attend, but the Director of the Royal Pavilion graciously greeted us on his behalf. It was Mr. Musgrave who later wrote the book *Life in Brighton* and as quoted below kindly included our student stunt.

An hour and half after the official greeting, and an impromptu press conference, along with formal introductions to academic dignitaries and their wives from the University of Sussex, as well as an interesting tour of the pavilion, which was a first for all of us, we were invited to "take tea" which was served from a beautiful silver service English tea. Because we were students from the College of Technology, none of the professors or their guests from the University of Sussex recognized us to sound the alarm.

We were asked by the Director of the pavilion if the prince would mind greeting a few of his personal friends. It was our privilege to meet Professor Asa Briggs of the University of Sussex, who was also visiting the Pavilion together with Professor Sir Hugh Trevor-Roper, who had been giving a lecture at the university.

After carefully checking that my professional makeup had not been transferred to the white gloves of one of the wives, I had shaken hands with, I marveled at my good fortune. It was at that point that I nearly "lost it." After shaking hands, one wife sweetly said, "Wasn't that nice of him dear to stop and shake hands with us?"

During the tour of the Royal Pavilion, we were mysteriously left alone for a few minutes and a thoughtful test was applied to us, as there was a question that we might be students. As the tour continued, we came around a corner and heard the sharp click of heels and witnessed a salute from a uniformed Royal Pavilion staff member. The click of his heels brought me to a stop and a response. I heard him say, "As-salaam ail akum" I responded as I had, all summer—I put my hands together in front of my chest, bowed and said, *"Ail akum as-salaam, Rafik!"* He said in Arabic, *"God be with you."* I said in return, *"God be with you, my friend." In the Providence of God, I had just returned from a three-month trip in the Middle East and had been hearing those words many times during the summer.*

We moved on, but I did manage to see a discrete "thumbs up" given by the staffer with his hand by his side. Maybe, that was the time when the silver service High Tea was rushed in for the "Prince," I do not know!

Another student, Ken, who was impersonating a travel representative from Frames Tours, took care of an unscripted moment. We were all seated around the tea-table, and it was my impression that nobody knew the proper etiquette on how to begin an English High Tea with a Saudi Prince. Ken was perfect and so suave. He solved the situation by standing up and saying, "Shall I be mother?" Meaning, "shall I pour the tea and get this show on the road." We were all relieved and enjoyed a very pleasant High Tea! After tea, we departed from the Pavilion in our borrowed black Cadillac.

We still had not been discovered. We were accepted for who we said we were. We drove out of the Royal pavilion grounds without being discovered or arrested, although the Director did note in an extensive recounting of the event in his book on Brighton (p. 427f.), that he had suspicions, but they were unconfirmed and my Arabic greeting to the staff member helped the successful stunt.

However, he noted: "What might well have aroused the most serious suspicions of all was the fact that the 'Prince' was if anything too regal, having rather more dignified reserve than is usually affected by visiting foreign royalties. The Director's son did point out that one should not have been taken in by an Arabian prince who arrived in a Cadillac that was at least three years old."

According to a local press report our student stunt had "the whole of Brighton laughing." A high honor indeed. We also got good reviews from the local press. My dad collected clippings from all the national English press except *The Times* of London, which did not cover the story. Finally, the president of the college, Dr. Watts, sent for me to come to his office. My classmates thought I was in trouble, but apparently, I was not. As I waited in front of the president's desk, he continued to finish what he was writing and then he looked up and spoke. Of course, I had no idea what he was about to say. With what I perceived as a wry smile, he looked at me and said, "Cook, you crook, well done! Would you like to become the captain of the College 'Tiddlywinks' team?" Of course, I accepted.

After my meeting with the president, I was introduced to four men from "the press." My inclination was that they were not "from the press." It was a cordial and appropriate meeting, with a photo session to satisfy their need to have a record of our meeting and pictures of us for their files.

I had purchased my Arab clothing during my summer sojourn in the Old City of Jerusalem close to the Damascus Gate in the Muslim quarter. We found inexpensive beds in a dormitory setting in a convent. This was also the area were an Arab tapped me on the shoulder and said, "Hallo Paddy!" I thought that line started with "Hallo John." The Arab turned out to be a fellow civil engineering student from Brighton College of Technology! We had just walked out of a restaurant after a bad meal, which he took us back to promising to resolve our problem since he "knew his way around Jerusalem."

In preparation for our stunt, we originally practiced with motorcycle outriders, but the collection of assorted motorcycles precluded any diplomatic aura so that idea was scrapped. However, the practice was helpful in that we discovered how powerful the brakes were on the Cadillac. None of us had cars with such powerful brakes!

I did tell my dad what we intended to do, and he seemed to take it in his stride. We also confided in one of Dad's Anglican Church wardens. We borrowed his beautiful leather briefcase, and he asked us what we planned to do with it. When we told him, he remained willing to lend it to us but there was considerable incredulity in his body language. One other person knew. The young mother, Judy in the basement apartment of my folk's house in Denmark Villas was a "Little Theatre" enthusiast and did a professional job of my makeup. Before perpetrating the stunt, I approached the *Brighton & Hove Herald* and told them in advance what we were planning to do, so that we would have our "Rag Week" promotional picture in the paper. That paper told other newspapers who ran with the story.

Another enjoyable student stunt we participated in was with a large group of students from Brighton College of Technology. Under cover of darkness, as silently as we knew how, we moved a hayrick at the local Agriculture College in Plumpton and moved it to the front entrance of the college. It blocked the main building for a short time until it was removed.

One of the social events that I wanted to go on at the College was a day away to play a soccer match against another college. But to sign up you had to commit to participate in the visiting College's "Dance and Bottle Party." I did not allow myself to think what that might entail. It took me a while to resolve the problem. Eventually, I decided to take a baby's bottle with a nipple on it, with milk in the bottle. Nobody had the courage to test what was in my bottle and when people asked me what I had in my bottle, I just said, "This is a man's drink and if you think that you are man enough to try it without me telling you what is in it, go ahead." Nobody took me up on my offer, so my problem was solved.

At that age, I certainly lacked the wisdom of Solomon and had not learned how to pray specific prayers to my heavenly Father. It took me far too long to make the connection between the biblical fact that God is omniscient (that He knows everything) and things I needed to know. Well, finally I discovered that if God knows everything then, "Da," how silly would I be not to ask him about everything! We should pray when we have no idea what to do—though probably not for stunts! After praying, an idea often comes to you.

Each year during Rag Week at the College of Technology there is the annual home-made boat race between the two piers. The Palace Pier and the West Pier. One reason you go to college is to learn what you do not know. Before we knew it, we thought that by building the longest boat in the race that when we lined up, we would already be ahead of anybody else. Yes, we were in front of everybody else, but what we did not know, because we were still learning how to build, was that the longest boat was too long to be maneuvered.

When we learned that our long raft was too long to steer, we had to paddle like crazy and head out to sea, then at some time we would all have to jump off our raft and face the other way and paddle like crazy back towards the finish line. Not all academic disciplines readily transfer to others. We may have been studying Building Construction, but it did resemble Naval Architecture!

Sailing and Sensibility

During my senior year of college, I took a small college sailboat out to sea off Brighton beach from the yacht club in Shoreham. It was a fearful day on the water. I took the boat out to sea using bad judgement. I sailed so far out into the English Channel that I could not see the power station back on land. Then the boat's tiller broke off and I became what is termed "a mariner in distress"—in my case, a foolish mariner in distress and not much of a mariner. I was, at best, a day sailor. Not long afterwards, an anchor arrived in the boat and dug into a seat. The good news was that it was attached to a rope!

I learned to sail on the Norfolk Broads as described earlier and did all my sailing on inland waters. I was totally ignorant of the warning messages of the flags flying in the harbor. I should never have left the harbor or taken the boat out into the open water. Thankfully, in the good providence of God, I was told later that the World Catamaran Champion, an Englishman was out at sea in the English Channel, sailing around in the storm. He threw the anchor to tow me back to land.

My problems arose because I took a college sailing dingy out at a time when my judgement was not sound. I was in the process of having a nervous breakdown. There were three main factors that went into that happening.

- One, I was physically exhausted from my 'happy go lucky' 30,000-mile road trip in the summer.
- Secondly, I had my first ever serious relationship with a lovely Christian girl come to an end. She later told me that she had become a Christian on one of our dates. We had gone to an evangelistic crusade in Brighton. In the good providence of God, she later married my good friend Korky.
- Thirdly my final exams were looming. The ending of my first serious relationship was very painful. I did not know how to deal with that. I could not figure out how long the pain would continue and that was a dark, confusing time, as others can probably relate to it or similar circumstances.

That loss of relationship has been a good lifetime lesson that Christians are not immune from depression.

But, back to the sailboat memories. I think my friends were not worried that I would get out of the harbor because there was no jib with the dingy and they could assume that I would not be able to sail out of the harbor without one. That part went fine. I sailed out to sea. In my unhealthy state of mind, I remember thinking that I was enjoying my sail so much that the idea of going all the way to France, probably 25 miles away was swirling around in my thinking. "Not smart, Patrick!"

I can imagine my friends saying, "I can't believe you didn't have a bottle of water with you! A reality check on my idea of maybe sailing over to France, the boat's tiller broke off. I do not believe that God had nothing to do with that. Not long after that I heard a distant voice which I barely understood. I looked up and was surprised by the size of the wavers around me. I had previously been looking down and "puking" in a plastic bucket as I was, as usual, being as sick as a pig on the open sea.

I understood my new and distant friend was saying in effect, "Lookout, I will try and throw you a rope." Almost at once an anchor arrived in the boat and dug into a seat. It was attached to a rope. Thinking about that, it was quite the throw! I continued vomiting into a plastic bucket, trying to fill it up, so I had not seen the anchor arrive in the boat. Again, in the good Providence of God, the anchor that saved me that day and allowed me to be towed back to the beach in Shoreham along the coast from Brighton, was thrown by one of the few who was qualified to sail in the storm.

As we approached the beach, despite calls from my rescuer not to get out of the boat, I jumped out and safely landed the boat on the shore without any extra damage. I could beach the small sailboat before stumbling up the beach into the arms of, can you guess? I stumbled into the arms of a retired sea captain! He and his wife kindly put me straight to bed and I woke up next morning to a wonderful English breakfast. My folks were of course glad to hear from me that morning.

They had heard on the news that many boats had been damaged and some even destroyed during the storm. I was totally ignorant and stubbornly rebellious taking the boat out of the harbor. All the proper flags were up warning sailors *NOT* to attempt to go out into the open sea. In the providence of God, He was watching over me and protecting me for His later purposes. To some of you, perhaps the story of Jonah comes to mind from the Old Testament. God was merciful to me and many others before me.

When I awoke in the sea captain's home the next morning, I casually flipped open a Bible and read these words from Ephesians 2:8–9. "For it is by grace you have been saved, through faith—and this is not from yourselves, it is the gift of God— not by works, so that no one can boast." I got the message, even in my foolish, stubborn attitude, God was merciful to me that day.

That passage in Ephesians refers to the doctrine of salvation. It is not meant to encourage foolish sailors! But it did for me and God in His mercy allowed me to get the message that He who created and sustains the universe and controls the storms on the mighty oceans had purposed for the British sailing champion to throw me an anchor and tow me back to land.

College Thesis: "Skills of Interviewing"

Interestingly, in my final year of college I was given permission to write my senior thesis on a subject that had nothing to do with what I had been studying for three years. I had been studying Building Construction for three years. Yet, I was given permission to write about, "The Techniques of Interviewing." Because I was not interested in writing about glass or concrete or some such subject, I argued that maybe I would end up being in personnel management in a building company. Thankfully, my idea was approved, and I graduated!

6

POST-COLLEGE BEGINNINGS: FITS AND STARTS (1964)

A Difficult Transition

The summer of 1964, after graduating from college, was a particularly difficult summer for me. I had not been "tracking" in my final year as a focused student. I was "out of it!" Because of my health I was not allowed to travel and use my last precious three-month summer holiday. I had to stay home and recover from an illness, that at the time, I did not think I had. Now, looking back, I think there were three heads that contributed to my breakdown. Much later I was convinced that the whole episode was also a spiritual battle. These three issues were part of it. I do not have any doubt about the spiritual battle and as I said, I understood this much later.

First, I was physically worn out from my exciting summer travelling 30,000 miles in the summer. Second, I thought I knew the Christian girl that I wanted to marry. I was wrong about that and the realization of it was very painful, and it took me too long to come to terms with that reality. Third, my final year I had not been able to focus on my studies properly as I should have. One accomplishment of that summer was that I taught myself to touch type—a skill that has served me well through the years and that I am using to write this book!

My First Job

I have never been interested in going back in time and re-living any part of my life. Leaving home and starting my first job was certainly in that category. I was fortunate and enjoyed living at home while I attended Brighton College of Technology. I had a great church, in Park Hill with pastor Derek Fortnam and his dear wife Barbara—Park Hill Evangelical Free Church, Kemptown, Brighton.

When I left home to go to my first job in the City of London, it was a hard adjustment, and I am glad I do not have to do that again. Unfortunately, in my immaturity, I had talked myself into a job that I was not qualified to hold. It took me three months to find that out. The company is a well-known and respected national building construction firm—Sir John Laing Construction Company. I was so fortunate to be hired by them. The Vice President of the firm asked me at my interview: "How much responsibility do you think that you can handle? You are a young inexperienced graduate." In my immaturity I replied, "I can handle as much responsibility as you choose to give me, on one condition, that there is someone above me to "carry the can," i.e., "accept responsibility for my actions."

Well, without realizing it, that put me even further out of my depth to begin with. I still had to struggle getting on the Tube in London's underground station as I delivered drawings for the company to architects and other construction companies around central London. As I sped along the rails I even wondered if I was going in the right direction! Most of the time I got it right, but I stressed over those simple responsibilities.

I left home and went to live by myself for the first time ever. While a student at Brighton College of Technology I was able to live at home. I was now alone in London, with a job that was too big for me, and I was living at the Salvation Army hostel and not fully healed from my breakdown. The Salvation Army is a wonderful ministry, but I was shockingly lonely without any confidence or money to speak of. I recall that most weekends I scurried back to Brighton taking the train for the safety of home.

Later, Dad arranged for me to stay with a godly family, Noel and Mary Gibson, from Golder's Green, in London. That was so comforting living in a godly home again. Noel worked for the Scripture Union in London.

My first day on the building site in Gracechurch Street upon-Cornhill London E.C.1. I went into the tearoom and read a letter from a construction worker thanking the men on site for all their encouragement while he was in the hospital. He had fallen on the site from a height and had to have a prosthetic leg fitted. An interesting fact. My first day on the building site in Gracechurch Street was adjacent to St Peters-upon-Cornhill, the Anglican church of which Dad was to be rector from 1965 until 1987.

The young surveyor on the site was also a recent graduate but unlike me he knew what he was doing. My first task was to climb a large ladder, 40 to 50ft high. I was to mark a line on the wall with a marker for him and the site agent. Until then I probably had a fear of heights but the thought that I was getting paid to go up the ladder took care of my previous fear and up I went. When I reached the top of the ladder where I was to make the necessary mark, I realized I could not turn around to see the agent.

My face was pretty much flat against the wall of an adjoining bank. Not only could I not see the surveyor to take instructions, but I could no longer hear him, because of the noise of all the city traffic! Then, I wished I were in a bad dream. I was not. I dropped my marker! Twenty minutes later I was back up the ladder. Now another problem prevented me from doing my job.

What I thought was a simple task of making a mark on a wall was not simple at all. While I was picking up my marker below a whole pile of timber had been piled up from a crane so that even if I could hear the agent, now I could not see him. I came down the ladder having failed what should have been a simple task. That was such an emotional issue that I do not remember anything else about my first day on the job. It was not a good start to my new job or my new career—and things did not get better in the following days.

After three months I was let go. Fired. Though I did not know it at the time, it was the best thing that could have happened to me. They were exceedingly kind and even understanding even though they were a large national corporate construction company. I think that they had figured out that I was not well and not qualified or experienced enough for the job I had talked myself into starting. My career in building construction was ended almost before it began!

Countryside and Coaches (1965)

After being "fired," "let go," or however you want to say it, in London, God arranged for me to go and live in the beautiful English countryside. My new address was "North Acres," Streat, Nr., Hassocks. Sussex. England. John and Val Eastwood invited me into their home to live with them. John and Val took over running the Norfolk Broads Camps after my dad had led the camps. It was a much-needed reprieve in my life when God had purposed that John and Val would play a pivotal role in my Christian journey.

Leaving home attempting to make my way in life, and setting out in life to "make it," was a painful and difficult time in my life. I am thankful that the Lord pulled me through that period in my life. The village of Streat, near Hassocks Sussex, was itself unique. As an English village it barely qualified. It had an Anglican church, a manor house, and a telephone kiosk.

However, there was no cricket field, shop, or pub. Most English villages have at least that! After the manor house, John and Val's house was the next largest. Over the years they devoted their time and resources to using the house in the Lord's work. Part of his ministry was restoring the large and beautiful Victorian house. John turned his hand to everything as the need arose.

My first few years after leaving London (1965–1970), would be years in which I alternated between driving and selling real estate. While living with John and Val I took a job as a coach driver driving 53-seater coaches for Plumpton Motor Coaches. I was thankful to drive for an old, established, local coach company. To get to work at the coach company, I had to walk from Streat along a beautiful lane through the fields. The route will always have a special place in my heart because of a blessed habit that developed I prayed every time I walked that route. It was about a half-hour walk each morning. Months after beginning at the coach company, as I was walking to work, I thought I heard the "sound of a rushing mighty wind." Well, I was not about to get caught up in a biblical experience, I turned around just in time to avoid being run over by a bicycle!

The first day at the coach company when we had our morning tea break, I decided that in this job I was going to deliberately be aggressive in my witness as a Christian, right up front. I introduced myself and went around the driver's tearoom, asking each driver about 11 of them, "Are you a Christian?" One by one they responded with awkwardness and some with red faces, each answering in the negative.

Each morning our first drive was to do the school run. Each driver had his route to collect local school children standing by the side of the road and take them to the local country school. Then on return to the garage our first task was to clean our coach inside and out. As I was praying and cleaning my coach the idea was given to me that if I cleaned my coach quickly, I could then offer to help clean another driver's coach. The idea being that who would refuse help to clean his coach? I would have private time to talk as we worked.

Driving the coach was a job filled with variety. One of my first trips was to take a coach load of British Army accountants to the firing range. I was proud that even though we were not at war I did not feel like a coach driver that day, I convinced myself that I was doing my part. I do not recall how I felt the next day when I had to take some of the accountants back to the firing range because they had not hit their targets!

On another trip I took a 53-seater coach to Holland filled with folks to see the Tulip fields. After a trip driving an empty coach, I would often turn on the coach microphone and sing. I pretended I was auditioning for some large appreciative audience. Of course, nobody ever heard me but since it was for my benefit, I thoroughly enjoyed the applause I thought I heard. A couple of times I was horrified when I discovered that I was tapping my foot on the accelerator pedal. I am not going to tell you how fast I was travelling the first time I realized what I was doing. At least I wasn't booed off the stage that I wasn't on!

There was quite a bit of variety in my trips. One lady getting off the coach after her sports team outing asked me if I finished my book that I had on the dashboard about Spirits. I was able to reply that it was a good Spirit and not to worry about me. It was a classic book written by the famous Welsh minister and physician, Dr. Martin Lloyd-Jones entitled, *Spiritual Depression.*

Another time either the drivers had played a trick on me as they often attempted to do, or I left my coach parked outside a diner and went inside for lunch without putting the hand brake on. When I came out after lunch, my coach had rolled back and was stopped by the car behind it. I never did find out if I had got out of the coach without putting the hand brake on. A few months later I drove home to visit Dad, and I looked at Dad's mail on the table by the front door and I saw a letter for me. It was telling me to appear in a court case in another town the next day. I scrambled and managed to get there on time only to find that my high-school headmaster was on the bench. That was a little embarrassing since I had graduated from college and was up for letting my coach roll back on the car behind!

One day I found myself at Wimbledon watching the All England, Lawn Tennis Club matches. Two coaches were ordered to carry young ladies from Roedean school (England's premier school for girls, near Rottingdean) to watch tennis at Wimbledon for the day. That was another day when I did not feel like a coach driver. Roedean School is the girls' equivalent of Eaton and Harrow schools for boys in England. The school buildings are set high up on a cliff between Brighton and

Rottingdean. The school is a majestic building overlooking the English Channel complete with a private tunnel and pathway to Brighton Beach for the students.

Another time, in 1966, I found myself with a ticket to Wembley soccer stadium in London for the 3rd place game of the 1966 World Cup. After the game I left early to get the coach parked near the exit so my passengers could find their coach quickly in the exiting crowds. While I was waiting, I was offered a ticket for 10 English pounds for the World Cup Soccer Final at Wembley soccer stadium for a few days later. England was to play Germany in a game for the World soccer Cup. For the price of the ticket, I took it, but I was not sure it was a valid ticket. Thankfully, it turned out to be a genuine ticket!

On the day of the World Cup Final, I took the train up from Brighton to London to watch the game. My space was behind the goal. I do not know how or why but I just "knew" that England was going to win. They did. They beat Germany 4–2. I was surrounded by hundreds of excited Brazilian fans all dressed in combinations of hats and scarves and yellow and green as far as the eye could see. I decided that when England scored a goal, I was going to confirm to myself that I did not have to do what everybody around me did. I was going to demonstrate to myself that I was an individual, made in the image of God. When England scored their first goal everybody around me shouted "GOAL!" in unison not to mention hugging and jumping up and down. I was different. I just said quietly to myself, "Well done chaps!" Very English.

It was easy being different. It was my choice! That was another subtle lesson I learned for life—we all have choices we must make.

On another trip, I drove folks to the British Museum in London to see an exhibit of the death mask of Tutankhamun—"King Tut."

As my passengers left the coach the teacher in charge of the day's outing insisted that I come in and see the display. I think she even offered to pay my entrance fee. She was a little taken aback when I declined her offer. I assumed that she thought it would be good for me and my education. It was the first week that it was displayed in England. She just stared at me when I told her that I had already seen it. "You couldn't have. This is the first time it has been displayed in England." When I explained that I had already seen it in Egypt, in the Valley of the Kings, she was dumfounded and just stared at me in disbelief.

When she got back in the coach and all her people were accounted for, she just asked me, "Driver, did you manage to find somewhere to have lunch?" I thanked her for asking and told her that I had a delightful lunch at the Hilton Hotel. She did it again. She just stared at me! My rationale was that the tip for the day would cover the fine three-course lunch. I only had to pay for myself. It didn't cost me anything to get there, and I was hungry.

What I did not tell her was that after lunch while I was waiting for her group, I found myself preaching at the famous free speech platform at Hyde Park Corner. I had never heard anyone preach at Hyde Park corner before, so I walked over for the experience. There was a man standing on a wooden box addressing the crowd of around 30 people. As I listened, because I had a good Sunday School teacher, I got confused about what he was saying. I plucked up courage and asked a question that was not answered. Then the speaker started talking about "his god." A couple of times I asked him. "What is the name of your god?" He did not answer. I finished with "Well, I don't know who your god is but whatever god you are talking about, He is not my God!" What happened next was totally unexpected. The speaker got off his wooden box and just walked away. What happened after that was even more of a surprise. The whole crowd turned around to face me as if I was now the preacher!

Instantly, I physically felt my legs buckle. I thought I was about to keel over. I do not even recall what I was enabled to say. Whatever it was lasted about 5 minutes. There was some appreciation for what I must have said, and I went on my way. That was not an ordinary day for a coach driver! Again, the memory of that experience is something that God would use many times through the decades that followed. Our experiences in life are not coincidental, they are providential.

My last Plumpton Motor Coach story caused me to think about offering myself to God for the gospel ministry.

On this final trip I took a coach full of ladies out for the day. It was a "Ladies Day Out" for a group of ladies from an Anglican church in mid-Sussex, England. I watched as the vicar tried to buy a packet of cigarettes for himself. He put his money into the machine, and not only did he not get his cigarettes he did not even get his money back. Throughout the day he was so unable to control his anger that it was clear, even to the coach driver, that he spoiled the day out for more than a few ladies. The whole point of the day was for the ladies of the church to have a pleasant day out. A drive in the country, a stop for lunch, and a stop later for tea and pastries.

When I returned home, I told my dad about the day and ended up by saying, something like this, "I hope you won't laugh at me but if that man can be a vicar what is to stop me offering myself to God asking him to admit me to the full-time gospel ministry? Dad was very sympathetic, and he quoted a similar situation to mine that caused him to pursue the ministry. We were similar. However, the difference was that Dad had a degree from the University of Cambridge in Economics. I was a coach driver with a Construction degree that enabled me to be fired after my first three months on the job. But the ministry seed had been planted and in God's time, it would bear fruit—it always does.

Later, I learned from Mark 5:1–20 that God is all powerful and He can save (regenerate) and use anybody! As I reflected on the above story later, I learned that Jesus did not come into the world to make bad people good. He came to make dead people alive!

The problem with our world is that we are not bad people trying to be good we are dead people who can only be made alive by Jesus Christ. "And you were dead in the trespasses and sins in which you once walked, following the course of this world, following the prince of the power of the air, the spirit that is now at work in the sons of disobedience among whom we all once lived in the passions of our flesh, carrying out the desires of the body and the mind, and were by nature children of wrath, like the rest of mankind. But God, being rich in mercy, because of the great love with which he loved us, even when we were dead in our trespasses, made us alive together with Christ by grace you have been saved" (Ephesians 2:1–5). Driving the coach was a good experience for me and helped prepare me for a life of talking with a wide variety of people about Jesus Christ. At the time, I did not realize how important the experiences I had as a coach driver would be in my future. God knew what He was doing day by day and mile by mile!

7

REAL ESTATE: THE FIRST TIME AROUND

Real Estate in the Historic Lanes of Brighton: (1964–1966)

In addition to driving a coach, because my corporate building construction career was clearly over, instead of going back to college to study for another vocation, the idea of selling houses seemed a reasonable way to go. Unfortunately, after selling a dozen or so properties I was bored selling houses. During the day I was in real estate. In the evening, I drove a taxi. It produced a little extra money, and I kept an eye on the new home "For Sale" signs.

One of the things that I liked about working in real estate was that I could use my MG to drive to the house and business appointments. Unknown to most, was the fact that I tried to arrange those appointments so that I could drive into the sun for those appointments.

I somewhat enjoyed the work, but it wasn't to last.

Just opposite the real estate office was an antiques business called Hawkins. The fact that shipments arrived in the middle of the night was known. What was less known was that in front of the business was a space with double yellow lines. Often the owner of the business would park his Rolls Royce on those lines. I did not think much of it until I got a ticket for doing the same thing. So, I went to pay for my ticket and asked the police why I got a ticket and Mr. Hawkins never seemed to get a ticket. I expected to pay my fine and made that clear. Within the hour Mr. Hawkins came across the road and threatened my boss! Not of much significance but it is something that I remember—and I am still careful where I park!

I recall two situations with clients when I thought that I had done all the necessary work to affect a sale. In both cases, I thought that all they had to do was sign the contract. That was not what happened. The next day my client asked if his mother-in-law could look at the house. The day after that I was told that the sale was off. What had happened was that his mother-in-law got off the bus and complained that she did not like having to walk up the hill to the house. I was beside myself.

I thought, "What is the matter with you people? Why on earth didn't you tell her to get off the bus at the top of the hill then all she had to do was walk down the hill to the house!" Ugh!

Another time, I thought I had done all the work to affect a sale, then the day before my contented client was due to sign the contract, he announced that he had to go in for eye surgery. He did not come in to sign the next day and I never saw him again. Ugh! Again!

My boss, Dennis Botting, was an extremely fair, honest, and compassionate man. He was a fine Christian gentleman and always treated me well and encouraged me in my work for him. His secretary, Nelle Capelin, was a lady from our church. I knew her because as Head Choir Boy I sang in the same church choir. They had been good companions over the years. It was a pressure-free atmosphere for me to learn more about real estate.

One Monday morning which I doubt I will ever forget and probably Mr. Botting would also not forget. I had to announce that I had been offered a new job. This is what happened. The previous Friday I was visiting with my friend Korky, who took my brother to Jerusalem on the back of his 650 Norton motorcycle.

Korky told me that Peter, who was our mechanic for our trip, was advertising in *The Times of London* newspaper for a driver to take a trip from King's Cross Railway Station in London to India and Nepal.

After leaving our 30,000-mile trip a couple of years earlier, Peter started running trips overland to the Holy Land and now, he wanted to expand his business. I jumped at the possibility. I drove back from London to Brighton and the next day, Saturday, drove up to London in my little British racing green, MG, and met with Peter, who gave me the job.

That was Saturday. I was to leave on Tuesday evening with Peter. I knew the route through Europe, Turkey and on to Tehran. Basically, you kept driving East and followed the telegraph poles. Of course, there were also signs along the way!

Well, as you might imagine, Dennis asked me on Monday morning, "When would you begin?" I replied, "Tomorrow evening I leave Kings Cross Railway station. Peter and I must pick up our 10 passengers for the 100-day round trip. Costing 155 English pounds for a 100-day round trip. Times and costs have changed in the world of travel! There was no tension in the air, just a pause in the conversation! I wondered what Dennis would say. What he said was, "Well if I were offered a job like that, I'd take it. Did you?" I think I gritted my teeth and said, "I did!"

Now I Needed a different set of skills for my new job!

8

EXPEDITIONS EAST (1966–1968)

If you spin a globe and then stop it with your index finger, you are likely to be pointing to a country or a region that I have travelled to at least once. That certainly was not my goal in life when I was a student and a young man, but my early experiences of long journeys were something that God used to prepare me for a lifetime of evangelism. We don't know how God is going to fit together the pieces of the puzzle that are our life experiences. Only God knows what the final image will be when all the pieces are in place and our life is ended. If we are open to His leadership, it will, however, be one that is pleasing to him.

King's Cross Railway Station London to India and Nepal

For two years I drove and led enthusiastic wanderers from England, across Europe, to India and Nepal and back to England. It would be difficult to do so today because of the political dynamics across the regions, but in the 1960s it was still possible for those who had an adventurous spirit and a flexible schedule. Safety was not as much a concern as it is today.

After my first trip to India and Nepal, my former traveling companion and now boss, Peter, continued to sell trips in London. On subsequent trips I would pick up 11 new passengers from King's Cross railway station. One security tip I learned, was to only take one set of car keys! It makes you careful about what you do with those keys! I was paid expenses and a wage into my bank account. It was a truly a remarkable time and what follows below are some of the episodes of those tens of thousands of miles. Every day brought a new challenge and a new experience.

Many of the folks who came on trips could have arranged their own private trips but to travel overland in the 1960s, it was necessary to purchase a year's insurance for Europe as well as a year's insurance for Asia. Most folks who traveled to India and Nepal traveled in a 4-seater Land Rover. For such a trip they just could not afford to purchase the insurance. That caused many interesting young people to come with us. I recall that the company mainly advertised our trips in the *Times* of London newspaper.

Quite a few of our passengers had parents or family members who had worked in India or Asia. After graduating from university, students often took a year off, a "gap year," before going into a bank or an office job. They travelled to India and Nepal to travel to countries that their parents had spoken about so much. In England it was not considered acceptable to drop out of university for a year. However, it was expected that you took time off between university and working for a living.

As noted above, I was paid wages directly into my bank and my expenses were covered for my trips. You might ask, "How did it work travelling with 11 passengers of whom you had never met?" On all the trips I took the template was the same. Everybody understood that we would all be together for 100 days, just over three months. We had to get along to get the most enjoyment and fulfillment from the trip, not to mention the investment of time and money.

Our philosophy on a trip was to do as much as possible and to see as much as possible during our travels. So, when everybody got home not only were they tired, but we wanted them all to realize that they saw more on our trip than any of the many other tour operators offered. For example, on my first trip we all agreed to squeeze a couple of extra nights in so we could sleep on a river boat in Srinagar, Kashmir. To make up for the extra time in Kashmir, which everybody thoroughly enjoyed, Peter and

I drove "non-stop" 4 hours on and 4 hours for almost a week. We drove from Kashmir to Jerusalem. It was about 2200 miles on less-than-ideal roads! We wanted to be in Bethlehem in time to sing carols in Bethlehem on Christmas Eve.

We made it on time, thanks in part to the Israeli Army escorting us back on the right road to Jerusalem. We were surrounded and questioned as to why we were where we were. As was expected they were courteous with their questions, but it was obvious we were in an area where we should not be. When we arrived in Jerusalem and after we parted good friends with our Israeli escort, we learned that nobody was singing carols in Bethlehem on Christmas Eve. Even so, it was a memorable Christmas.

"Watch Out!" Letter

As we traveled overland from country to country, we would call into the British Embassies or Consulates, to collect our mail. At one stop, we had received a letter from Rev. Fred Preston, a former British Army parachute chaplain, telling us to be careful driving in Iran. He warned us to expect that the Iranian children were trained to fake being run over as we drove through the small towns and villages. He explained that as we drove slowly through the village the child would use his hand to slap the back of the car and then roll in the dust to fake being hit by our passing car. He was right, we experienced a couple of such incidents just as he described!

Driving through a village we heard a bang at the back of the car. Looking in the wing mirror we saw a child rolling in the dust grabbing his ankle.

I mention this story as when we were trying to leave an Iranian town, we found that many of the towns were laid out on the same town plan. That is, a roundabout entering the main street with a roundabout at the end of the town. On one occasion, as usual, we were surrounded by local folks who wanted to look in the windows of the Land Rover at the ladies and whatever else they were interested in. We made it quite clear when we were ready to leave and pull away from the sidewalk. Nobody moved. Eventually, I had to put the flashing lights on to emphasize that we were pulling away and for folks to move out of the way. Eventually we started the engine. Again, nothing happened. We then turned on the Maserati air horns. Most folks moved out of the way. It was hard to not get the message!

However, there was one man, who refused to take his foot from under the front wheel. His eyes were defiant. I made it quite clear that if he did not move his foot out of the way of our front wheel, he was going to have an "Owie." If I had spoken his language, I would have told him that I was going to run over his foot. It was not going to be as bad as it sounds as the road surface was soft dirt. But he was going to get his "Owie." With the engine running the flashing lights on and the air horn howling its piercing sound I pulled away. He remained in place and earned himself his "Owie!" His mother never told him that to have your foot run over by a Land Rover was a bad idea.

Pulling away and looking in my wing mirror it did not surprise me to see the man rolling on the ground apparently in pain. Considering all the clear and obvious warnings and the time it took to leave the curb I planned to drive off. Right at the same moment I saw a local policeman pushing his bike towards me. I decided to stop and explain what happened. The policeman wanted me to come with him! I had forgotten I did not speak Farsi!

He took Peter and me up some stairs to a room that appeared to be the office of the chief of the local police. There were three telephones on the man's desk, two of which were in use. Something was going on, but we never discovered what was happening. However, after about half-an-hour with repeated questions by us as to what was happening and repeated answers by the chief of police saying, "a moment, a moment, a moment." It dawned on us that the man probably did not speak a word of English.

Again, we were in a hurry to try and reach Jerusalem for Christmas. We were driving 4 hours on and 4 hours off so every hour delay for us was 50 miles that we had to catch up. We were driving from Kashmir to Bethlehem to get there to sing carols on Christmas Eve. Finally, I cannot remember our reasoning, but we both got up, shook hands with the chief of police, thanked him and took off down the stairs. It did not take him long to let out an almighty shout. 3 or 4 armed police with rusty old .303 rifles rushed up past us. Of course, we "egged" them on. That part was fine, but when we got to the Land Rover, we had to wait for a Christian doctor who was on the trip and who had gone off to buy some sugar for the missionaries in Nepal. We also had to pull up the legs of the Sleep Mobile (camper) we were towing behind our Land Rover.

The doctor showed up and the legs were up on the Sleep Mobile, we were ready to drive away but the chief of Police who was a large man was now sitting in the passenger seat. In his hands were a whole sheaf of papers. We were correct. He did not speak English. We at least got that right. Now it seemed that all he wanted was for us to sign some papers. I'm not sure how we decided but one of us signed some papers as "Happy Christmas" and the other signed some papers as "Happy New Year."

Now the police chief had calmed down considerably and kept repeating "OK, OK, OK." We were pleased for him that he thought he had accomplished something of importance without being able to speak English. We thanked him again and drove out of town westward following the telegraph poles. Pilots of previous generations were known to say that sometimes they flew railroad tracks, following them to their destination. Well, we drove telegraph poles!

Towing Hook and a Snow Drift

On another trip driving through the Taurus Mountains in Turkey with the Sleep Mobile in tow, the towing hook broke. I had been driving on compacted ice and snow with the Sleep Mobile for about ten days and was used to the conditions and was thankful that we saw very few other vehicles on the road.

One of the advantages of driving with the Sleep Mobile in tow was that there was a handbrake lever that was attached to a steel cable that acted as a vacuum operated break on the two wheels of the Sleep Mobile. What that meant was that if I needed to slow down, I could activate the air brake. In effect it would drag the Sleep Mobile behind and was a great way to be able to slow down in these snow and icy-road conditions. I was careful to take the line of the road around corners. Then a potential disaster happened. After driving uphill, I had kept the line of the road as usual but coming over the hill the road seemed to take an unexpected turn in the other direction. I overreacted too quickly to change direction.

Long story short, we ended up in a snow back high up in the Taurus Mountains in the early afternoon. The Land Rover ended up on its side on the icy road with the towing hook snapped. The Sleep Mobile was still on its chassis but was resting in a snowbank by the side of the road at about 45 degrees. Thankfully, nobody was hurt.

The mercy that God providentially arranged was that when we looked around outside, the snowbank was the only one around. If it had not been there, we could have had a "roly poly" down the mountain that likely none of us would have lived to talk about. As I mentioned there was extraordinarily little traffic on the road at that time of year and at that altitude so it was not as dangerous as you might think to be driving. However, that snowbank turned out to be a blessed miracle of God's protection.

Later in the afternoon a Turkish truck stopped, and we arranged that it would take the ladies and some of the men to a Turkish army base for the night. Thankfully, that turned out to be a good solution. Three of us stayed with the Land Rover and the Sleep Mobile that night. One was our Australian architect rugby player and another, an English cosmetic salesman from Bury St. Edmunds. We slept in the "Snow Mobile "which was lying in the snow at about 40 degrees all night.

Before nightfall, a NATO Jeep stopped to see if we needed any help. I think they were a little puzzled to see us out in the weather! We explained the situation that Peter had sent us with a spare towing hook, but I did ask their advice. "If we dug a hole in the ice and pulled the Land Rover

over so that a wheel caught in the hole we had dug, would that damage the other wheels or the bearings when they hit the ground?"

The 4 men in the Jeep, all assured us that it would not. We went to sleep, eventually, because I recall it was an exceptionally long night before we had all finished telling stories to each other!

In the morning, we managed to pull the Land Rover back on its 4 wheels and with our new towing hook drove the Sleep Mobile carefully and successfully back onto the road.

We drove carefully on and found the Turkish army base. I say carefully as although the Sleep Mobile box had remained on the chassis it was balancing and not fixed any more to the chassis with the 4 U-bolts that were designed to stabilize it. The impact had sheered the U-bolts that held the box to the chassis. Mercifully the Sleep Mobile was balancing on the chassis and was drivable. Again, thankfully all was well with the rest of the group, so we all set off again.

During the 10-hour day while we were driving, I had someone watching out of the back window the box balancing on the chassis. I wanted to be sure it did not move! If it had moved off the chassis, we would have had a major problem. Maybe it was the stress, but I had a terrible headache the whole day but at least when we pulled into a small Turkish village for the night the box was still on the chassis.

I doubt if you can imagine what I discovered. It certainly amazed me. Before going in for the night I had a quick look under the vehicle to check tires and springs etc. The last thing I did before going into the hotel was touch the back of the box with my index finger. Just by doing that the box moved! In the providence of God, it was safe, but it was balancing right on the fulcrum. My index finger told me that it was on the chassis, but only just!

Problem Solved in a Turkish Lumber Yard

I was so concerned about our situation, but it was solved after breakfast in the local Turkish lumber yard. Again, it is clear to me that almighty God was looking out for us all in this situation. Also, for some reason Peter had sent me off on the trip with a spare 2-inch towing hook packed on the roof of the Land Rover!

I came out next morning into the street, again I probably prayed but if I did not, I should have because I had no idea how to fix the situation. If I did, I do not have any memory of what I prayed for. A Turkish man approached me in the street. He was beckoning me to follow him. That had happened several times to me particularly in Istanbul, but I waved him off. Then he waved me to get into the Land Rover and follow Him. That I did assent to. At the end of the street, we turned right into a lumber yard. About 20 Turks armed with 2 x 4's started levering the chassis, jumping up and down as a team. I saw what they were trying to do. It looked like they knew what they were doing. No instructions seemed to be given and suddenly, the chassis fell into place. The problem was solved!

All we needed to do was to drill four more sets of holes in the box, place 4 more U-bolts through them, and tighten the bolts underneath. Once done, we were good to go! We settled on a reasonable price and off we went as if we had just filled up with gas. I take no credit for solving the problem. I did not even have an idea of what to do but God had purposed to work in the minds of others that we did not know to solve our problem. A good Providence for sure!

Rough Roads and Tea

Back to the dusty roads of Iran and Iraq—It was like driving over sheets of corrugated iron. The corrugations were caused by the heavy drumming of the axles of the big international trucks and their trailers that they towed behind them. Once then, in the middle of nowhere, there was a sentry hut and a pole across the road. It was a roadblock. At first, we had no idea what the purpose of it was. We assumed that if the roadblock were not there, there would be two more Iraqis or Iranians without a job. Of course, we stopped while they tried to explain why we had to sign their book and record the method of transport. That was not close to being successful. We looked in their book to find that we had just missed Prince Phillip and Dame Sybil Thorndyke riding a tandem. I would have loved to see that. That would have been quite the picture!

Another example of God's good providence was while driving in the southern Iranian desert, in a sandstorm towards Isfahan. Foolishly or not, my practice when I had to drive in a sandstorm was to keep going. I have never had to stop driving because of a sandstorm. It seemed to me that if I was still able to drive that is what I did. If the sandstorm stopped my vehicle, I would pray and do what I could do at that time rather than risk unseen problems while uncovering the engine to see if all was well—as if I had the ability to do that anyway. I did not. It seemed like we had been driving for hours. I suspect we could have all enjoyed a break, but in the present circumstances, that was not likely to happen. The visibility was almost non-existent. Then, unexpectedly, we came alongside a mud hut that was a chi-shed.

As we slowed down, sure enough it was a very welcome site. The idea of a break to stretch our legs and get a cup of tea with sugar, no milk, was most welcome. I was probably the most comfortable person inside the Land Rover because I had my own seat. There were two other passengers in the front seat and then behind us there was a bench seat for three more passengers. In the back of the 12-seater Land Rover there was seating for 6 bodies. Two bench seats for three people, facing each other. You get the picture. An opportunity to stretch legs and a bathroom break was always welcome. Travelling as we did, any time that we wanted to stop for a break or for the night, we did so.

As usual before I followed everybody, I walked round the vehicle, checking the tires. Being in Iran with its corrugated dirt road system I also checked the springs. God was looking after me in a special way that day. The bolt going through the end of the spring was literally about to drop out. For a moment I thought about what we would have done if we had not been led to stop right there at this moment. Of course, the

Chi-shed had a lot to do with it, humanly speaking but it was God who caused all the details to come together at this time and in this place.

Not being a mechanic, but having some measure of creativity, I went and produced a hammer and simply banged the bolt back into place. At least my "solution" meant that I could go in and join the group over tea and not give a thought as to how to fix it right then and there. I am sure I stripped the threads of the bolt but at least we could drive on and look for an Iranian shop with a spring. There were always plenty of those!

Carpets on the ground covering the dirt floor, and warm tea in glass cups in our hands with plenty of smoke in the air. It was a welcome break from following the telegraph poles and bouncing up and down on the corrugated road surface. It was no big surprise that nobody could understand us or what we were saying. But with plenty of smiles and many O.K.'s and thumbs up signals, it was not long before we were on our way again. We never did find out where everybody came from who was "stuffed" into that tiny roadside café. We had not seen any buildings or mud huts for quite a while.

I often wondered why the Lord took us to the city of Isfahan in Iran. Later, when I was on the Brighton seafront, I found out the reason. I was listening to David Fanstone, who was a member at Bishop Hannington Church Hove, the church where Dad was the vicar. David was also the Director of Open-Air Campaigners in England (now OAC Ministries). David's father, retired Wing Commander Fanstone, was definitely 'a one off' Englishman. He and Dad were a pair. The story goes that the wing commander mortgaged his house late in life to buy a sea-front property overlooking Brighton beach.

The purpose of that bold decision was to purchase a hostel for international students to have a Christian atmosphere and experience, while studying in Brighton. Muslims lived there in "Friendship House." There was a time when the wardens of the house were wondering why the monthly water bill was so high. The reason was that the Muslim students did not like to wash in standing water. They believed it was better to wash in running water. Who could argue about that?

And the Isfahan connection? Once, after a street meeting, an open-air evangelistic meeting on Brighton seafront, I found myself standing next to an Iranian student. I was prompted to ask him, "Is that merchant in Isfahan still in business, the one that sells delicate filigree butterflies with the blue stones for eyes? He suddenly came alive and stared at me with an interested intensity. "How do you know about that shop he asked?" Who on earth, I thought, would have started a conversation by asking such a question? Try God. We talked about the message of the meeting for a significant amount of time. Another seed of truth planted in a man known unto God.

The Isfahan story is a good tale, but for me it is more than that. It is an example of how God uses seemingly inconsequential circumstances and incidents in our lives—often, years later—for His purposes. Remembering that, or realizing it for the first time, enables us to live each day knowing that it is not simply "another day" or "an ordinary day." Rather, each day is one given to us by God and one in which He will work His purpose for us and for the world whether we see it or understand or not in those moments. God can and will use something from your past in your future in unexpected ways!

From Isfahan to Istanbul

Why did I pick up a hardback copy of the *Larousse Gastronomique* encyclopedia for a dollar from a street vendor in Istanbul? Maybe, because he only wanted a dollar for it. We also used it to pass around the Land Rover on our long journeys through the northern and southern deserts of Iran. When all you see for days is blue sky, sand, and telegraph poles, it becomes a treat to flip through colored pictures of succulent food dishes from around the world!

Once when I was in Istanbul, I met an American G.I. travelling and I noticed that he had cash sticking out of his back pocket. I went up to mention it to him and he said, "I know, I have been robbed so many times while travelling so I put fake money in my back pocket to vex the thieves. I asked him what he studied at college. He told me that he had studied American History.

I cannot explain why but I asked him. "If you studied American History, what did you do in the afternoon?" I thought that was funny. He did not! I do not know what kind of a day he had had but it became clear that was pretty much the end of our conversation. Sometimes it is hard to know when to end a conversation. I had help with this conversation!

It was a great help for me to be able to take my first expedition trip with Peter. I was not and am not a mechanic. Subsequently I was given a new Land Rover for each trip or one that was in excellent condition. Every 2,000 miles or so I had to get the Land Rover serviced. My first service call was in Istanbul, Turkey. Peter also showed me how to change an oil seal on the Land Rover as they had a habit of leaking with the oil damaging the brakes. Somehow, I managed all those trips and all those miles—surely the angels were working overtime on my behalf!

9

LEARNING THE HARD WAY

Decades of traveling in countries near and far has taught me to expect the unexpected. You never know what is around the next bend, over the hill, or awaiting you down the road. Challenges of language differences, cultural differences, and weariness from travel can make even the smallest difficulty a major concern. Simple daily tasks and routines that we take for granted can suddenly become a major frustration. It is easier to solve problems from the comfort of home, but that is exactly where the traveler is not!

Troubles at the Bulgarian Border

In addition to changing an oil seal on the Land Rover, the other mechanical responsibility I had was when I arrived from England at the Bulgarian border. This was long before the Berlin Wall came down and communist nations began to move toward democracy. At the border, or just over the border, it was necessary to do a procedure to change the timing on the Land Rover because the gasoline was much weaker in quality in that part of the world.

On one occasion I replaced the distributor cap, 180 degrees out from what it should have been. As a result, I could not start the Land Rover that was parked in front of the main entrance of the customs shed with the two-way traffic between Turkey and Bulgaria. My idea was to park the Land Rover in a place that the authorities wanted me gone as soon as possible. The time that I could not start the Land Rover was when the Bulgarian chief of customs was most angry with me. It took so many hours before getting our visas etc. that I was frustrated. So, I went behind the counter and took my passport because I knew that I could not move the unit until I had purchased what I thought I needed—a new distributor.

I planned to leave Bulgaria to buy a distributor in Turkey, but the consequences of my actions infuriated the grumpy Chief of Police. He told me to follow him. I just stood there saying, "No thank you!" Remember I assumed I was safe staying in the open area where travelers who were coming and going could see me. Later an attractive German-speaking girl came up to me and asked me to come with her. For some reason I did not see a problem doing that! She showed me into a room which belonged to the Chief of Police. This was a time where the Australian expression that someone is "Blue Mad," really applied. The Bulgarian Chief of Police started shouting at me beckoning that he wanted my passport.

Not speaking any languages and certainly not Bulgarian, I retrieved my passport from behind the counter and gestured with my hands, "a moment, a moment, calm down." All the time trying to calm the situation and trying to indicate that to obey the chief and move the Land Rover unit from outside the front entrance I needed to go back into Turkey to buy an electric part so I could start the vehicle and move it.

If you do not speak the language of the country that you are in, you are likely to have misunderstandings. This was one of those times! However, I thought that this was different. The Chief of Police began to lather at the mouth in his anger and charged at me. I was able to step aside but he was so angry that he could not stop himself. He smashed into a plate glass door and glass shattered all around us.

He shouted for backup and about 6 Bulgarian soldiers rushed in with rusty old looking .303 rifles. It did not take me long to grasp that they were all pointing at me. Oh, the humor of God. At that moment I thought about sending a postcard home to Mum saying, "The weather is fine. I wish you were here!" As I started to laugh, I realized that I was on the floor being kicked. I felt the kicks of course, but fortunately they did not appear life threatening. Though they were harsh and painful.

When I awoke, I was sitting in a chair in the office of the Chief of Police. I was shaking and I must have fallen badly as I had a swelling on my elbow as big as a golf ball. To my amazement I noticed that the Chief's office door was ajar, and I could see my friends at the front counter. Turning to the Police Chief, I pointed at the clock behind the Chief on the wall and made a horrific expression. As he turned to see what caused my expression I jumped up and ran for the door and tried to jump over the front counter into the safety of the public area where my friends were standing. What I did not realize was that after my "roly poly" in the Chief's office I did not have a lot of energy that I could draw on. Consequently, there was no way I came close to clearing the front counter. I did manage to get over the counter but in doing so I smashed the glass shield which shattered into the area where the waiting travelers were congregated.

What happened next thankfully, was a good surprise for me. Fred, the Australian architect who liked his beer, saw the Chief of Police come flying out of his office. Fred greeted him with a flying horizontal rugby tackle, placing his head squarely in the Chief's belly and decked him. Fred was angry with the Chief as he speculated about what had just gone on in his office.

Fortuitously, a translator appeared at that moment. The Chief was trying to make me pay for the damage to his office glass door. I told him that if I had broken it would have certainly paid to have it fixed. However, because I did not break the door, I did not understand why he wanted me to pay for it. I do not think he liked that! I told him that because I did not break it, I would not be paying for it.

Amazingly, for his own reasons, he gave me a stamp in my passport that banned me from ever going through Bulgaria again. We were told that we would not be able to leave the customs area until a coach load of officials arrived from Sofia. On no account were we to talk to anyone about what just happened. We talked carefully to all who would listen. It was decided that two of us get out of the customs area and file a complaint in the Greek consulate in Thessaloniki.

But first the officials came from Sofia. The officials told me that I would have to go to jail. I told them that their idea was not a good one because as the leader of the trip I had all the money in the form of American Travelers' checks. If I were in jail, I could not sign the checks and they would have to house and feed all the 11 passengers and fly all 11 passengers' home to England and then, some to Australia. Then in the good providence of God I said, "You see that young man with the red hair? Trust me you need to treat him very well." I was able to explain that Henry's father was the British Ambassador in Nepal.

The night before we were allowed to leave the country and head out through Greece, two of us left the compound and filed an official complaint at the consulate in Thessaloniki. The consulate officials told us that we were the first people who had ever filed an official complaint. He was sure that travelers were having trouble at this customs point, but he had no proof. However, he advised us to take up the matter with Britain and Bulgaria when we got home. He thought we would get a clearer hearing if there were only two parties involved. To include Greece as well, in his opinion, would complicate the situation.

When I was back in England, I was at a real estate seminar, and I asked the lawyer teaching us if he would write a letter to the Bulgarian Embassy in London. He did so, and eventually he read to me the letter that he received back from the embassy. It said that the reason I had troubles at the border was because I attacked 6 armed guards. That's not how I remembered it; but then, I had been kicked quite a few times!

Incidentally, God answered prayer because when I replaced the distributor after all the ruckus, I must have put it back the correct way. We were then able to drive off and be on our way! Not far down the road in Greece we were stopped by roadside police and asked to empty all the suitcases off the roof rack. We had a lot of trouble with roof racks on the corrugated roads and therefore I only allowed myself to get up on the roof. However, after the last few days, I was the one with the *least* amount of energy to do that. Since the official was not looking, I dropped the first suitcase on top of him. With profuse apologies uttered by me we were eventually waved onward in our journey. Later, along the roadside, I stopped the car and fell asleep—it was much needed!

Ramadan in Pakistan

On another trip we arrived in Lahore, Pakistan only to find that it was the time of the holiday of Ramadan. That means that everything was shut down to celebrate Ramadan. For us that meant that we would have to camp on our favorite campsite in Lahore—the cricket pitch. (Cricket is taken as seriously, if not more seriously in Pakistan and India as it is in Britain!)

Well, not wanting to stay in Lahore for three days the idea came to us to go to the British consulate to ask if it would be possible to collect our mail. On arriving we talked with the 3rd Secretary's wife. I did not want to be dishonest, but we did not want to wait until after Ramadan to pick up our mail. I found myself saying, "We have a young lady on the trip who has a boyfriend and there is a 50% chance that he might make a proposal of marriage by mail and the proposal could be in the consulate waiting to be collected. Is there any possibility that we could get our mail today instead of waiting in Lahore until after Ramadan?" She appeared very understanding and went inside. Thankfully, and a little surprised, I saw her coming out of the consulate with a pile of mail for us!

After thanking her for her kindness we took off and had a group meal at the "Silver Grill," which was my Chinese restaurant of choice in Lahore. Yes, Chinese food in Pakistan! We had some good food and good sleep and set off in the morning in the direction of India and Nepal. As driver expedition leader, the company had set me a manageable but tight schedule for the trip, so any unexpected delay was not welcome. Because I was a child of God and made in His image, I was counting on creativity to help me overcome unexpected problems along the way. As usual, God was faithful, and we did not lose two days travelling time—nor was there a letter proposing marriage.

Down by the River Side

If you are in India one of the things you do is, visit the Ganges River. We left the Land Rover by the Ganges and ended up in a restaurant some distance away near a university. We were aware that at the time we were in the area that the Indian students were protesting the use of the English language. Because we had English lettering on the side of the Land Rover it was of some concern to us, but we did not know enough to worry about our situation. We were young *and* foolish!

The restaurant owner received a telephone call warning him that a mob of Indian students was on its way to his restaurant, because somehow, they knew he had English tourists inside. Eventually we realized that we were in a little more trouble than we wanted to be in. When the mob arrived, a large pole was pushed through the front window of the restaurant and to protect ourselves we had to turn the large table on its side and get behind it.

Again, I was thankful that Peter was on my first trip as it was decided that the two of us go out onto the roof and make our way back to the Ganges River where we had left the Land Rover. As we came around a corner, we saw a large angry mob of Indian students approaching. We needed a miracle to get back to the vehicle.

Our situation was such that we had mud walls on either side of us and we did not know how we were going to avoid trouble. Then an amazing thing happened, some might call it a miracle. Right beside us, a badly painted dilapidated door opened, and without coming out the occupant feverishly beckoned for us to come through his door, which we did. Phew, that was close! Eventually we made our way back to the Land Rover by the Ganges and started to drive through the narrow streets towards the restaurant.

We soon caught up with the mob from which we had previously escaped. We had a decision to make. To pick up our team before the mob got to the restaurant, we had to get there before they did. To do that we would have to pass them. To do that we attempted to drive slowly and carefully right through the crowd which was more of a mob than a crowd. That wasn't working well and the longer we were in the mob, the more danger we faced. So, we chose another course of action. To help us we turned on the orange flashing lights and turned on the Maserati air horns, revved the engine and took off at speed. That option worked!

I do not remember what speed we managed to achieve, but thankfully, it was fast enough for all the mob to scatter and flatten themselves against the mud walls of the street to let us through. A thankful delivery to be sure! We got to the restaurant before the mob, collected the tea and drove away safely—no injuries to occupants or demonstrators! I do not remember praying about what to do; it all happened so quickly. But we were thankful for the way our return to the restaurant worked out so well!

Today, I know better. Whenever there is a demonstration, a mob, or an excited crowd, safety is in the opposite direction. It is never worth taking a risk to see "what it's all about."

A Country Like No Other

One of the delights of driving to India and Nepal, and there were many, was that we always drove through Afghanistan. Every trip was an adventure. Unfortunately, such an adventure could not be done today.

Afghanistan in the 1960s was very different than the war-torn Afghanistan we know of today. It was safer for Westerners and its majestic views and cultural heritage were a joy to experience. You also drive through Kabul. As you enter Afghanistan from the west the first significant town you come to, is Herat.

Here's a bit of a tangent—it was remarkable that the main road was one of the finest surfaces that I had ever driven on. I later found out that the Americans and the Soviets had completed it with their aid programs. I believe the Americans built the section of road in western Afghanistan from Herat to Kandahar in the south and the Soviets built the section of road from Kandahar in the south to Kabul the capital in the east. Such were the machinations of the Cold War.

The whole road made a giant u-shaped highway of the highest quality. We arrived in Herat on the western edge of Afghanistan late in the evening and we were all hungry, so we stopped at a mud hut-type building. We were enchanted with the little border town. The town appeared to be fifty years or more behind the times. There were people and horses, but not too many vehicles. I was hungry, but the cleanliness of the kitchen was a concern to me. Eventually, after thinking that a friendly egg would probably appear on my plate untouched by hands, I ordered four of them and an Afghan flat bread, along with a cup of tea without milk or sugar. I was so hungry after eating them that I ordered another four. It is a historical fact that for the first time ever in my life I sat down and ate twelve fried eggs for dinner that night! I can even brag that it happened in the town of Herat in Afghanistan.

Driving into the center of Kabul was always a memorable occasion. In 1966, there was one main restaurant, and it was a magnificent buffet-style restaurant. Every time we stopped in Kabul, that was where we ate. Three times on different trips we met Steve K. an American G.I. His father was working in Kabul with the Ford Foundation. There is no space on these pages for all the tangents with Steve—his stories are another book!

Upon arrival in Kabul, we would make our way to the British Consulate and camp outside the building and collect our mail. There was a house next to the compound owned by a hospitable Afghan who was an International pharmaceutical salesman. Once, all 12 of us were invited into his home for a meal. We all sat on the floor, with our shoes off but at a table where we stretched our legs out under the low-slung table. (I later met up with him by arrangement once in London.) The table had a heavy carpet-like fabric for a tablecloth. We all sat on the floor with our feet stretched out under the table. In the middle of the low-slung table there was a fire of hot ashes that warmed our feet. A little smoke arose through the hole above the fire. Talk about bragging of ordering a dozen eggs for dinner! With the variety of foods set out for our enjoyment I was able to eat two dozen roast potatoes. Of course, they were "ladies-sized" potatoes. They were oh so good!

Icebound in the Hindu Kush

From Kabul, we traveled north towards Mazar-e Sharif. In that area the mountains produce a valley so that there is not much sunshine that shines down on the frozen river in the valley. That being the case, it is easy to understand that the river could overflow the road and then freeze over on the road. We thought that we were driving on the ice. We were, but under the ice was the river and not the road! Sure enough, we found a thin spot and broke through the ice. It took us a week before we could dig it out and drive away.

As we looked at our Land Rover, stuck in the ice, we started to walk away and down the mountain. It was a week before we came back to the Land Rover. That night we stayed in the first mud hut that we came to. And yes, it was a long walk!

It was providential that we met the Afghan living next to the consulate in Kabul because later we came back to him, and he helped us with a letter from the Afghan Minister of Tourism to instruct the nearest military base to give us assistance to get the Land Rover out of the ice and on the road again.

Before we landed in the frozen river with the Land Rover, I remember it was bitterly cold as we drove north from Kabul. Finally, we arrived at a recommended lodging place. When we got there, we were aware that the menu might be sparse. Imagine how we felt when we were told that at 6:30 pm on a cold icy night that the chef had gone home, and the kitchen was closed. We offered to pay for the basic amount of food whatever they had. For some reason, the manager was most unhelpful and even a little hostile. Eventually we told him that if he did not provide a basic meal that we would go into the village, buy some eggs and potatoes, and come back and set fire to some old furniture from the hotel and cook it ourselves—not the best tourist manners!

On the way down the mountain and with our Land Rover set in ice, we settled for the first mud hut that we saw. We thought that we had ordered a modest meal of eggs, bread, and warm tea. However, after over an hour of waiting we went into the kitchen and gestured with our hands asking "where is the meal that we asked for? We have all the money that we need to pay you well. Where is the food?" It turns out that it appeared that they did not have enough food to feed four us. I think we each ended up with a small cup of warm tea and a small piece of Afghan flat bread—a minimal but welcome meal!

When we arrived back in Kabul, we met with our friend who lived next door to the Consulate. He introduced us to the Afghan Minister of Tourism, and he wrote a letter that we could present to the nearest army base to help us get the Land Rover back on the road. Steve, the American whose dad worked in Kabul for the Ford Foundation, gave me a couple of American parkas and head gear. As Brits we chuckled over the 13 instructions, on how to put on an American army hat, that were sowed into the hat.

We returned to the Land Rover via a truck with a barrel of oil along with a truck load of Afghans and their animals. We actually paid for the truck ride and the barrel of oil. A strange accident sent the barrel of oil rolling down the hill into welcome hands in a village below on a bend going up the mountain. Following that, I decided to collect all the money that had been collected from the now-filled-up truck of all the people who paid to share the ride up the mountain. All the money was held by one man who collected it all.

I asked him if I could see the money which he then produced. I then stuffed it all in my pocket and promptly "fell asleep." Yes, I kept it because we had already paid for the truck and the oil. As we went into the nearest Army base to where the Land Rover was stuck in the ice, we tried to find somebody we could show them the letter from the Minister of Tourism that asked them to help us.

Despite the powerful letter of introduction from the Afghan minister of Tourism, I could not get anybody to speak to me. Finally, I went into an office of the Army officer who looked like he was the commander of the base. He would not even look up and speak to me. I found a raw egg, and to get his attention, I cracked it open on his desk in front of him. He looked at me.

I handed him the letter and a few things began to happen. Peter was on this trip, and he fixed the punctured hydraulic brake pipe on a truck we were given. Initially it looked like we could not use the truck because of the punctured hydraulic break pipe. Thankfully, Peter was able to plug the hole and wrap the metal of a baked beans tin around the repair. There was no AAA service in Afghanistan!

What I did not realize is that the parka that Steve K. had given me in Kabul had "U.S. Army" embroidered on the chest and the nearest military base was a Soviet base. Sometimes I wonder why God keeps rescuing me from situations like this! More seriously, one thing this entire incident demonstrates and why it is worth recounting is that God cares for us even when our unusual or difficult circumstances are "self-inflicted."

When we finally got back to the Land Rover, the river around the two wheels had frozen solid so all we had to do was to dig a little and free the wheels from the ice. The key was put into the ignition and the Land Rover's engine started the first time. With that encouragement, we were able to drive back onto the ice-covered road. This was a great way to build a resume as a driver, but not one that I would recommend!

The Border between India and Nepal

The clarity of the atmosphere in Nepal was the finest that I have ever experienced. It was practically impossible to capture on film the clarity and the crisp freshness of the air and thus the sharpness of the images photographed, even with the best available Hasselblad camera. The heights and vastness of what one sees is remarkable. For the beauty of nature and God's creation, I think there is little that compares to watching a sunrise over Mt. Everest. What I experienced as I travelled in Nepal was stunning. It is a beautiful region of the world.

One of the most interesting experiences I remember having in Nepal, and particularly the capital of Katmandu, was made possible by my time earlier in Iran. (It really is a small world sometimes!)

While I was waiting for the completion of the servicing of the Land Rover in Tehran, I was walking around in the streets, and I bought a copy of *Time* magazine from a street vendor. There was a page-long article about the "Wild Boar Inn" in Katmandu and its owner.

His name was Boris and he was commonly known as Boris of Nepal. It mentioned that Boris was the first white Russian who entered Nepal. His desire was to build the "Wild Boar Inn," which he did. In those days, all the distinctive furniture for the interior of the inn had to be carried into Nepal on the back of elephants because there were no roads for any other form of transport to be practical. The last sentence of the article read as I recall, "If you are ever in Katmandu drop in. We would love to meet you."

I kept the article, and I eventually knocked on the large wooden front door of the Wild Boar Inn in Katmandu. I was warmly welcomed and was amazed at the atmosphere and the uniqueness of the interesting décor that made the Wild Boar Inn so distinctive. I enjoyed meeting Boris and told him why I knocked on his door. He invited me to stay for the evening meal which he went off to prepare. I do not recall what was on the menu, but it was different and delicious.

One of the other dinner guests was an English lady who I talked with while Boris was off in his kitchen. She told me that she had come out from England to arrange the details for the first production of the Cambridge Repertory Company's performance of a Shakspearian play. She had been sent to make all the necessary arrangements for the first performance of Shakespeare, in Nepal.

During dinner she invited me to attend the performance. I remember writing home to my folks on a postcard saying that the weather was beautiful and that I had been seated four rows behind the king of Nepal at a Shakespearian production. I think Mother thought that I was smoking something!

While walking around Katmandu I came across a community of Tibetan monks. Their leader asked me to take a roll of highly colored fabric to the Dalai Lama on my way home. The Dalai Lama was (and is) in religious and political exile in India. I do not recall what place along my route home that I met up with the man who served as the intermediary to whom I gave the fabric for presentation to the Dalai Lama. I transported the roll of fabric without thinking that it might be a problem. It wasn't and I never looked to see if I was carrying a roll of fabric with anything inside it. I do remember that the person to whom I gave it was ostentatiously thankful as if I had delivered a holy relic—perhaps I had!

10

A SEASON OF TRANSITION

Real Estate—The Second Time Around: 1968–1970

After my two years of traveling and driving, to India and Nepal, I vowed to myself that I would *never* go back to selling real estate. As I prayed to God to do what He wanted me to do, He directed me back to real estate and yes, Dennis Botting was gracious enough to take me back! After Stephen Botting's I went to work for a bigger and well-respected firm in the Brighton and Hove area, Eric Marchant's. During my time at Eric Marchant's, I bought a 4-story terraced house, for 1,500 English pounds. It's amazing to think of those prices in today's market!

In the basement there was a business tenant of long standing who paid rent. The house was 7 Market Street, Brighton, off Western Road. Western Road is the premier shopping street in Brighton. Looking back to that time it is hard to believe that I only paid 1,500 English pounds to own my first house. It had a great location. It was also only a few blocks from the famous Brighton beach and the sea front of the English Channel resort town. I was one of the first to paint the front of my house, and soon a few others in the street followed.

At the time I was a member of Park Hill Evangelical Free Church in Kemp Town, Brighton. Pastor Derek Fortnam and his wife Barbara were very faithful in the Lord's work. They trusted and believed the Bible. A group of well-established folks were in the congregation, and many students found a warm and solid example of how to live the Christian life. Reading Holy Scripture, practicing evangelism, and prayer were all encouraged as part of living a Christian life. We often had all-night prayer meetings. We sang praises to God and prayed. Being young, it seemed normal to go to the church we loved, to pray to the God we loved, who loved us so much, and to sing with our friends as a church.

The Toll House in Linfield

During one spell in real estate, before I bought my house in Brighton, I had a delightful period when I lived in the historic Toll House in Lindfield Sussex. My brother Peter shared the accommodation with a dedicated schoolteacher called Bill. The drive to Brighton each morning was delightful. At one point I thought I could enjoy working in real estate if I could have such a beautiful drive each day. The drive started in the heart of the Sussex County side in "stockbroker" country. I suppose it gave me the impression that I was a successful businessman with a sporty little British racing green MG.

I joined an MG car club and periodically we would meet in a country pub at different locations. I do not recall ever talking about cars, but I did enjoy driving around the English countryside to the different venues!

From the Lindfield house, I also recall washing my hair and going across the road to dry my hair under the exit heater of the local grocery store. Different and the price was right! Being too frugal? Probably.

One of my managers, a decent man but not a Christian man, was what I would call a "Hoover Salesman." By that I mean, that he could sell ice to an Eskimo standing in his own back yard. Whether the Eskimo wanted it or needed it. Bosses love the sales figures of folks like that. In my opinion he was a sales manager who still had things to learn about managing folks. He always seemed to leave you with the feeling that whatever your philosophy of selling was, using it, you never sold enough houses to satisfy what he wanted you to sell, to make the department he managed look good.

Often, I could observe that he would sell people an expensive house that they really did not want. Even with my inexperience I discerned that the client had been persuaded to buy what they really did not want. Then low and behold, back they came six months later time asking him to sell their property and help them buy what they now thought they wanted. He was driven by his sales figures. Well, to be fair that was what his job description entailed. I understood that, but I could not and would not operate that way. Often a competing agent would come in and ask to borrow a key to a house for sale and the manager would look at me and say, "That key is out isn't it, Paddy?" I would not know so I would go and look. Many times, I would find the key. Well, the competing agent took the key, and my manager would not look good.

Then, if the competing agent's client bought the house our company would only get 50% of the commission. I would then believe that we made a 50% commission. My manager would see it as we lost 50% of a future commission.

Eventually things came to a head between us. One afternoon, my manager asked me to stay after work. That evening I particularly wanted to get home promptly to watch what I would call an important European Soccer match. Well, for almost an hour I had to listen to my manager telling me in any number of ways that I just did not sell enough houses for him. In fact, I could not even get a word in edgeways. Finally, I asked if I could speak.

"Is it my turn to tell you what I think of you?"

"Yes, yes, yes."

"I have three things to say. 1. I don't trust you; 2. You don't tell the truth, and 3. You couldn't manage a sausage!" Well, you guessed it. I got home in time to see the game!

The next morning, I had to meet with the boss. He was a fine and a fare man and well respected in the town. He thanked me for being me but added that "I wish you also had the manager's sales figures. You understand that I must let you go?" "Yes, sir," I replied, and I thanked him for the work he had given me. I did not have the wisdom or confidence to ask if I was making enough money in my sales to pay my wages and the cost of being with the company. I had always assumed that I covered the cost of being there.

A year later, when I was home from travelling abroad, I dropped by the front office to say, "Hallo." I was welcomed warmly by the front office staff, and I will never forget what came out of the manager's mouth. He was not a Christian but what came out of his mouth were these words. "Paddy, you were not predestined to sell houses, were you?" We agreed on that. *Real estate was not for me*. Although while working in real estate I was able to buy a small, terraced Regency style 4-story house for 1,500 English pounds. It was also close to the office. If I had been able to keep it as an investment, it would be worth a fortune today.

At one point, I thought that there might be an opportunity for officer training in the British Army and that, perhaps, it would be a good fit—if the boot fits, wear it. However, after a weekend of field training and exposure to a variety of military activities and challenges, life in the military was not to be for me. In the good providence of God, He closed the door to me going into the British Army. While in school or shortly after school, some young people are fortunate to know exactly what they want to pursue as their life's work—or what God wants them to pursue. Others of us test the waters and try several things before we settle down. I was among the latter. Each has its benefits and each has its challenges. I believe however, that if we are honestly pursuing things that are in accordance with our interests, ideas, skills, and dreams—and we are doing so in a relationship with God and obedience to His Word, He will guide our steps "Show me the path where I should go, Lord; point out the right road for me to walk. Psalm 25:4" Knowing Who controls the future is more important than knowing the future.

11

STORMS OF EMOTION (1969–1970)

As we go through the seasons of life, each one of us experiences personal storms of emotion, health, family, vocation, relationships, and a score of other things. Some will be small spiritual squalls; others will be gale-force storms. We experience emotionally and spiritually what mariners warn of physically—rocks and shoals. It is during those storms that we come to appreciate fully the words of the psalmist: "Out of the depths I cry to you, O Lord!" (Psalm 130:8, ESV). Some of my storms came in 1969 and 1970—suddenly and unexpectedly.

One, not Two

The first happened while I was working in real estate in Brighton selling houses. It was with more thanks that I can express even now, that God and my older brother Peter, my only sibling was used by God to introduce me to the ministry of Dr. Francis and Edith Schaeffer at L'Abri Fellowship in Switzerland in the latter part of 1971 after my storms. I was a survivor of an emotional and spiritual shipwreck. (I grieve that there is nothing that is comparable to L'Abri for my children's generation, to experience God, like I did in my desperate time of need.) To this day, my time in the chalet of Udo and Debbie Middleman at Swiss L'Abri in Cheseires during the last 3 months before Christmas in 1971, with Udo & Debbie (Schaeffer), remains without equal, the most beautiful expression of Christianity that I have ever experienced. (More on that in a few pages.)

I do not want to spend a great deal of time on this difficult part of my story. It was so painful that I suppressed it and have limited memories that I can recall and not many that I understand.

While I was working in the Lanes of Brighton, I got to be very friendly with a young lady who I enjoyed being with. Over time, our friendship grew, and we decided to get married. I had a house, and I knew how to be a hard worker.

In 1969 we were married. Dad married us in St Peters-upon-Cornhill in London E.C.1. My wife was interestingly sociable and easy to be with. We enjoyed our new friendship. I was 25 years old. We took our honeymoon in Northern Ireland with accommodation provided by relatives on Mum's side.

After two or three weeks of marriage back in Brighton, my wife up and left and I have never seen her since. I never suspected foul play in her case. My speculation as to what happened is just that, speculation. I concluded that there are some people who are incapable of being able to commit to a close relationship that is required for a healthy marriage.

The verse that gave me immense comfort during those five long years was, Lamentations 3:35: "The Lord is good to those who wait for him, to the soul who seeks him." As I think of that verse, of how God was so comforting to me all those years of loneliness and waiting, I know and testify that God cares about us as individuals. He comforted me. He has blessed me more than I ever could have imagined. I can say through the hurt: "It was worth the wait!"

As painful as it was during those five years, God used that storm in my life for good. He revealed Himself to me as the personal God who exists and is knowable and who provides for His children. It is beautiful. He adopts new Christians into His family and *never* un-adopts them. *That is a real inheritance.* It is in fact an eternal inheritance. It is good for this life and the next life!

I learned that contentment in this life will never come from any of the things in this world. True contentment comes only from the Lord Jesus Christ, the only true and living God. God himself had to come from Heaven for that to happen here on Earth.

I remember one night crying myself to sleep remembering that God claimed to be a God of comfort. In my tears and anguish, I asked Him to comfort me and prove Himself. I recall that my prayer was clear and specific. I knew that God claimed to be a God of all comfort and a friend of sinners.

Imagine my amazement when a strange peace came upon me, and I was comforted! The good news out of this awful five-year experience was that I realized, for the first time in my life, that God really was all that He said he was. He could be trusted.

During those years, a few godly friends suggested I might think about having a Christian lady for a friend. I did not agree. It was easier to be faithful to my marriage vows until I was legally free of those vows.

After five years our paths never crossed, and I was legally enabled by the law in England to file for an uncontested divorce. The divorce was granted in 1974. I believe that is all I can write at this time about that very confusing, painful, and dark time. Yet even in the darkness, God was present. He was there for me, and He is and will be there for you as well.

Iron Sharpens Iron

During the storms of my life God has always blessed me with devout, kind, and godly friends to listen to me, to give me solace and strength, to pray for me and encourage me, and to give me physical and spiritual respite. In Proverbs 27:17, we read "As iron sharpens iron, so a person sharpens his friend" (NET).

Three couples are intertwined with my story throughout the decades and each person has a special place in my heart. The first couple I thank God for is Derek and Barbara Fortnam, Derek being my faithful pastor.

At this time in my story, in the good providence of God I was blessed to be worshipping at Park Hill Evangelical Free Church in Kemptown, Brighton. Pastor Derek Fortnam and Barbara became part of my life. Derek, as I write this page is still faithfully preaching the gospel at Park Hill Kemp town, Brighton, 58 years later.

The second couple is John and Val Eastwood, who took me into their family after I left (school) college and when I worked for Plumpton Motor Coach Company. To live in a Christian family without having to find an apartment where I could walk to work was a great providence. They also were exceedingly kind to me and understanding of my situation after college and my breakdown from which I was still healing. It was a great blessing for me to live with their family and not alone in an apartment! I was so thankful to have a great church, Park Hill Evangelical Free Church, at this time in my life.

It was at that church that God purposed for me to meet a unique and special person and couple—Laurie and Elvira Mckintosh. Laurie was a great a gift from God to be my godly mentor through this difficult time and teaching me by example, how to talk to people outside the church, about Jesus. Laurie is from Australia and Elvira is from Mexico. All six dear friends were in my prayers daily. Pastor Derek is 91. I phoned him recently.

Laurie came to England in the first wave of staff members of Campus Crusade for Christ (now Cru). He was the director of the work based in Brighton. Over the years, he had been a civil engineer, anthropologist, farmer, and translator with Wycliffe Bible Translators. He also had strong strands of theology and philosophy within him and all of those combined to make a passionate and interesting communicator.

I saw him primarily as a loving and compassionate evangelist. As the Brits would say, "Laurie was no dip stick!" He had a delightful and energetic love for talking to people about Jesus wherever he went. *One of the greatest blessings of my life was the Lord bringing Laurie and Elvira McIntosh into my life.*

Laurie was around 6 ft. 6" tall. He had a long black beard that made him look like a rabbi. He had an infectious smile that you had to notice.

Elvira was Mexican and so Laurie would often be wearing an orange blanket. All Laurie had to do to draw a crowd was to stop and hold up his hands. I heard one small child say, "Mummy, is that God?"

Laurie was the "ultimate Arminian Evangelist." He probably was until he died recently. His love for the lost wandering souls approached the compassion that I observed watching Dr. Francis Schaeffer talk to students.

During my time getting to know Laurie, Laurie's brother, Malcolm in Australia, was looking for a hired hand. His father Mr. Mac. and mother, sold their homestead, in New South Wales, Australia and moved up to 500 acres of dust just outside Bourke, New South Wales, on the edge of the outback. Mr. Mac was having health concerns and Malcolm was looking for somebody to step in and help with his innovative fresh ice-cold milk project. Malcom had irrigated 500 acres of dust form the nearby Darling River.

Restless and ready for an adventure, I decided I was the person Malcom was looking for to help with the dairy business and volunteered my services. A new adventure was about to begin!

Headed Down Under

When I left to go to Australia, Mum sold my Regency terraced house close to Brighton Beach for me. I think she must have sold my precious MG as well. The extra pain for Mum was that I think she knew that she would never see me again. She died while I was in Australia. She must have known that I wanted to get as far away from Brighton and all my pain, but she knew as I found out later, my pain went with me. She knew that as we said "goodbye," for what was to be the last time, but I didn't know that then.

Saying goodbye to Dad before leaving for Southampton docks to sail to Australia, Laurie came with me to see me off. However, God was still my heavenly father and although Mum and Dad could not come with me to Australia, He could and of course He was there to greet me and remind me that He was my heavenly Father. More later.

Three, not Four

As I wrote earlier in the book, my mother died at age 50 while I was in Bourke, Australia. Our family of my father, my mother, my brother, and me was now a family of three. It was the second great storm of these years.

In Australia I went into the post office once a week. There was always a delay in news. When I started making plans to go home for the funeral, the funeral had already happened. However, I was able to make a telephone call home on the morning of Mum's memorial service, so Dad was able to include that in the service. The loss of her to me, our, family, the church, and her community was enormous. Through God's grace we endured the grief and sorrow. Recently, I discovered a postcard from my Mum with a picture of Brighton Beach. "Hope you are enjoying your trip. We are all thinking of you. Thanks for your letters. Love from all of us at home. Mum & Pop and all." Decades later, memories of her and her love of life, family, friends, and God still comfort me.

12

"ONCE A JOLLY SWAGMAN," AUSTRALIA AND BACK (1970)

At the end of my time with Laurie and Elvira in Brighton I set off for Australia via the famous Southampton docks where I boarded the SS *Arcadia,* a ship launched in 1953 for the P&O Cruises line, bound for Sydney, Australia. I paid around 270 English pounds for a 4 and a half-week one-way trip to Sydney, Australia.

It was not until Laurie was walking back down the gang plank in Southampton that he told me who was meeting me in Sydney Harbor. "Look for Bob, he will be waiting for you in Sydney when your ship docks." I hollered back "Bob who? What does he look like? How will I recognize him?" Finally, the secret was revealed. As Laurie stepped off the gang plank, after saying goodbye and praying for me, he shouted at me. "You just can't miss Bob."

I was picturing thousands of folks meeting the ship waving and being covered in ticker tape. "Bob is a bald-headed Indian!" Sure, enough when I arrived in Sydney Harbor there were thousands of folks surrounded by ticker tape and there was Bob, amongst them. Just as Laurie had said, "A bald-headed Indian!" So, I shouted down, "Hallo Bob." Right away I could see him wave and thought I faintly heard him shout back, "Hallo Paddy!"

Southampton to Sydney

The trip from Southampton to Sydney was to take 4 and a half weeks. There were planned stops along the way in the Canary Islands, Tenerife, and Johannesburg, South Africa. Thanks to the ministry of Parkhill Evangelical Church, in Brighton, I was substantially in the healing process but there remained a deep hurt and grief in my heart. Being a child of God I also had a solid measure of peace with God that is expressed in Psalm 23. I knew and experienced God's presence and promises that God the Good Shepherd would *lead* me, *guide* me, and provide for me.

Having spent much time in the healing process with Laurie at Park Hill, it did not surprise me when I realized that I would have a captive audience for four and a half weeks to talk to people about Jesus on board the SS *Arcadia*. I was given permission by the captain to hold a Christian meeting on board the ship. The first evening some 25 folks showed up expressing a desire to be part of such a group. When I announced that we would meet for fellowship, Bible reading, prayer, encouragement, and witnessing, our confined congregation's numbers changed dramatically to 4 or 5 folks! Each Sunday on board the ship, the captain held a brief traditional worship service, for which I was thankful. Worship services held on ships, whether commercial or military, are known as "Divine Services" and have a long, unique, and honored place in maritime history.

During one of our meetings, we witnessed a burial at sea, seeing a flag-draped coffin go over the side of the ship from our meeting room. Later in the cruise I approached a lady looking over the side of the ship and opened my conversation with something like, "beautiful view, isn't it?" Unfortunately, the lady was trying to deal in her own strength with the memory of her husband dying on a previous cruise and being buried at sea, his body in a flag-draped coffin, going over the side. The Lord was faithful, even though I do not remember any of the conversations that followed.

That brief conversation is a good reminder and illustration that in God's providence, even a brief conversation or a passing few words can be important as we interact with others. Your next conversation may be a salvation seed being planted in the life of someone for whom Christ died. Our words matter!

Each dining table in the elegant dining hall on SS *Arcadia* seated 10 people. We were the same 10 people at each meal. It was requested and assumed that at every meal we would be appropriately dressed. We all dressed for dinner. We certainly had enough time to dress appropriately for each meal. There were three such meals each day and memorably there were 10 courses for each formal meal. Dinning was a grand ordeal.

For the first 10 days of the 4-and-a-half-week cruise I faithfully fulfilled my culinary responsibility. That not being my usual eating habit, I chose to take a break from some formal meals. Then, after a while, I realized that I would likely never have this opportunity again, so I faithfully returned to the formal meals with thankfulness. One of the young ladies on my table was the secretary to the architect of the Sydney Opera House who regularly traveled from England to Sydney. There were some great table conversations!

Welcome to Australia!

In addition to Bob, who I mentioned above, when I stepped off the gangplank in Sydney, God had arranged for two bikers to be at the bottom of the ramp. For most of us, that would be an unusual welcome anywhere in the world! The first thing that I focused on in Sydney, was a laminated Bible verse hanging from the handlebars of one of the men's huge motorcycle. It was, "Have I not commanded you? Be strong and courageous. Do not be afraid; do not be discouraged, for the Lord your God will be with you wherever you go" (Joshua 1:9).

This verse was a needed and timely reminder. My heavenly Father was there with me.

As I stepped off the ship, it hit me that I was miles away from home, I was still hurting badly and grieving strongly, and the only person I was about to know humanly speaking was Bob. That is why that verse was so powerful then and why it is still so meaningful today. I often sign my e-mails, "Firmly in His grip, Paddy, Josh. 1:9."

God's provision for work in the Australian bush came as a welcome "valve" for my agonizing pain and grief. If you are born in Europe or England, going to Australia appears to be going to the end of the Earth. At the time I think I was also looking to "get as far away" from my deep agonizing pain and hurt. I knew that running away to Australia, I could never run far enough away to escape my pain, yet in my weaker moments I was going to try! I didn't, but should have remembered Psalm 139:7 "Where shall I go from your Spirit? Or where shall I flee from your presence?" I wasn't trying to flee God; I was trying to flee my pain. In so doing, I forgot that God would be with me in my pain—regardless of my location or my circumstances. That is a thought that can bring comfort to anyone, anywhere, anytime.

First Stop, Maroubra!

I was not to be staying with my new friend, Bob. He introduced me to a Charismatic Christian family to stay with who lived a few miles south in Maroubra for 3 weeks before catching the train up to Bourke in New South Wales. I had arrived at Christmastime, and spending Christmas Day on Bondi Beach was different! Christmas dinner on a sun-drenched beach took some processing. Cooling off from the scorching heat from the Australian sun by swimming in the ocean was no problem. That was a delight. Eating Christmas pudding, an English tradition at Christmas, in the sunshine was different!

My host was zealously active in the Charismatic and 'Healing' lifestyle. He told me he thought that God was calling him into the healing ministry. Because we seemed to go to charismatic meetings every night, I wondered if he might be trying to get fired from his job so that he could take that as a sign that God was calling him into a full-time ministry.

The first evening in his home he asked me if I had anything that I needed healing. I thought of an old soccer injury on one of my knees. So, I said sure. It was an odd atmosphere in his living room as a couple of black cats kept darting around the room. I have no interest in cats. After his prayer he asked me how it was. Fine, I thought. Well, in the morning I had to tell him that I had given him the wrong leg!

On another occasion we were at an evening meeting, and the person at the podium was claiming that he had the gift of healing. His line was that "if you have the faith, I have the gift of healing, so with my gift and your faith, come up and be healed."

After urgent appeals for folks to come forward to be healed nobody moved. There was a man behind me who only had one eye. Admittedly it was not in the middle of his head it was in the correct position, so it did not have to be moved, it just had to be healed. So, I asked him, "Why don't you go up and get healed?" The man sadly confessed that he did not have enough faith.

Again, because nobody took up the offer to go up to be healed, it was announced that as a friend, if you had faith, you could stand in for a friend. So, I turned around and asked the one-eyed man, "Would you like me to go up and stand in for you? I have the faith." He said that would be fine with him, so I set off up the aisle in front of a crowd of around 500 folks.

When I approached the speaker, he asked me what it was that needed to be healed. I told him I was fine but the man behind me only has one eye, and you said I could stand in for him. "You have the gift; I have the faith!" Well, I made my first known error in Australia. When he said quietly under his breath, almost like a practiced ventriloquist, so that only the two of us heard, that he could not do it, I returned to my seat. I think what I should have done is take his microphone and repeated my question. "You have the gift, and I have the faith, could you please heal my friend's eyesight?" I hesitated and did not have the courage, so I lamely walked back to my seat. If I were in a similar situation today, I certainly would not have walked away! This time in Maroubra was the first time in my life I had ever been with Charismatics. I grew up as an Anglican choirboy!

At an inter-church service in Brighton years ago the evangelist claimed to have similar gifts to those mentioned above. He repeatedly called for folks to come forward to "decide for Christ." For a significant length of time nobody moved. We had all been instructed to keep our eyes shut. Not me! I kept my eyes open to observe what happened. Eventually a man walked awkwardly up the center isle showing body language that he needed to make it to the bathroom. When he turned right to walk out of the room the evangelist called after him admonishing him from tuning away from Christ. Ugh!

Traveling North by Train to Bourke, New South Wales

Riding the train is usually restful and soon it was a part of a new adventure in my story. The 500-mile train ride was uneventful and pleasant as I watched the new countryside speed by. The train was so ancient that it never occurred to me that it had air conditioning so when I got off the train in Bourke, I nearly fell over with the onslaught of heat that hit me standing on the platform. It must have been around 110° F. Welcome to your new home!

I was enjoying the adventure of my current journey as we drove along the dusty dirt road on the way out of town to "Lodebar Dairy." Laurie's brother, Malcom, was educated as an agriculturist. His folks had sold their place down south in New South Wales and had purchased 500 acres of dust adjoining the Darling River. There is only one reference in the Bible to "Lodebar" (2 Samuel 9:5, "Lo-debar"). It means in Hebrew, "a place of no pasture." Since the Mac's bought 500 acres of dust a few miles outside Bourke, it was an obvious name for their new home!

Becoming a Milkman in the Bush

Bourke, New South Wales, has a population of about 2,000, is considered to represent the edge of the settled agricultural districts and the gateway to the

Outback that lies north and west of the town. This is reflected in a traditional east coast Australian expression "back o' Bourke," referring to the Outback. The Outback is the vast, remote interior in Australia. "The Outback" is more remote than those areas named "the bush," by which Australians mean any location outside of an urban area—that's most of Australia!

One reason for the Macs moving up north to Bourke was so that they could minister the good news of the gospel to the Aborigines on the local reserve. Sunday afternoon was taken up with entertaining all the local children who managed to clamber on the back of Mr. Mac's flat-bed truck before leaving Bourke after their brethren worship service. At "Lodebar," Mrs. Mac taught them a Sunday School lesson and then followed a supervised swim in the nearby Darling River.

Sunday evening was always embarrassing to me as Mr. Mac drove down to the Aboriginal reserve and "Hollered" at the folks on the reserve with a loudspeaker standing on top of the back of his flat-bed truck. I never saw any Aborigines come out of their tents. I assumed that they were either out, preoccupied, asleep, or not interested. Mr. Mac was not what I called a sensitive evangelist. The only way I could get him to stop hounding me around the kitchen table was to read my Bible. I read my Bible all the way through twice while I was with them at Lodebar Dairy. That part was, of course, a blessing.

It was challenging out there. The main family living area of the "Lodebar Estate" was a corrugated iron structure with a concrete floor, with a single air conditioner unit hanging from a window. The size of the structure was about 15 ft. x 12 ft. We had a table in the middle with 4 chairs, a two-ring gas fired stove top, a bookcase, and a kitchen cabinet, and that was it.

Malcom lived in an upturned water-tank. The Macs lived in a small caravan without wheels. I had a metal bed and a tin trunk for my belongings. I had a tent that did not reach the ground and a rusty scaffold pole with one end resting in a fork of a tree. When a snake killed one of the cows, I had corrugated sheets fitted on the ground and above the bottom of the hanging tent.

Each morning, I had tea, a friend egg and toast. For lunch it was often lamb. Mrs. Mac had a small patch of manicured lawn. In one corner of it there was the bathroom which was an upturned water tank with no ceiling. An upturned water tank housed the shower. Hot water came via an outside Gigee wood fire (Gigee wood is very susceptible to fire). To shut off the hot water, you had to go outside and kick out the fire—but at least there *was* hot water!

In that part of the world the living accommodations are modest as the land must produce a living before money can be invested in the home on the property. They took to heart Proverbs 24:7 and 24:27: "Prepare your work outside; get everything ready for yourself in the field, and after that build your house" (ESV) and "Develop your business first before building your house."

Before I arrived in Bourke there had been no significant rain for 7 years. That is a dry spell indeed! In Bourke, hats are sold that have strings with corks hanging around the brim. When people ask what the corks on strings are for, the local response is, "They are there to keep the flies and mosquitos away." Whether or not it works is a matter of opinion.

The property of Lodebar Dairy was originally 500 acres of dust. Ingeniously the Macs had irrigated their land from the Darling River. Malcom amazed the locals by getting three crops of lush green grass when others only managed two.

The milking shed was the finest building on the property in keeping with the land having to produce before spending money on personal accommodation. It was a block building with a concrete floor and a corrugated tin roof. Since the milk prior to the Macs coming to Bourke was put on the train in Dubbo, 200 miles south, and sour by the time it arrived in Bourke, it was no surprise that when Malcom started offering fresh ice cold non-pasteurized milk to the 2,000 folks of Bourke, he did a roaring trade.

My job after breakfast was to work in the dairy, carton up the ice-cold milk and pack the waxed cardboard cartons into cardboard boxes to be placed under a tarpaulin on my milk truck. Then, after lunch, I delivered the milk throughout the town, and it arrived cold. The folks were delighted.

Each Saturday night I would take a milk churn full of beautiful cold milk to the only soda bar in town. In the process I got addicted to a large glass of crushed ice saturated pineapple juice each week. There was nothing else to spend my money on in town.

When I drove home from my milk round in Bourke, when we did have rain, I would leave the tarmac road and go onto the property. I had to make sure that I put the truck into the ruts on the soft sandy ground and drive slowly making sure to take my hands off the steering wheel and let the ruts get me safely home.

One Sunday I walked home from Bourke to Lodebar Dairy. Mr. Mac was a fascinating character, but his theology was flawed in several areas. The little Brethren Fellowship only had 5 members. Mr. and Mrs. Mac, Malcom and one local Aboriginal couple. I went into church with them but on the Sunday that they had The Lord's Supper Mr. Mac was overly concerned that I was coming to church that Sunday. He told me that it would not be possible for me to join them for the Lord's Super (that is a brethren practice of "closed Communion"). I told him I was coming to church anyway. To cut a long story short, I decided that rather than 'fight it out' I would walk home. However, I told him that if any of the locals asked why I was walking home I planned to tell them. Nobody asked me.

It was so hot that after a few miles I passed a neighbor's property, who had an orange farm that produced rows and rows of orange trees. I planned to "steal" an orange and then on the way into Bourke the next day, as I drove into town for my milk delivery round, I was planning to drop by and confess my sin and ask what the farmer thought I should do now that I had told him.

For some reason I was not able to take an orange. When the Mac's got home I told them, and they told me that "If you had taken an orange and the farmer had seen you, you would have walked home with a bullet in your leg!"

My time in Australia was filled with new experiences. I had never ridden a motorcycle but one day Malcom asked me to go and find the cows on the motorcycle. I was impressed with my performance. I never fell off, but I also never found the sheep! On another occasion, one morning, Malcom asked me to milk a cow. What he did not tell me was that a cow with mastitis produces blue milk. When I tried to milk the cow, it produced blue milk. Obviously, I did not receive the cow-milking gift in Australia!

Aussie Hospitality

There were a couple of American families who came out to Bourke together—the Busters and the Boons. They grew cotton and did very well at it. The Busters had a biplane on their property to use because the area was so large. It was always fun to go to a barbeque at their home. A healthy bush fire was built with a large quarter inch steel plate placed on top of the fire and large steaks and good things were just thrown onto the hot metal slab.

Once, after the wedding of a young couple in the church, along with the Buster's and the Boon's fellowship in Bourke, I saw Australian hospitality at work. The first day of their honeymoon, one of the church members tapped gingerly on their front door, later after an interval another person arrived to wish the young couple well. Then another, and then a few more. The young couple hosted over 100 thirsty church members for tea!

As a bit of an aside, but an important one, I have observed and been the recipient of gracious hospitality in many cultures and many countries—and often from complete strangers.

I have received nourishment, rest, shelter, assistance, companionship, and been treated as a friend or family member by people who shared from their abundance, and who shared from their scarcity. I have been honored and humbled more times than I can count. There are many verses in the

Bible that speak of hospitality, and it is a virtue and a way of honoring God. I think especially of Hebrews 13:2: "Do not neglect to show hospitality to strangers, for thereby some have entertained angels unawares" (ESV). How different at times might we have acted or reacted if we knew that we were speaking with an angel?

Laurie and Elvira eventually arrived home in Australia and came to live in Bourke. I was thinking they would be there 6 months after I arrived, but instead, they arrived the day I was leaving Australia. I was in Sydney waiting to leave when they showed up. I was hiding behind the door to give Laurie a surprise. I should have known better as it was around 25 minutes that he took to talk to the taxi driver about his eternal home, i.e., where he was planning to live in the next life. (In one sense it is a lot easier deciding where you are going to live in the next life as unlike earth with all the countries, cities, and different addresses, the next life there are only two addresses from which to choose!) It was wonderful and an encouragement and blessing to see them, but I was only able to say two things—"Hello!" and "Goodbye!"

Australia was good work and a good experience. I learned a lot and I saw the hard work of others and the pride that comes from such work. The Aussies are wonderful people who have unique history that has shaped the nation and the people with great pride—and rightly so.

Homeward Bound

Laurie and Elvira came to see me off at the airport in Sydney. I flew from Sydney to Gatwick Airport in England with a stopover in Adelaide, Australia to pick up some passengers, and then on to an overnight stop, in Singapore. Laurie prayed for me and my trip home. I was the last one on the plane, not because of the prayer, but because I had forgotten to collect some paperwork!

When I sat in my seat on the plane (the dreaded "middle seat"), I was next to an insurance agent in the aisle seat, and an Englishman, in the window seat, who I learned later lived 10 minutes away from where I lived back home. When we were up in the air I started to talk to the man in the aisle, seat.

I asked him what he did for a living. He told me that he was an insurance agent. When I asked him what his territory was, he told me his "patch" was the Southern Hemisphere! In that era, when many people selling insurance were doing it door-to-door, that was *some* territory!

I looked at him and asked him why, if his territory was the Southern Hemisphere, was he travelling coach and sitting next to me, and not in first class. He told me that he loved his family and with all the savings that he accumulated by travelling coach he created a holiday travel fund.

I was prompted to say, "Well, if you love your family, what have you told them about Jesus?" He told me that he had sent his daughter to see the Roman Catholic priest I playfully took hold of his shirt collar, like Laurie used to do, and said, "I thought you said you loved your family!" He replied, "I do love my family." So, I said, "If you love your family how do you know that the priest is going to tell your daughter the truth? As a father, it is your responsibility, to know the truth, so you can check out the priest! The subject had been raised and an encouraging conversation continued for a couple of hours.

When the plane had a brief stop in Adelaide, he was received on the tarmac by a line of 8 smartly dressed businessman lined up to be introduced to him. We had planned to talk some more but he had warned me that it might not be possible as he may have to meet some folks.

Later my insurance agent friend asked if I would carry my duty-free allowance of cigarettes through customs and deliver it to his hotel. I said, "Sure." I was thinking it may be another opportunity for a cup of tea and a conversation with him and maybe others. As it turned out, I was able to give him my cigarette allowance, so I did not need to go to his hotel.

After about half an hour break in conversation, I turned to my window seat traveler and before I could say a word, he already had fingers in his ears shaking his head he said, "I don't want to have a conversation with you! I don't want to talk about what you were talking about!" I told him that I would respect his desire.

After a reasonable amount of time, I was unsettled in my soul and was prompted to say, "Do you mind if I ask you a question?" He was OK with that. So, I went ahead: "Why don't you want to talk about it?" Instead of talking for two hours *he talked* for nearly three hours. That was an even more interesting conversation!

Family, Early Years, and Ministry Beginnings

Paddy with Mum, Dad, and Older Brother, Peter

Sailing on the Norfolk Broads as a Youth

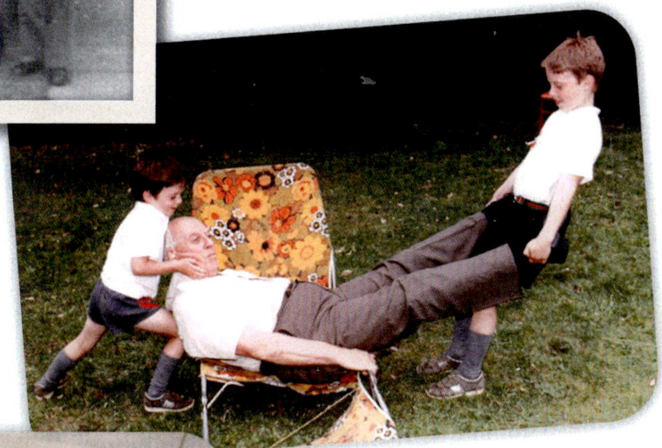

Grandsons Stephen and Andrew Playing with "Pop Cook"

Summer Days of Camping and Sailing

Peter (18) and I (16) Drove to Nice, France in Search of Adventure

Paddy's Prank Handshake with Clifford Musgrave

Early Morning View of the Sun Rising Over Mt. Everest

On the Border Between India and Nepal, 1965

My 1953 MG TD that I bought for 200 pounds.

The Toll House in Linfield, Sussex—
My First Rental Apartment

Frozen in a river in the Hindu Kush,
Afghanistan—it was a long week!

Paddy, the Milk Delivery Man in New South Wales, Australia.

Paddy's College Surveying Class

Necessary Dip in the Nile

Snow-Covered Mt. Ararat

Tibetan Monk in Nepal

Francis Schaeffer at Swiss L'Abri in 1971, Húemoz, Switzerland. He was a spiritual lifeline for me.

Edith Schaeffer and Companion, 2005

Korky—God's providence in my life.

Laurie McIntosh—he taught me how to evangelize.

The Early Years Together
1979 in Grand Cayman Island

Pastor Derek Fortnam

John Eastwood—A great blessing to me through the years.

Dad's London Church,
St Peter-upon Cornill

Dad with Margaret Thatcher

Mum and Dad, in a photo I took at the front door of our home in 24 Denmark Villas, Hove. Sussex. England.

My Brother Peter on the Queen Mary off to Brandeis University

Elizabeth (Betty) Ferguson Cook. Died Aged 50, 11th February, 1971.

Paddy Rowing Sheila on Lake Manitou

A Younger Sheila
(Drawn by Matthew Cook)

Paddy & Sheila's Wedding Day in St. Louis in 1975.

A traditional Grand Cayman house. In the U.K. we cut the grass. In Grand Cayman they rake the sand!

Seven Mile Beach on Grand Cayman Island

13

SINGAPORE STOPOVER

This episode in my travels was part of the return trip from Australia, but it deserves its own chapter. Singapore of the 21st century is very different than Singapore of more than half a century ago. Today, officially The Republic of Singapore, a city state and island nation, is a magnificent international city that rivals and exceeds any and many other cities around the globe. It is truly an amazing place. In the era of the 1970s, it was a stopover location for many travelers because long-distance flights were not as they are today. The capabilities were different—and the city was different!

When I was established in my hotel in Singapore, with free coupons for my stay, my dinner and breakfast, I decided that I wanted to go for a short walk. I put on my only brown summer suit and was enjoying the clean cool air outside my luxury hotel. As I looked out on my surroundings, I saw an incredibly clean and attractive part of town (as it all is today). So much so, I was prompted to pray that God would not lead me into temptation from which He would not deliver me. It was and is as basic as, "Lord, when I have the opportunity to sin, don't let me have the inclination; and when I have the inclination to sin, don't give me the opportunity."

No one in Singapore knew me and no one in Singapore cared about what I might or might not do during my night out. Nobody I knew would know what I did, or that I was a Christian and that my dad was a prominent Anglican clergyman—except, of course, God! As I considered the situation I was in, it occurred to me that whatever I did I was well prayed for before I left Sydney and I knew that when I got back to my church in

Park Hill, Brighton they would want to know who I talked to on my trip home. So, I asked God to use me as He had purposed to use me.

As I stood on the sidewalk in front of my hotel in Singapore, my thoughts turned to a story my dad told me about a close friend of his, who was an English Bishop. He had been known to minister in the red-light district in Soho, London. He would purpose to spend some time occasionally to reach out to prostitutes and plan to talk to them about the beauty of Jesus who came to save us from our sins. When the prostitute wanted to begin plying her trade, he told her that he always insisted that before he did anything of significance, he had a cup of tea. As tea was being made, he began to ply his trade of evangelism!

I confess, I thought that whatever God had purposed for my evening in Singapore, he would be faithful and provide a way out if I found myself needing and wanting one. I was at peace in Singapore. God's Word teaches us that God will never cause us to sin. In every situation, he will provide a way out. There will be a way that he will provide that we can go so we do not have to sin. I mention this as I was aware of the temptations that were in even such a pleasant and clean place as Singapore.

What happened next is hard to believe. I was a clean, well-dressed tourist outside an expensive hotel courtesy of Swiss Air with a coupon for dinner at the hotel and a coupon for breakfast. However, I did not have a cent on me! I may have looked like a "well-heeled" businessman, but I wasn't one!

A taxi driver pulled up to the curb and said, "You like nice clean girls Mister, you get massage?" I do not know what possessed me, well I do, it was the Holy Spirit who had possessed me. What I said was, "I do like nice clean girls, and I'll give them the message." He seemed pleased with what I answered and offered me a ride. Analyzing the conversation later I could not believe I said what I said. That often happens to me. I am talking to someone, and I say something I have never said before. Sometimes the conversation goes on for so long that I am afraid I will not remember the good lines that I was given!

My taxi driver drove me through the city and finally pulled up at the curb. I was still at peace. We went into a building that I soon discovered was a brothel. I was introduced to an attractive young lady. We sat down in a nice room. It was then that I was taken off guard! Her first words were, "How long do you want?" I was enabled to quickly scramble my words."Oh, I don't think you understand. I've come here to tell you about Jesus to give you a message!" That was not what she wanted to hear, and I was quickly dispatched! Well, there were 5 or 7 such "ladies that I then was introduced to and each time I explained that I had come to talk to them about Jesus and give them the message.

Eventually, the manager came to me to ask why none of his pretty ladies were good enough for me. I told him that his taxi driver friend had asked me if I liked nice clean girls. I told him that is exactly what I like, nice clean girls—but these were not that. I do not remember what he said next, but it was clear that it was time to leave. As I got back into the taxi, I thanked God that he had watched over me, and I had not been 'rolled' two floors below ground. I confronted the taxi driver again and told him that I like nice, clean girls. I guess he took that to mean he needed to take me to another place where "nice clean girls" could be found.

The next situation was an entire floor of a high-rise building somewhere in Singapore. He left me in the room as he went over to the bar in the middle of the room where a crowd of what he thought were nice clean girls were standing. After a few minutes they all turned around and looked in my direction and started to laugh. I have a good sense of humor and like a joke, so I went over to the group and asked what the joke was. I am not sure, but I think I may have been the joke. I never found out. The driver whisked me out of there also.

The only thing that made me feel bad was that I did not have any money to pay the taxi driver. I did not think it was part of the service of the hotel to provide the taxi for me although it did cross my mind.

As I said goodbye to the taxi driver, I pressed him again and said, "you told me, they were nice clean girls. They were not. They were dirty girls! I am not going to pay you." Well, I could not pay him. I was not going to give him either of my meal coupons. On reflection it would have been better if I could have paid him. That way I could have used the opportunity to talk at length to him. I did not own a credit card then.

In the first situation I did offer to take the girls out of the brothel across the road to the American embassy but none of them took me up on my offer. A couple came close, but they were scared. They were afraid that they were not allowed to leave. That was the *first* reason that they gave for not coming. The *second* reason was that they needed the money to send home to their family in another country. That is very common. Girls and young women are enticed to a country with the promise of good employment. However, once there, they are forced into prostitution. The saddest was the *third* reason. They said they were looking for a husband. When I arrived home in Brighton from Australia, I knew that my church would want to have news of my time there and the trip home. I reported—even the sad circumstances during the Singapore stopover.

Why tell this story? It wasn't the first or last time that I was in the same or a similar situation. It is common in many parts of the world. The circumstances of the prostitutes and the plying of "the oldest profession" is well-known and sadly, repeated in cities around the globe too many times to count every day and every night. Prostitution and all that goes with it, human trafficking, substance abuse, physical abuse, and even slavery are horrible—but very real. And every person involved in these activities, willingly or unwillingly, is a person for whom Jesus died.

It was wonderful to finally land back in England. I was home and back in my home church Park Hill Evangelical Free Church, Brighton. It was so good to be back at Park Hill again. They asked me to tell them some of what happened on the way home and of course I relayed what had happened, while also giving current news of Laurie and Elvira. God had been at work in my life as well as in the lives of others and there was much to tell and much to hear. The earlier storms of emotion were subsiding and there was a season of growth commencing.

— 14 —

BEACH EVANGELISM AND ARREST

Returning from Australia, for three months I could afford to read and study in the morning and in the afternoon, I went out and about and found people to talk to about Jesus. My pleasant lifestyle was made possible because in Bourke, I had nothing to spend my money on. That is except for my ice-cold pineapple crush each Saturday evening. (I did buy a rugged pair of Australian bush shorts that lasted for years).

Preaching and Arrest

Brighton is a famous seaside resort in England. It is the sight of the Royal Pavilion, but also like many seaside areas where tourists go for sun and swimming, it attracts a wide array of people. Over the decades and more than two centuries, Brighton has had a famous, but checkered history. (It was there in the late 18th century that the Prince Regent (later King George IV) brought his mistress Maria Fitzherbert.) Brighton is also the 1930s setting for Graham Greene's famous murder novel *Brighton Rock* (1938). When Britons think of a day or a week at the beach, it is often Brighton that forms the images.

One memorable day, I went down to Brighton Beach with my friend Jim. He had become a Christian and previously, had been living on the beach. It was the day before my brother Peter's wedding to marry Nancy Nordquist. She was from Minneapolis and had met at Swiss L'Abri.

Jim and I decided to go down to the part of the beach that Jim had recently left, where he was known. Jim was the kind of guy who even on a crowded bus with him in the front of the bus and me at the back, both of us standing, shouted out, "Hey Paddy, you think these people know anything about Jesus?" He was not an introvert! In the circumstances, I quickly told Jim that the next stop was ours and that he should make his way past everybody else standing at the back of the bus so that we could get off!

Once on the promenade at Brighton Beach, I went up to a man eating his lunch on the promenade and asked him, "Do you mind if I ask you how long you will need to finish your lunch?" He seemed pleasant but surprised by my question. "Why are you asking me that question?" I told him that when he had finished his lunch I was planning to stand right where he was as it was an ideal place for me to preach to the passing crowds.

There was a plethora of ideal acoustical aids in the immediate architecture of where we were. There was a tunnel, a three-tiered promenade with railings to lean on, along with a brick wall from which to bounce the sound of my voice. I give this background to mention another instance of God's care of me. At this point, I had not been to seminary; but I had been attending Park Hill Evangelical Church in Kemp Town, Brighton.

I went with Jim, a friend from church, down to Brighton Beach. The police allowed the hippies to openly congregate on this beach. It saved the police time when the police needed to pick them up. I was later told. Jim became a Christian and had previously been one of the hippies on the beach. He had cut his hair and bought a suit from the Brighton Railway Lost Property. (Remember, this was the early 1970s!) Jim wanted to return to the beach to give his testimony.

After the man finished his lunch, I began to speak, where he had been standing. I sang scripture verses and played my 12-string Gibson guitar. Then Jim would give part of his testimony. The whole event lasted close to three hours. At times there appeared to be around 400 bystanders.

I presumed they were holidaymakers walking along the promenade in Brighton who were watching other holidaymakers doing the same.

Several incidents from that day stand out particularly. The first was when a man came up behind me as I was speaking and told me to move on as I was standing on his drug patch where he did his drug transactions. He was wearing the type of shirt that the Italian gondoliers in Venice wear. For a reason known only to God, I spoke up to the crowd and said, "There is a man behind me in a blue and white gondolier's shirt with a knife in my back telling me that this is his drug patch." As I turned around, he was running off along the promenade.

The second incident was that in the process of speaking so much, I suddenly lost my voice. A man from the crowd approached me and offered me a drink from an open Pepsi can. Without thinking about how silly I was accepting the drink from a stranger. I took a sip, and my voice returned. Do not ask any questions because I do not have any answers about the event.

Then something else unexpected happened. A lady had for some time been quoting the Lord's Prayer to the crowd while she continued encircling Jim and me. I could not understand a word of what she had been saying. If it was a satanic hex that she was attempting to put on us, it did not work. I had never had anything like this happen to me, so I just vowed that I would not go home before she did.

I speculate that what happened next was that in frustration, she called the police and filed a complaint. If not her, perhaps someone else did because an officer approached me and told me to move on. We talked for a moment, and I told him that I was aware of the local law concerning street preachers. It was my clear understanding that obstruction was caused only when a preacher's crowd would not let a couple comfortably walk through the crowd arm in arm, so I carried on saying we could talk later but I thought everything was in order, legally.

Minutes passed, then two or three police cars came screeching to a halt. The next thing I knew was that a policeman came up to me and put what I now know to be a "chokehold" on me. I subsequently learned that the idea of a chokehold was to put pressure on my Adam's apple and both carotid arteries on my neck. Doing so prevents air and blood from passing through the neck. They knew what they were doing—it worked! I say that because for the first time in my life I was unable to breathe and was surprised how my body reacted. In an instant I was free, and the policeman was on the ground.

I still do not know how I was free, and the policeman was on his back on the promenade, with me standing over him, free and un-harmed. I quickly stood and put my hands on my head. This is what I think happened. I had learned some basic moves at a judo class in Brighton as a teenager. I was never awarded a higher belt than the white belt I was given to tie my judo jacket around me. However, I have always remembered two things that have stood me in good stead in life. First, that if your attacker is off balance, you can push him over while he is off balance. Second, when you fall, if you tuck your chin to your chest as you fall your head does not flop back and hit itself on the ground. Looking down at my "attacking" policeman, I put my hands on my head and waited for what came next. Next for me was the policeman putting me on the ground and kneeing me in the stomach. I remember telling him that if he was trying to make me swear, I do not do that! I think the fact that I was able to free myself so quickly was a good providence. It was also good for my health, because I was breathing fresh sea air on Brighton Beach!

Jim was standing by and said, "'ere, what are you doing with my friend. I believe the same as he does?" Jim managed to pass my guitar to someone before he was hustled into the police car as well. I know one thing for sure—that night the policeman and I were both sore. The difference was, he went home, and we went to jail! That may be one of the few things I have in common with the Apostle Paul; we both went to jail for preaching the gospel!

On the way to the police station in the police car, the policeman tried to mess with my mind with questions:

"How old are you? When were you born? What is your birthday? That does not add up!"

"Yes, it does" I replied.

"Where do you live? There is no such address!"

"Yes, there is. Hove Woolworths is at the bottom of my road and Hove Railway Station is at the top of my street and your police station is right behind my house!"

In my cell I had taken the trouble to take my shirt off as it was clean and pressed. Even though I had been on the ground wearing it, I did not want to sleep in it and appeared disheveled the next morning in court!

In the morning, as Jim and I were being led up the stairs to our court appearance, the same policeman kept questioning me:

"What are you going to plead?"

"I don't know I've never done this before but if you are going to be in court, you'll know then."

He did not like that answer and asked again. I told him I did not know what was going to happen.

When the judge opened the hearing, the policeman stood up. I still remember the policeman's name and number. We were shocked as he started to lie and said we were out of control and used bad language. Both Jim and I, without coordinating our movements, could not believe he could lie, in court to a judge. We both stared at him. It was still in a culture that when we both stared at him, he turned as red as a beetroot.

The judge quickly had us stand up before him and said, "I do have to charge you both 10 pounds each for, I do not remember for what, but you are both free to go as somebody has already paid both of your fines." I don't know who paid the fines.

When I returned home and told Dad where I was, he was not a happy dad. He said, "I thought you were going to take pictures at your brother's wedding?" "I am" I replied. "What time is the wedding?" "The wedding is at 12:00 noon!" "Well, it is only 11:00 am. I should be in time." Thankfully,

I was! I can also say, one of the few things I have in common with the Apostle Paul is that we both went to jail for preaching the gospel!

The Importance of Evangelism

Christians should not forget the command of Jesus in Matthew 28:12–16:

> Now the eleven disciples went to Galilee, to the mountain to which Jesus had directed them. And when they saw him they worshiped him, but some doubted. And Jesus came and said to them, "All authority in heaven and on earth has been given to me. Go therefore and make disciples of all nations, baptizing them in[a] the name of the Father and of the Son and of the Holy Spirit, teaching them to observe all that I have commanded you. And behold, I am with you always, to the end of the age" (ESV)

Evangelism is not an option; it is a command from Jesus. It is not an elective. It is a command from, the most high God.

As an aside, I commend to anyone interested in evangelism the book *A Certain Sound: A Primer on Open Air Preaching* by Tran Denton and Scott Smith. Scott is a respected REF evangelist and is a great example of a godly preacher with biblical knowledge and zeal. As he acknowledges the encouragement from his wife, he cites his wife, who tells him, "You can't plow a field by turning it over in your mind." Scott is devoted and called to open air preaching. He is faithful and good at what he does! He has been given a godly talent for open air preaching. Part of his ministry is to mentor young men who are interested in open air preaching. It is a book worth reading more than once!

People often ask me, "What is the best method of evangelism?" I usually reply, "After dinner evangelism!" Then they ask me, "How does that work?" I reply. "You take me out to dinner, and I'll show you."

Let me give you another suggestion. Sunday evening after church is another great time to talk to people about Jesus. One evening after church a group of us from Park Hill were walking down a hill and we passed an open window that happened to be the window of a pub. As we were passing the open window, we heard someone inside calling out, "I'll take requests. Is there anyone out there who would like to come and sing?" I was prompted to put my head in the window, and I said, "would you like us to come inside and sing for you?" "Yes, come on in!" "If we come in, how do we know that you really want us to sing to you?"

What happened next was quite the invitation. The man stood in front of the crowd sitting down in the pub looking at the stage where he was standing. None of them gave the impression that they were thirsty! They had been drinking much of the evening it seemed. The man began a chant, banging his own beer mug on a table, "Do we want them to come in and sing?" Everybody roared for us to come in. "How will we know that you will like what we will sing? Again, "Will we like what they will sing?" The enthusiasm for us to come in and sing what we wanted compelled us to go inside. Suddenly, we had to come up with something to sing. I ended up singing a chorus I learned in Australia.

Unbelievably they loved it and were chanting and banging their beer mugs in unison, "Sing us another, Sing us another!" We decided to all sing "He's Got the Whole World in His Hands." When we announced what we were going to sing, a drunken man with wobbly legs stood up and was about to shower us with a glass carbonated soda fountain. He never made it. Another patron stood up and 'decked' him. This was our last song as we could not think of anything else that we all knew. As I looked out into the crowd, many of them had tears streaming down their cheeks.

I tell this story because it occurred after a day of sound Bible worship both morning and evening as we were all close to the Lord, having received many blessings during the day. We had taken in and now it was natural to give out. God used the event to soften hearts, but we have no idea what was accomplished except that we had been invited to witness, and we believed that in a small way, we had been found faithful in doing so. I believe this witness illustrates that Sunday really is the "Market Day of the soul."

We should never forget Isaiah 55:11:

> " ... so shall my word be that goes out from my mouth;
> it shall not return to me empty,
> but it shall accomplish that which I purpose,
> and shall succeed in the thing for which I sent it" (ESV).

On another occasion, my friend Nigel Goodwin gave a wonderfully encouraging talk about witnessing in Brighton and challenged us to come to a pop music festival being held at Plumpton racetrack. The track was near Plumpton Motor Coaches where I used to work. (It was Nigel who I first saw who signed his letters "In his grip.")

At a subsequent planning meeting for the event the discussion revolved around what to wear for the event. What should we wear to "fit in"? Was that even important? If it was important, why was it important?

It surprised me how much time was given to stressing about what we ought to wear to this new witnessing opportunity. I was prompted to say, "I don't think it matters what we wear. However, it does matter what we say!" At the end of the meeting, I announced that I was going to wear my only three-piece suit. "I believe I will talk to more people than you could imagine with my witnessing outfit!" Over my suit I wore a black ski jacket. Walking around the pop festival site amongst all sorts of garb, it struck me that I looked like a detective.

It's good I wasn't a detective. My first conversation followed a drug deal that I witnessed! I wandered over to the group and said, "I saw what you were doing, would you like to talk about it?" The response surprised me. "Yes, sir!" I think they thought I was a cop. I witnessed to them for about an hour.

As I left, somebody in the group asked me if I was a cop and I replied something to the effect that they didn't need to know what I did for a living. I chose to wear my only three-piece suit along with a black ski jacket. Humanly speaking, it may have been a key to all my conversations.

My time of respite at home after Australia was good and needed. I was able to reconnect with my church and recharge my spiritual batteries. I needed it—my next trip was not to the beaches, but to the mountains of Switzerland.

15

"I LIFT UP MY EYES TO THE MOUNTAINS ..."

In 1955, Francis and Edith Schaeffer were serving as missionaries in Huémoz-sur-Ollon, Switzerland. They decided to open their home to people who were seeking philosophical, theological, and biblical answers to questions of purpose, meaning, and direction in life. Francis Schaeffer was a Presbyterian pastor with a love for people, God's Word, and the quest for truth. They named their ministry "L'Abri Fellowship" (French for "shelter"). Through their ministry and writings, they influenced thousands of people in Switzerland, England, the United States, and elsewhere.

I will always be grateful to my brother Peter for telling me I ought to go to L'Abri in Huémoz, Switzerland. He knew I was "messed up." Looking back, I lived my life based on my feelings, how I felt at any given time. That is not a recipe for success. I didn't know how to use sound moral and biblical reasoning to direct my life.

I had also read Edith Schaeffer's book *L'Abri* (1969) that told the story of their ministry. It is a beautiful story how God lead, guided, and provided, for Francis and Edith Schaeffer, who He called to minister in Switzerland, after World War II. It is the kind of book where you sit in front of a dancing log fire, drinking hot chocolate on a snowy winter's night.

The cover art for the book was designed by Elder Ted Smith of Grace and Peace Fellowship church in St. Louis and I was captivated by it. The cover of the book attracted me to go to L'Abri in Heumoz, Switzerland.

It was the thought of meeting all those interesting looking people in another country that attracted me to L'Abri. It was not at all the thought of getting "sorted," as the Brits would say. My older brother Peter encouraged me to go to L'Abri. He had been there, and he knew that L'Abri would help me. An older brother has a unique perspective on how "messed up" his younger brother is at times.

In the late summer of 1971, I set off for Swiss L'Abri. In my naiveté, I took a copy of Dr. Schaeffer's book, *The God Who is There,* thinking that with my new adventurous spirit that included a "quest" for knowledge and culture, that I would read the book on the ferry going across the English Channel.

I forgot two things. *First,* I am almost always seasick crossing the English Channel and, *second,* apart from faithfully reading my childhood comics namely, *The Dandy, The Beano* and *Tiger,* and reading a few books about the exploits of the French Resistance fighters in World War II, at 30 years of age I had never read a serious book. In view of my sparse literary history, I think I continued my new journey encouraged that I had read a whole page of such a profound book. No comment on how much I understood. Later I discovered that there was an explanation of Dr. Schaeffer's words in the back of his book!

The only two questions that I asked Sheila before I asked her to marry me were, one, "Do you get seasick?" Secondly, "Do you have good teeth?" Sheila wanted to know why I asked if she got seasick?" I told her that I always get seasick if I am not on an inland waterway. If we got married and had children I would disappear below, and she would have to totally take care of the children while we crossed the English Channel. I think she was so taken aback with my first question we did not get to the second question!

I arrived at L'Abri after riding the bus up the mountain from the historic town of Aigle. I was anxious because I feared that I might not know where to get off the bus. However, the bus driver was so used to seeing people arrive from all over the world that when we stopped outside

Chalet Les Melezes, he said something like, "this stop is probably where you want to get off."

Once at L'Abri, when I talked to the person "on the door" his name was Rob Burkham. Imagine my disbelief when Rob told me that there was no room for me at L'Abri. I do not recall having any negative thoughts upon hearing that news. I was still enjoying the adventure of arriving in Switzerland. Rob looked like a hippie who had recently arrived from the East looking to re-habilitate himself at L'Abri as so many before him had done.

I understood that there was no register of names and addresses of folks who had booked appointments to arrive for their time at L'Abri. God was the One who chose who came to L'Abri and who did not. I was warmly welcomed into the L'Abri community by all who I met, and it was arranged for me to be given accommodation in a local pension in the village of Huémoz, a short walk down the hill.

My family had the privilege of knowing members of the Guinness family. I understood that a third of the family was involved in investment banking; approximately another third was involved with making the world-famous Guinness beer in Dublin, Ireland; and the other third went into Christian ministry.

When I arrived at Swiss L'Abri, Os Guinness was a worker at L'Abri. Os is a prolific Christian writer and thinker and at the time that I arrived at L'Abri he was working on his book, *The Dust of Death* (1973). What I could not know at the time was that a year later, Sheila, my future wife, would arrive at Swiss L'Abri. Sheila came with her Swiss friend Laurence, and they would be assigned to work together on translating a section of the book into French. Later still I would visit Sheila and Laurence in Toronto, Canada.

When I arrived, the L'Abri community was praying for Os because he was working on a section of his book dealing with the occult and the expected spiritual battles were in full swing. The devil is historically real and immensely powerful. However, in the big picture Satan is the biggest loser who was ever created. Although his power is real, and needs to be acknowledged and respected, Satan can do nothing that our Heavenly Father will not allow him to do.

It was my privilege to be part of the small number of students (I like that word) that Os chose to see and work with at that time. Os thought that I should stay at L'Abri, even though there was "no room." He told me to talk to the Lord and ask him what He thought and decide if I thought that I should stay and then report back. I had never been taught to decide and so the thought of making a list of "pros" and "cons" and attempting to make an informed decision was not in my playbook. My response was to go for a walk up the mountain towards Cheseires. On the way up, the road towards Cheseires I said to the Lord, "Lord if that cloud passes the sun before I count to ten, I will know that you want me to stay at L'Abri." It did, so I reported back to Os that I had "decided" that I should stay at L'Abri. It was in 2016, that I was able to tell Os in Chattanooga, Tennessee, that since he did not ask me how I decided, it never occurred to me to tell him! It certainly was not the most biblical or spiritually mature way to make such a decision, but it was the best way I knew at the time—and fortunately, it wasn't a rain cloud!

Once again, my heavenly Father loving drew me along on the journey that he had purposed for me to take. There will be other examples in the book where the Lord had to do the same again! One can begin to understand how correct my brother Peter was when he encouraged me to go to L'Abri to get "sorted." My first day as a student in Farrell House, my tutor was a delightful Englishman by the name of Donald Drew. Donald was a much-loved godly public-school teacher in England. (That would be a private boarding school in American English.) He gave me my assignment, which to my delight I understood and felt confident that I could carry out. All I had to do was choose a book to read. Any book, it did not matter which book. Just choose a book and read it. There would be no test. I did not have to understand anything in it that I read. The assignment was to remember the book I was reading so that I could read every word of it and remember the title each day so that I could return to it.

The book I chose was a classic church history book (though I did not know it at the time) by Swiss historian and theologian Merle D'Aubigné *The History of the Reformation in the Sixteenth Century.* Originally published in French in five volumes over two decades in the mid-1800s, I think the abridged version that I read in English had 637 pages. Quite enough for me as one making his first foray into such material!

I eventually successfully completed the assignment. Each morning, I read along with all the other students; I felt like a million dollars! It was amazing. Columns of information began to form in my mind and then a few beams began to connect some of the columns to each other. Information was beginning to form in my mind and was being added to some of the columns that were forming. What was happening was that I was in the beginning stages of forming a framework of truth. That journey continues to the present.

My months at L'Abri were inspirational, formative, and healing. I was blessed as much by what I saw and experienced as I was by what I heard and learned. Switzerland was beautiful, but L'Abri was life-changing for me. The wall on the left-hand side of the chapel at L'Abri was glass. I never saw anyone look out at the Swiss Alps while Dr. Schaeffer was preaching or teaching.

I believe that Francis Schaeffer's personality, compassion, and ministry arose in God's timing for unique and turbulent times in Europe and the United States in the second half of the twentieth century. He had many critics and many admirers, but no one doubted his sincerity.

Of course, his appearance—a goatee and longish hair and unique style of dressing—like a Swiss farmer, wearing knickers, knee socks and an alpine hiking outfit, and walking boots, made him stand out in any American crowd—even in the 1960s and 1970s!

Looking at pictures of him today always reminds me of when I was in Indiana, a few years after leaving L'Abri, listening to him answering questions. He spoke to a packed audience of around

8,000 people. He was alone on a flood lite stage sitting on a refectory table with his hands under his thighs swinging his legs comfortably.

An irate lady approached one of eight microphones, and her question was, "Dr. Schaeffer, could you tell us why you wear those ridiculous knickers?" He sweetly and clearly replied, "Yes, there are two reasons really. I like them and they are comfortable." Then with his gracious body language he indicated he was ready for the next question from another microphone. Such was his character and style.

I believe that L'Abri was, and still is to this day, the finest example of what godly, authentic Christianity looks like. I experienced the full beauty of it in Udo and Debbie Middleman's chalet. After three months, I left Swiss L'Abri just before Christmas 1971. I thoroughly enjoyed my time in the home of Udo and Debbie Middleman in Cheseires, in the canton of Vaud. Udo's father was a diplomat. I had never met anybody as brilliant as Udo. The fact we became friends over time was more than someone like me could have ever expected.

A Return Visit

Some years later after leaving L'Abri, I was on a mission trip in Austria, Germany, and Switzerland with my son Stephen and I was very pleased that we were able to visit Udo and Debbie, and that Stephen could meet this gracious and remarkable couple.

A couple of free days opened on a trip with Stephen, and we set off across Austria headed for Switzerland. I wanted Stephen to meet Udo and Debbie. Udo held summer seminars and Stephen is quite a student. We stopped for lunch at a delightful location. I ordered a Vienna schnitzel with a fried egg on top, with French fries and mushrooms. (Isn't it interesting how we can forget so many things in life and yet remember meals from years ago? Indeed, we may not "live by bread alone," but it seems that rarely do we forget it!)

When we got near Gruyere, we stopped at what turned out to be the nearest family hotel to Udo's chalet. We did not realize it at the time, but it was the height of the ski-season and there were no rooms available anywhere. We spoke to the Swiss proprietor who told us, "It is most unlikely that you will find a room in the area at this time of year." He did not have a room either. He asked us how long we needed the room. We told him that it would be just for one night. He stated that he did have a small attic room we could use. We looked at it and took it. It was beautifully Swiss.

At breakfast, the next morning we talked to a Scottish family with six children. Being Scottish and having six children in and of itself was interesting! When we discovered that the father's name was John Calvin we were surprised once more! He was quick to tell us that he was not religious and was not related to John Calvin, so we came back down to earth. After breakfast I went upstairs to our room and got a couple of books to give him. We then set off to find Udo's chalet.

Previously, Stephen and I had tried to find Udo's house in Gruyere. I had never been there, and we did not know it, but we were quite close. Eventually we discovered that to find someone's house in that part of Switzerland it was best to go to the local post office. They gave us directions to the plot rather than the house number. The access road to their beautiful home was too steep to drive up in the snow, without chains on our rental car.

Having gone to the post office in the morning for directions to the chalet, we had more confidence that we would find Udo's chalet. I had sent an e-mail but did not receive a reply. We also called and still we did not hear from Udo. We assumed he was away. When we found the house and saw no evidence of anyone being home, we took the liberty of taking pictures and I walked around the back to enjoy the view when Stephen called out that he thought that he had seen movement behind one of the curtains. To our delight and surprise Udo appeared at the front door and as he was going to his car explained why he had not responded to our e-mail, or our phone calls.

Once a year the family got together, and it was a "sacred time" for Udo and Debbie which they had to guard and keep free from students and guests as they were always immersed by students with needs and questions year-round. Unknowingly, we had arrived at such a time. Of course, we understood and were delighted to have a few minutes to say "hello" and have Stephen meet them both. We saw Udo drive off in his car and as he disappeared down the steep snowy road, he passed Mrs. Schaeffer and her companion. That is when, as Stephen and I were walking down the hill, we were privileged to stop and talk to Mrs. Schaeffer for a couple of minutes.

Stephen and I did not have chains on our rental car, so we had walked up to Udo and Debbie's chalet. We helped each other slip and slide up to Udo's house, yet here was Mrs. Schaeffer walking up the hill unaided except for her cane walking with her companion, at age 94!

As she stopped in front of us, I took the opportunity to thank her for her wonderful talks on prayer that I had been so blessed by at L'Abri that she was so well known for giving on Monday's day of prayer each week. She graciously gave permission for me to take a picture. However, my camera jammed, so I asked Stephen to take a picture. It was such a beautiful memory, and I was so thankful that we could take a picture. Probably too many times that day, I had to check with Stephen that he still had the photo and had not deleted it. Stephen being Stephen, jokingly told me that if the photo was so valuable should we think about auctioning it on eBay. Ugh! Such an inappropriate idea, let alone one that should have been uttered!

I, like many other people, have been influenced dramatically by the person, ministry, and writings of Francis and Edith Schaeffer and the L'Abri Fellowship. They have been transformative personally, intellectually, and spiritually. Dr. Schaeffer frequently said, "There is only one reason to believe Christianity: because it's true." That statement sums up so much of my own life and thought.

The ministry of the Schaeffer's as I understood and experienced it was to proclaim and demonstrate that God exists, God is personal, and that God provides for His People—and to do so in a context of true Christian love.

Their ministry helped me begin to develop a biblical worldview that was consistent, comprehensive, non-contradictory—and grounded in Christian love. It is Christian love, as Jesus spoke in John 13:34–35 and John 17:21 that is the true"mark of the Christian" (See Francis Schaeffer's small but influential book by this same title). It is more than kindness; more than compassion; and more than empathy—but it entails all these things. I have adopted a similar position for my PEF/REF ministry.

As noted earlier, to this day my 3 months in 1971 at L'Abri just before Christmas was and remains, the most beautiful expression of Christianity that I have ever experienced. I cannot capture in words the beauty, the peace, the gentle liveliness of the community living and working in their home. There was security and a loveliness that just was throughout the home.

I encourage you to read the works of Francis and Edith Schaeffer and especially *L'Abri* by Edith Schaeffer. You will be blessed to read it. When I give this book to people in the US or in Europe I say,"This book needs to be read in front of an open fire with a cup of hot chocolate preferably with snow falling outside and snow on the ground."

In the providence of God, what prompted me to go to L'Abri was that my brother Peter encouraged me to go and the cover on the book,"L'Abri." I was interested in meeting all those interesting looking people pictured on the cover of"L'Abri," standing outside the church in the Swiss Alps.

Quite simply the writings of the Schaeffer's and the ministry of L'Abri changed my life. With a biblical framework and guided by the inerrant Word of God in the Bible, I now had a compass for my journeys that pointed True North.

16

A TIME OF TRANSITION

Although I didn't know it at the time, the months after leaving Switzerland were to be months of transition during which God strengthened me and guided me toward theological education and full-time ministry. There is no doubt in my mind that God was guiding my steps.

Brighton Buses and Taxi Evening Trips

When I returned to England from Swiss L'Abri for Christmas 1971, I took a job again as a bus driver on Brighton & Hove bus company. Still in existence today, it was founded in 1884 when the transportation was "horse buses" known as horse-drawn omnibuses. In 1916, the horse buses were replaced with motor buses. By the time I was driving for them, it was a subsidiary of the National Bus Company. The horses were long gone and that was probably best for me, the horses, and the company!

One morning early, it was my turn to pick up the drivers for the first shift of the day. A policeman stepped off the pavement and stopped me for speeding in the Old Steine, Brighton. It was around 4:30 a.m. and there I was in my little British racing green MG. The only thing, in my favor was that my bus driver's uniform was showing under my open coat. I was admonished as a bus driver and thankfully the policeman used his discretion and showed me mercy and let me off with a warning. For a short while, I was given the nickname of "Three Wheel Harry." I was asked to move a double-decker bus in the garage. On the front of the bus was a printed plaque with the words: "Working on the bus."

I assumed that I was to move the bus to where it was to be worked on by the mechanic. I do not know if you have ever experienced the sensation of driving a double-decker bus with only three wheels on it. It was early in the morning and the mercy of the situation was that there was nobody under the bus working on it!

Another time in Brighton near a roundabout called "The 7 Dials," I was perplexed to see my conductor outside on the pavement waving frantically at me. I did not have any idea what he was saying but finally he gave me the thumbs up sign. I think he thought by doing that I would understand what he said and what he was about to do. I did not. We had been in a traffic jam for a while and he had got off the bus and was trying to tell me not to move, I got that right as I could not move at all and had not for some time.

Eventually, as if all stuck together, the traffic began to crawl in a slow caravan towards the bottom of the hill. A short while later, imagine my confusion when I saw my bus conductor outside on the pavement, again waving frantically. He looked out of breath. There was a reason for that too! At the top of the hill, he decided that we had been stuck in traffic for so long that he was going into the newsagent to buy a fresh pack of cigarettes. The timing was bad for both of us. As I began to inch the bus forward, glad that the traffic had begun to move, I did not realize that I no longer had a conductor. He was buying his cigarettes, and he did not realize that he no longer had a bus to hop back on!

Because I had time on my hands after work during the day, I took a night job driving a taxi around Brighton and Hove. I do not recall any specific stories from my taxi driving in the evenings, except I did keep an eye open for the new "For Sale signs" going up on new houses for sale. It also became clear that along with being a bartender, which I never tried, taxi drivers could also bring up any subject and it was acceptable to talk about it with the passenger.

I knew the town well. When I was arrested with Jim for witnessing on the beach and the policeman in the car on the way to the police station tried to tell me that there was no such road as Denmark Villas, Hove, the road that I told him was where I lived. I was able with confidence to tell him that he was wrong. It did not strengthen his argument for him to be reminded that his police station was on the next road east of my house. Of course, whether I should have corrected him is probably debatable!

I do recall one time when I had to do a three-point turn on a road. That was a clue for me that I had taken a wrong turn! The reason for the three-point turn was that there was a quaint old bridge that was not going to let me drive my double-decker bus underneath it. All in all, things went well enough on the buses and there were no bridges damaged—at least by me!

English L'Abri (1972–1973)

When I returned to England from Swiss L'Abri for Christmas 1971, what a delight to learn that there was an English L'Abri in Greatham, Hampshire. During that time, I was driving buses again, and while visiting John and Val, I met a young lady called Jill. Imagine my delight when she told me that there was an English L'Abri in Greatham, Hampshire. With Jill, the daughter in the home where John and Val often met with their youth group, "biker and scooter" ministry, I visited English L'Abri.

Driving a double-decker bus is an honest job but the thought that I could visit L'Abri in Hampshire on the weekends lifted my spirits, as I drove my bus. One weekend Jill took me to Greatham and introduced me to English L'Abri. At English L'Abri I had the privilege of meeting and getting to know Ranald Macauley and Jerram Barrs and Jerram's brother John who eventually joined me as a student at Covenant Seminary with his wife Jill. Still later, Ranald's brother John Macauley became a student at Covenant Seminary with his wife Heidi.

Later I "got off the buses" and was privileged to be invited to what turned out to be 11 months working in the English community at L'Abri in Greatham, Hampshire. I was not officially what L'Abri called a helper but with my construction degree my function was to work on the house for my half-day work period and then eventually work full-time during the 11-month period when the stables were re-roofed and then on the larger project of remodeling the barn, and the pump house.

One story that I must include during my time at English L'Abri was with a real Englishman, Tom (known affectionately as, 'Tommy Hardin'). Tom lived with us for a while until he was able to buy a home. He was a brick layer by profession (mason for American readers) with considerable site experience. For many of the 11 months I spent at English L'Abri there was much remodeling work to be done. I used my building construction degree to help with a project to renovate the pump house.

We had the luxury of working with an architect and an unusually knowledgeable surveyor, Richard Greaves, who took responsibility for our work himself, so we basically had to concentrate on producing the work and the finished project. For several weeks, under his supervision Tom and I underpinned the whole of the pump house. We could never have done it without Richard's oversight and experience. It was fun driving the small Kubota (and easier than a bus) to dig out below ground level and move the soil and then excavate the individual segments to be underpinned.

The site conditions revealed a situation that at first sight seemed to contradict the Bible. The Bible speaks about building your house on the rock and not upon the sand (Matthew 4:24–27). When we excavated each separate section to be underpinned, we discovered that we would be building on sand. However, it was not the kind of sand that comes to mind when you think of the kind of sandy soil that you are not to build on. The sand was so tightly packed or compressed that if you wanted to stick a half-inch piece of reinforcing bar into it, you had to do it with a two-pound hammer.

We learned about "pudzles" from Surveyor Richard. Pudzles can be likened to streaks of raspberry in vanilla ice-cream. The pudzles were dark brown while the sand on site was light brown with brown steaks running through it. The biblical principles were not violated here because the biblical principle was to build on firm ground. This sand offered a firm and ready to build on foundation.

One morning Tom and I were working on laying the drains up to the pump house and a young American student came to look at our work. We gathered he had just come from a high-powered lecture inside the Manor House. He looked down on us and said in an affected voice, "How are you brothers walking with the Lord today?" Tom replied with wisdom and candor "We're fine mate! It's 's people that we have trouble with! We are walking with the Lord, just fine!"

As a workman, Tom could use his hands and his brain. Manual laborers or craftsmen like Tom, often were looked down on as second-class citizens. To be a craftsman and use your hands makes you, I believe, smarter than office workers. If an office worker makes a mistake, he can throw his work in a waste-paper basket, and nobody needs to know. If a craftsman omits to think and plan it is very noticeable and often expensive to correct a mistake like excavating on a site at the wrong address. And regardless of our views, we must always remember that what is most important is God's perspective. God looks at the heart, not the hands (1 Samuel 16:7)

Interestingly, the construction site that I was assigned to for my first job after college was the site next to St Peters-upon-Cornhill in London. Later when Dad became the Anglican Rector of St Peters-upon-Cornhill, one of the references that he was able to use, was that of the chief of the City of London Police. Father had ministered to him while he was convalescing at, I believe at the time, the only police convalescent home in the country. It was in Brighton. Dad was chaplain to it. I remember Dad saying, "If you want to see things happen in a 'hurry,' mistering the gospel, offer to do ministry with police officers. They know all about sin, you do not have to teach them much about sin. They work with it every day. They just want to know the solution for it!"

During these months, as I grew more in my faith and looked toward the future, I thought a few times that I would like to apply to go to Bible college. However, that was not to be my next journey. God had something else planned for me. At the end of my time at English L'Abri in 1973, I boarded a plane in Gatwick Airport, for St. Louis, Missouri in the United States of America to attend Covenant Theological Seminary.

17

GOING TO AMERICA

Covenant Theological Seminary, St. Louis (1973–1977)

On leaving English L'Abri, having bought my one-way ticket to St. Louis, Missouri, I boarded a plane in London for America. I arrived in St. Louis in the summer of 1973 with $70.00 in my pocket. I had thought that I should go to Bible School. However, Ranald and Jerram at English L'Abri, encouraged me to go to seminary.

In following their advice, I learned a tremendous biblical lesson regarding seeking and following wise counsel—listen carefully and prayerfully to those who are more mature in the faith. The theme of the Book of Proverbs is skillful living in a foolish world and doing so according to biblical wisdom. It has many verses regarding seeking wise counsel. Two that standout to me are:

"The way of a fool is right in his own eyes,
but a wise man listens to advice."
Proverbs 12:15 (ESV)

and

"Without counsel plans fail, but with many advisers they succeed.
"Proverbs 15:22 (ESV)

God never leaves us without guidance from the Bible.

Also, while I was at English L'Abri a couple Bob and Caroline Stuart from Texas visited L'Abri and Caroline stayed on for a few weeks. She was convinced that God wanted me to go to Seminary. So, I said if I get accepted, would it be all right if I phoned you and ask that you sponsor me. I was not convinced as much as she was that God wanted me to go to Seminary. When I did get accepted, I called her from English L'Abri and she called up to Bob and said, "It is Paddy. He got accepted for a seminary in America. Is it all right if we sponsor him?" Bob needed more information, but it was decided that they would sponsor me. Bob had a patent on a diamond bit drill. I think he worked for himself in the oil business. However, after a few months his circumstance changed, and he could not in good conscience continue to promise to sponsor me. He had to bow out. That was to my advantage. I was already at school. I was granted permission to work while I was a student.

When you have great decisions to make, seek godly counsel. Listen to the perspective of other Christians—God places people in our lives for a purpose! The reason that I chose Covenant Seminary was that Dr. Schaeffer had introduced me to the concept of biblical inerrancy. I had never heard the word before in England. When I understood the term and what it meant, it became essential that I find the right seminary at which to study. I had to find a seminary with a faculty, where all the professors believed in the inerrancy of Scripture. At the time, Covenant was first on Dr. Schaffer's recommended short list.

I was anxious that I would not fail as a student. I had basically failed as a student every other time I tried to be one. The day I took the eleven-plus exam in Junior School, I did not really know how important it was. The fact that the whole of the school soccer team that I captained failed the exam softened the blow from the result that I had failed it. Perhaps we all should have played less soccer and studied more! I discovered that passing or failing the eleven-plus exam determined in the UK whether you went on to a grammar school and then higher education or stayed on the vocational track.

Summer Greek

When I arrived at Covenant Seminary, in St. Louis, I had been out of school for 10 years. I had not studied the humanities or the classics. I studied Building Construction. I had never studied a language, and my first class started on Monday, and I arrived in St. Louis on Wednesday morning. I was already late! I was met at the airport by Fred MacFarlane, a senior at the seminary. What confused me was that we went to Dunkin' Donuts for breakfast. I was used to eating something savory for breakfast and something sweet in the afternoon. This was the first of many things I was to learn in the United States!

Coming straight from the UK I assumed that I had arrived in the afternoon. Eating donuts enforced that perception for me. My first class at Covenant in the summer of 1973 was designed to cover the normal first year Greek course of study in 6 weeks. I had to pass the class before starting seminary. I was already two days late for my intense immersion into studying my first foreign language—not a great start to my new academic endeavor!

The person who greeted me in the doorway of my Greek class was none other than Rob Burkham, who I met at the door of Swiss L'Abri, two years earlier when I met him at the door at Swiss L'Abri it was his job to screen the students who arrived and were either unexpected or expected. No appointment book was kept at L'Abri to show who would be arriving and there was certainly no record of how long anyone would stay when they arrived. The policy at L'Abri was to pray that God would send the students that God had purposed to come to L'Abri and ask him to keep those away who he had not purposed to come.

Rob said to me that he had wondered how many Paddy Cooks there were as he heard my name called on Monday and Tuesday and nobody answered. He asked me where I was staying. I told him I had no idea. He invited me to stay with him. After class we went back to his apartment in the area known as Grace and Peace. We got home about 11.30 a.m. He fixed us lunch and finished the day's homework before we ate. I felt guilty taking time away from studying to go to the bathroom!

For the next six weeks it was early in the morning each day before I got to bed. Class started at 8 am. It puzzled me how Rob could do his homework so quickly. Although he gave the impression that he was a recovering hippie, Rob had a degree from Princeton in Oriental languages. Who knew? I just assumed that I was still a bad student.

Later in the week after class we visited Covenant Seminary Bookshop on campus. Rob wanted to buy some books. Then he handed me an open check. I think he thought that I had dropped it. I told him it was not mine. He assured me it was mine and that he wanted to give it to me to buy books. I had assumed I would borrow books. When I look back over my ministry, I often wondered how much Rob's thoughtful gift shaped that part of my future ministry. On the way home he stopped at his bank. I was shocked that he went to the drive through window and did not even get out of the car. The US was not the UK!

God had provided a place to stay for summer school and even a ride to school. It took nearly 10 years before I could travel highway I-40 without flipping my Greek vocabulary cards and not feel guilty.

At the end of the summer, I had to leave Rob's apartment as he was getting married. What I did not know was that a young lady named Sheila, who I later married, was invited to his wedding. However, she was not able to attend because her older brother Duncan was getting married the same day. I also did not know that just as Rob and I were at L'Abri together, a year later Sheila and Lynn were at Swiss L'Abri together. It was only later when Sheila came to visit Lynn, Rob's wife, that I met Sheila at Grace and Peace Church.

I was struggling with my summer school Greek requirements. So much so that I called home and spoke to Dad to tell him that if I failed summer school Greek, I did not have enough money to come home. So, he told me I had to pass! Fatherly tough love! The rest of the time he kept saying, "You better ring off now it must be costing you a lot of money to call from America." Those were the days at home in the UK when there was a money box by the phone and even one in the bathroom for the bath!

The professor for our summer school Greek class was Juan Mesus. Dr. Schaeffer said of Juan that his mind was one of the brightest that he had ever debated. Juan understood that I had been at L'Abri, and I ended up for a week or so each night walking across town to save money for my tuition. He was a great encouragement. Juan spoke 16 languages fluently—which did not help me directly or my self-esteem. You can imagine my joy when I learned at the end of the summer that I had passed summer school Greek. I got a D+. I have never jumped so high as when I heard the news. Despite the D+ I was so thankful and rather proud of myself if you can figure that one out!

Juan had an amazing testimony of how he became a Christian. He was walking in the streets of Paris, France, while he was a student at the Sorbonne studying Existentialism. A young girl approached him on the street and told him that Jesus had a wonderful plan for his life. Leaving aside here the theology of Campus Crusade for Christ, Juan being an intellectual, his mind was always working. He did not have a category to know where to fit this Jesus into his thinking. Eventually God led him to L'Abri and Dr. Schaeffer. When I discovered that Juan got dizzy standing on a chair fitting in a light bulb for some reason, I felt better about myself. I could do that.

Years later, having lost touch with Juan. I found myself talking to an Italian in Italy. For some reason known unto God, I asked him if he had ever heard the name Juan Mesus. This was the answer that I was given. "I cannot verify this, but I was told that Juan had or was still working for the CIA." Either way, what is important for me is the role model and friend that he became to me—not because of who I was but because of who we were—brothers in Christ who God brought together for a season. Be aware of the people God brings into your life; they are they by providence, not by circumstance!

Seminary and Becoming Presbyterian

After leaving Rob's apartment and my free ride to seminary all summer I was offered room and board at Skip and Margo Todd's apartment. They were members of Grace and Peace. All I had to do was come up with $10 a week. In the providence of God, around the same time I was offered a job, at Grace and Peace Church for $10 a week cleaning the sanctuary between services sweeping and sometimes mopping the floor. Since it was an inner-city ministry, I acquired another skill. I learned how to scrape chewing gum and bubble gum off the floor and sometimes off the chairs.

Again, in the good providence of God I was offered a ride to seminary each day by a Canadian student, Gene Haas. Gene had two other Canadian seminary students in the apartment. Amazingly my daily ride to seminary carried on all through seminary until I married Sheila in the summer of 1975. We then bought our first black Beetle VW together. As I will discuss below, we were married after my second year of seminary and before my final year. My senior year at seminary we decided that I would split the year in two six-month semesters. We were married at Concordia Seminary in St. Louis by Dr. Will Barker. I remember early on in my time at Covenant saying to Dr. Barker that I liked what I was being taught. However, I was anxious that I would never know enough to become a Presbyterian. He assured me that eventually I would know enough to become a Presbyterian. He was a great encouragement to me as a young seminarian. He even traveled to Grand Cayman Island in 1978 to take part in my ordination service. However, after the service he appropriately admonished me over an incident during the service. Little Andrew, our first son, got loose and climbed out of my arms. Rather than disrupt the seriousness of the moment I let him continue. I got that wrong!

Because I love to travel and meet new people, I always accepted a ride to presbytery meetings. It gave me a break from the academic atmosphere, and it was so interesting traveling with the professors to different cities in the Mid-West. I remember stopping for lunch at McDonalds.

Dr. Wilbur Wallis, my Greek professor, was ordering his lunch in front of me. I could not believe how he ordered. He said, "Do you by chance have a hamburger with everything on it." I piped up and said, "Dr. Wallis, you wouldn't let me speak like that." He graciously rephrased his order to, "Do you, in the good providence of God have a hamburger with everything on it!" So, I said to him, "So you *can* teach an ole dog new tricks?" He told me that with the Holy Spirit all things are possible!

He was such a dear man. In Greek class he asked me how I was doing with studying Greek. I assured him that I was praying a lot about my Greek. Later I was able to tell him that a significant prayer about my Greek had been answered. He was genuinely pleased when I told him that I had married Sheila who was a linguist!

Sheila had lived in Switzerland for five years and was a student at the University of Neuchatel. We reconnected in Toronto in the summer of 1974, after I had finished my summer work on a property in Maine for Andy and Peasy Love. Sheila and I had been writing to each other but after arriving in Toronto we became engaged in 36 hours! It was arranged with Dr. Barker that Sheila could come to study at the seminary and audit classes. Three weeks later she began taking Greek and Hebrew. At the end of the first month of class, Sheila's first week of Hebrew, Sheila got an A.

When Sheila came down from Canada and audited classes at the seminary she lived in the neighborhood with Peter and Linda Vaughn who were members at Grace and Peace. After school she would come home and cook a meal for Tom and me. That was always welcome. Sheila was a great cook before becoming a lifelong Cook!

Grace and Peace Church in St. Louis was pastored by Egon Middelmann the brother of Udo, who married Dr. Schaeffer's daughter Debbie. I stayed with Udo and Debbie in their chalet during my stay at Swiss L'Abri. Grace and Peace was planted in the neighborhood to be a witness to the local community. It was basically a safe community, unlike what is happening today in some inner cities, but there were robberies and problems with some locals that encouraged ladies to be accompanied in the neighborhood. We never really were affected although one beautiful summer evening I was walking Sheila home across the neighborhood to Peter and Linda's when on the other side of the road walking towards us were five men walking wearing long trench coats. Because it was a beautiful summer evening, instantly I was prompted to think that they were up to no good and were likely carrying long guns and were possibly gunslingers (perhaps a bit of English fascination with the American West).

Again, I was prompted to cross over the road with Sheila and walk straight up to them and asked them for the correct time. They gave it to me and thankfully we all continued our separate ways.

After living at Skip and Margo's apartment I shared an apartment with Tom Heyse, who was also at Swiss L'Abri and a member of Grace and Peace. Tom had a degree in film but started at a local television station, "Channel 2," basically as a coffee boy. He had a great testimony just sticking with his job and was promoted up the ladder. By that time God had provided me with a regular Saturday job where I was able to earn $10 an hour, working for Andy and Peasy. That was an encouraging leap from $10 a week to $10 an hour! I understood that they had five properties so there was plenty of work maintaining them and as it turned out, job security in a foreign land!

Tom and I had a great time as roommates. Early on in our relationship I was studying for exams and there was a commotion on the corner across the street. I opened the window and hollered out. "Hey, how am I supposed to study for my exams with you all making so much noise?" Then I realized that the pop sound was not caused by fireworks. There was a shootout on our corner. Either the folks were bad shots, or they were using blanks as nobody fell over and eventually all was quiet again.

One time we got a telephone call from a stranger. The caller had dialed a wrong number. He started out by saying, "Hey man do you have the stuff I need some badly." We arranged to meet him in St. Louis on a certain corner, and we were to give him the "High Beams!" Tom, but specially me chuckled over the need to give him the "High Beams." We ended up bringing him home to our apartment. It was unusual but after a short conversation and not being able to give him his "stuff" he became belligerent. His behavior became so bad that I had to scream at him, "In the name of the Father and of the Son and of the Holy Ghost, get out of my house!" He did and we dropped him off someplace.

One of my close friends at seminary was Dan Wachsmuth. Previously he had studied law and gone to Swiss L'Abri. His parents had an old and established oyster bar in Portland, Oregon. He took an apartment a few houses down from where Tom and I lived. God used Dan to help me see the reality and power of praying specifically. As I have often said, "We pray God bless all the missionaries, He will. However, we will never know what happened because of those prayers. We believe that not only does God love to hear our prayers, but that He loves to answer our prayers far more than we are willing to pray those prayers. Also, if we pray specifically, for example, "Dear God, will you allow Harry in Bulgaria to buy a bicycle so that he can get his shopping done more quickly" and Harry gets his bicycle, it is such an encouragement to Harry and of course to us!

Dan and I decided to get together each weeknight around 10:00 pm, for a hot drink and 15 to 20 minutes to pray. One of the first specific prayers that we prayed together was answered! I will never forget that experience. His sister in Portland was having a bad time in life so we specifically prayed that she would come to St. Louis so she could come to visit Grace and Peace. Three weeks later Dan came rushing round to the apartment with the good news. "We need to go down to the Greyhound Station right now. My sister just arrived in St. Louis!" Whoa!

Dan and I both worked on Saturdays for Andy and Peasy on their grand house on Westmoreland Street in St. Louis. At some point I went out on my own and Dan often worked with me painting houses. Later, Dan married Becky, daughter of Ted and Gladys Smith.

It was six months after they had been married that Becky was concerned that whenever Dan and I worked together he did not seem to have an appetite to eat the home-cooked meals that Becky had prepared. We pushed ourselves painting so I introduced Dan to my habit of stopping by Dunkin' Donuts for coffee and a couple of donuts with the false rationale that we would unwind by doing that before arriving home. I had to confess to Becky that it was my fault.

My First Christmas in America

My first Christmas in America was in Oyster Bay, Long Island. David Rowley, who I have known since the summers spent sailing on the Norfolk Broads, invited me up to Oyster Bay for Christmas. Some friends of his were at English L'Abri who knew Governor Nelson Rockefeller. It was arranged that Randy and Joan Nabors, and I were to drive up to New York for Christmas after our seminary exams.

My last exam of the semester was my first Hebrew exam at seminary. Self-disclosure here. Basically, I am a "C" student. I say that because the only "A's" I ever got throughout my schooling were at Covenant Seminary. I was given an "A" for counseling and an "A" for a mid-term Hebrew vocabulary test. Although, I graduated from seminary with an M.Div. and a very welcome spattering of "B's." Now I think about it, from the time I left seminary in 1977 until now, 48 years later, nobody has ever asked me what my grades were in any part of my schooling! It's a bit like the t-shirt one sometimes sees in mail order catalogs that reads "Another successful day without Algebra!"

My first Hebrew language trauma happened the morning of our trip to New York. I stayed up most of the night before my first Hebrew exam which was the last day of the semester before Christmas, thinking to myself that I might even be able to say, "I've got this!" Then I heard somebody shout out in our apartment building, "SNOW DAY!" I always liked it when the snow fell in England growing up because it usually meant no school that day. As it began to sink in that in America a snow day meant the same thing I began to panic. My panic began as I could not hold the information that I had crammed into my little brain, i.e., the Hebrew I thought I needed for my first Hebrew exam, over the Christmas holidays!

I had discovered that foreign languages were not part of my gifting. My headmaster in high school gave his reason for not letting us learn a foreign language by saying, "When you can speak English properly, then you can learn a foreign language." Later I learned that if he had allowed us to learn a foreign language it could have helped us with our English. With a somewhat pictorial memory I did find studying Hebrew was a little easier than Greek. What followed next was a series of events that allowed us to arrive in New Jersey that evening and Oyster Bay the next day.

I walked from my apartment through the neighborhood to Randy and Joan's house to press him to get me up to the seminary so I could take the Hebrew exam before we left for New York. He gave me the impression that he had forgotten that we had a Hebrew exam that day. Then he told me that he did not have any snow tires for the trip.

However, he went to his mailbox and received a letter with money in it so now he did have money for snow tires. We barely made it to the garage through the snow and he borrowed my Hebrew textbook to prepare for the exam while the four snow tires were fitted. We both eventually set off to the seminary with another student and arrived in time to take the exam.

However, we had to walk from the seminary car park across the campus to Dr. Laird Harris's house and persuade him to let us take the exam, which he agreed to.

The snow was knee deep on campus so the three of us, the only three that took the exam before Christmas, took the exam with very wet feet and legs. I think that we all dropped a grade when we eventually heard our results. The fact that I passed my first Hebrew exam was all that I wanted. Frankly, it amazed me that I had a grade to drop down to and still passed. I was well pleased! After being out of school for 10 years and never having studied a language, I had chosen to embark on beginning both Greek and Hebrew in my first semester. I was more than well pleased that I had passed my first Hebrew exam! Now I did not have to attempt to hold all that Hebrew in my head over Christmas.

We could now head off on our adventure to New York. We did, and the weather was atrocious. It rained and snowed the whole way. Randy did all the driving. The traffic and the roads were bad, but the Lord allowed us to arrive safely that evening in New Jersey and arrive the next day on time in Oyster Bay.

The next day we drove to Long Island and arrived in Oyster Bay. I was amazed at the size of the houses. Most of them seemed to have multiple cameras set up at the front gates that led to so many grand houses. Armed with my degree in Building Construction, I knew that they were grand houses! When I arrived at David's house, he quickly took note of my wardrobe and arranged for me to go with him to get a more suitable outfit for my new surroundings and the people that we would meet at the party that we had been invited to. Imagine the adjustment I had to make. David chose white trousers with a colorful tartan that made my eyes buzz. I was thankful that I had tartan trousers and not a Scottish kilt to wear in my new surroundings. We met interesting folks at the party and people just accepted my dress, that Englishmen wore colorful tartan trousers.

Seminary Studies

Back at Seminary in St. Louis I was thankful that I lived off campus and had a great church, to attend with so many folks who had been to L'Abri. It was a help in my adjusting to being in America. I was also thankful that I could be a full-time student. I admire students who were not able to be in the academic atmosphere of studying on campus. I do not believe that I could be an online student. Then, as I discovered later in my ministry it was such a privilege and blessing for international students to study in America at seminary. With the first student of my PEF ministry, Bertie from Duress, Albania, I wanted him to have the same blessings that I had experienced as an international student.

Most people told me that the last thing that I needed to do was to bring an international student to America. They never leave. I weighed that but I also asked myself, "where in Albania will Bertie get his reformed theological education from if he stays in Albania?"

I was convinced that Bertie should come to America for his theological training. One of my goals in ministry has been to look for and find international students who can go back to their own countries equipped to be confessional, reformed Presbyterian ministers of the gospel. In all my travels I knew that everybody seemed to know what a Pentecostal is and what a Baptist is and believes. However, when I mentioned that I was a Presbyterian they did not appear to have a clue about what I was talking about. So, I resolved to offer myself to God to do something about that. I was not qualified to assume that role but in the providence of God he heard my prayer and decided to help me do something about the situation.

One huge advantage of studying on campus is that you meet like-minded students who often become friends for life. You also meet good professors who introduce you to the great tools for learning—sound theological books. It puzzles me that more students do not consider working their way through seminary. Suppose it takes you 7 years instead of 4 years to finish school. You will get to know 7 years of students instead of 4!

I discovered that for me the best place to study out of class was in the seminary library. There was quiet and with the academic atmosphere it helped keep me focused. Everybody was so friendly, and I made so many friends that I decided that to get more work done and a little less fellowshipping, I should go and study in the library of Concordia Seminary. That turned out to be a good move. Eventually though, although it took a little longer, I needed to find a place where I could just study. The solution was to study in the library of Washington University in St. Louis. This time I chose to take a copy of a large book written by G. C. Berkouwer, in his series *Studies in Dogmatics*. It was his book on the theology of sin (known as the doctrine of hamartiology). On the book cover the word "sin" was written in large capital letters on the spine of the book. Studying at Washington University was the answer to studying and being undisturbed. It took me a while to realize that putting a big book with "SIN" written in large 2" letters on a table for 10 was probably the reason why I was able to study alone!

For me, a highlight of each day at seminary was the chapel service. *I always went to chapel.* I enjoyed the break from the academic classroom setting. Again, the Lord showed me how essential it was to develop the habit of regular devotions and worship. I also like to sing. I usually had a quick conversation with somebody and the whole "package" of events refreshed me for the next class. This was another example of God providentially carrying me along to fit in with His plan to prepare me for the gospel ministry.

One of the young women (Stephanie Witherspoon) at English L'Abri while I was there lived in Memphis. I believe she and her family won a contest that allowed her to travel to England and visit L'Abri.

Stephanie's parents were very hospitable, so she used to say to folks that "if you are ever in Memphis drop by. We are always having missionary families stay with us." So, one day while I was in seminary I decided to go to Memphis—about 300 miles away.

As I set out from St. Louis it was a terrible day for hitch-hiking. It was cold, wet, and windy. As I stood by the side of the road, I had another fear overwhelm me. I was going to visit a Christian family because I was depressed. I realized that the last thing that I wanted to do at the time was to witness about Jesus. I was not ashamed of Him I just did not want to do it. Conversations I had, often included, "Why are you here?" "I am a student." "What are you studying?" "Theology." I remember that day never feeling so weak and down cast. Thankfully, I did not have to wait long for a ride.

A trucker stopped and I got in the cab of his truck thankful that I was out of the cold wind and rain in a warm cab. He was a big man, and I mean big! And as the Australians would say the trucker was "blue mad!" I did not even have to start the conversation. He was grumbling out loud.

So, I said, "What's up?" He was grumbling about the price of prostitutes in St. Louis. "You do not have to pay for that." (*If you are married.*) "You do not have to pay for that?" "You don't?" he replied.

"By the way, where are you going?"

"Memphis."

"I can drop you at the door. I am going through Memphis."

"I'm going to see a friend and visit her family."

"Does she have a friend for me?"

"I'm sure she does, she is very friendly."

"Can you introduce me to her?"

"No. I cannot!" "Why not?" Pause.

"I cannot because you are not man enough to handle her!"

I do not know what the Australians say after being "blue mad" because that is what happened next. For the first time in my life, I thought I had "gone too far." The veins on the trucker's head started to bulge and he was seething with rage. I was thinking I might need to jump out of the cab, but we were going too fast for that. Then, this happened.

He burst into tears and began sobbing. The trucker started to fall apart before my eyes. The testimony of the trucker was that he was the oldest of seven siblings. His father was a Baptist pastor, and all the family were walking with the Lord. He admitted to being the black sheep of the family. We talked all the way to Memphis, and we prayed before I jumped out of the cab thanking him for the ride. I was a few blocks from the home of my friend. The scripture that came to mind was, "For the sake of Christ, then, I am content with weaknesses, insults, hardships, persecutions, and calamities, "...for when I am weak, then I am strong" (2 Corinthians 12:10).

"Day of Evangelism"

Dr. George Knight, New Testament professor at Covenant Seminary helped instigate a "Day of Evangelism" once each semester during my time at Covenant. It was my desire to have an open-air meeting on the campus of Washington University. Growing up in Brighton, England it was a common sight to see in an English sea-side town. My thought was to arrange an open-air meeting once each semester down at Washington University in St. Louis. As I asked students if they would be interested; I was hit by what I named the "seminary alibi."

The seminary alibi went like this: "If I don't come with you to Wash U. God will forgive me, right?" "Right." "But if I don't get my Hebrew paper turned in tomorrow, I am going to have an "F" on my resume for eternity."

I went to see Dr. Knight. I sensed that even though it was a great alibi, I sensed that many of the students that I asked were not really interested in reaching out with the gospel or talking to people about Jesus outside the church. Dr. Knight solved the problem by arranging to have a "day of evangelism." What that means is that everybody had a free day from classes to do evangelism. Some instruction was given, and the day was set.

I started off the day being encouraged as I was approached by Howard, a fellow student. I am not sure why Howard was even at seminary. On the day of evangelism, he came to me and asked me what I thought he should do. I knew that Howard was likely not a believer so instead of asking him what his spiritual gifts were, I was prompted to ask him what he liked to do. He told me that he liked looking at plants and reading books. *I told him I did not know what he should do but I knew someone who did.* So, we prayed. I asked God to help Howard know what he should do for the day. i.e., Show him whether to go off and look at plants or go off and look at a book.

Well, at the end of the day I saw Howard coming towards me with a sort of smile on his face. I remember saying ironically, "Howard, *what in the world* happen to you today?" Howard told me that he had two conversations about Jesus during the day?" I told Howard that in my book he got himself an A+, twice. I asked him if he wanted to tell me what happened but both conversations as he said were disasters. Later I discovered that the first conversation was in a library. Someone came in and could not figure out how to use the card system. For some reason, known to God, Howard offered to help him.

As he was helping him, he remembered what I had said, that if you are having a conversation with someone you can choose to change the subject. Howard tried and failed miserably. His second conversation happened as a student entered the library and was obviously stressed and angry. It turned out that the student's professor, who was not a believer, was punishing the student. His punishment was that he had to write a five-page paper on the New Testament. When Howard discovered that, again, for some reason, since he was studying the New Testament at seminary he offered to help. Again, he tried to witness and again made such a mess of it that it was a while later that I heard his embarrassing story of the second conversation.

In both cases, I told Howard that if I were grading his day's work, of course I was not, I would have given him an A+ plus, and another A+ for his second conversation. When I am talking to non-believers I sometimes say, "You know, you should really relax. I do not have any power over you. All I can do is give you information. I do not even have the power to convince you of what I am saying. Even if I know more than you in one respect it is of little consequence. Again, I can only give you information. That's it!"

Back to Howard. Neither he nor I can save anyone—but grasp this. Neither of us can send someone to hell either. Regeneration is 100% God's work. Saving a person from their sins is 100% God's work. This is the amazing story for me that I learned on the seminary's first "Day of Evangelism." Howard likely overcame his fear of talking to people about Jesus outside the church for the first time in his life. It does not matter that on both occasions it ended in disaster. Howard has the rest of his life to get better at talking to people about Jesus. No eternal damage was done! Howard had cast off and set sail on his lifelong adventure in talking about Jesus.

Many folks hesitate to even begin to witness about Jesus. They are terrified that when they say the wrong thing that the other person will go to hell because they were given the wrong information. Another problem is that they think that there are 3,000 questions that they do not know the answer to. It rarely happens but even when someone asks you a question. You can say, "Nobody has ever asked me that question. I don't know the answer. What I do know is that for every honest question there is an honest answer. I'll find the answer and get back to you." In fact, there are about 12 answers in my experience that you are likely to be asked. "Old chestnut questions" as the Brits might say.

The work of saving a person from their sins or regeneration, is 100% God's work! What that means is, after Howard and I prayed Howard broke new ground and twice he tried his hand at witnessing. On his own admission both times ended in disaster. What was amazing was that Howard who was introspective shy and even awkward socially, literally stepped out in faith on the Seminary's first "Day of Evangelism." Howard demonstrated in effect that you can steer a moving ship, but you cannot steer a ship that is not moving.

A Bride for Life

Sheila and I were married during the summer of 1975. I had completed two of my three years of seminary so we decided that my last year I would split into two six-month semesters.

Andy and Peasy hosted our wedding reception in their beautiful home in St. Louis and allowed us to have a ten-day honeymoon in their home in Maine, which was called "Munasca." I worked on the house and Sheila did sewing for Peasy.

The house sat on an ocean front in a beautiful location on the edge of the Atlantic Ocean, in Maine. "Munasca" was the home I had worked on the summer I met Sheila up in Toronto, Canada. Eating at their dining room table and looking out the window it was easy to imagine that you were eating at the captain's table looking out on the Atlantic Ocean. But I am getting ahead of myself with the story!

In the summer of 1974, I drove up with Brent Yule in Peasy's truck and we drove up to Maine from St. Louis. As we drove north on Route 1, we picked up a set of Queen Anne chairs that Peasy had bought, or she was having restored. Driving up Route 1, I never drove for so long without seeing a blade of grass. I finished my work on "Munasca" in good time and asked if they wanted me also to paint the outside of their home. It was a delight as the house was on the edge of the Atlantic Ocean and on each of the three floors you could step out of a window onto the roof below and walk all around the house with the sun and the sea breezes all around you. All I had to do was go out a window on the roof and walk around the house painting in the sunshine with the refreshing Atlantic breezes. It was a treat to go to work.

On the way home from Maine, I had Brent drop me off at a Greyhound Bus station and I went up to Toronto to visit Sheila. I knew it would be a good time as she shared a house with three other girls one of whom was Laurence, the girl who was at Swiss L'Abri with Sheila, while they both worked on translating part of a section Os Guinness's book, *The Dust of Death*.

Sheila met me at the bus station in Toronto and we walked back to the house. As soon as we entered the kitchen in the house, one of her girlfriends asked me before I even sat down. "What do you think Sheila should do with her life?" I was a little taken aback and managed to answer, "Oh I think that she should live it!" That appeared to be an acceptable answer. Well, as I recall we got engaged in 36 hours after she met me at the bus station!

We had been writing to each other for a year or so. With all my travels I have experienced, how nice it is to get a letter from a relative or a friend. On Sunday afternoons I often sat down to write letters. Sheila had committed to working at a Teen Challenge center in St Catherine's and it turned out to be a lonely and difficult situation. We both looked forward to receiving letters from each other.

Sheila was working at the University in Toronto in the housing department. We went up to the library and apparently, were sitting too close to each other. So, we got the impression that we should go outside and find a bench to sit on. We had been reading about Martin Luther who was explaining a couple of reasons why he decided to get married which were to "vex the pope and shame the devil." I was so excited about falling in love with Sheila and getting engaged that I do not remember how I got home to St. Louis. Did I hitch-hike or catch a bus? I have no idea!

Dr. Will Barker gave permission and arranged for Sheila to attend seminary, as an auditing student. So, some three weeks after the semester began Sheila started classes. After her first week she took a Hebrew test and produced an A. The rest of the class were taking the exam at the end of their first month.

Sheila was able to live in the Grace and Peace neighborhood and stayed with Peter and Linda Vaughn. Peter was at seminary with me. Peter would later organize my Workshop on Reformed Evangelism that I had written. Sheila would ride with us to school, attend classes, and go to work for Dr. Shearer. Sheila would then come back to the apartment, and then later I would walk her back to Peter and Linda's.

Sheila and I went to her cousin David's wedding at Lake Manitou, Québec. Sheila's dad built a house on the edge of the lake, in this idyllic setting. Of course, I smartened up to meet Sheila's folks and to attend David's wedding. Sheila and her family spent many happy holidays at Manitou. I'm glad I was able visit Manitou and understand why they had so many holidays there.

We were married on June 7th, 1975, in the Chapel of Concordia Seminary. Sheila's mum, (Elspeth Byers) made Sheila's wedding dress. She sewed for the Missouri Repertory Co. for their productions. None of my family were able to be present in St. Louis for our wedding. However, we were able to visit them in England six months later for 6 weeks. We also were able to travel to N. Ireland to visit my mum's family.

We rented a car and travelled through the English countryside stopping for leisurely coffee, pastries and meat pies and Pub lunches. We travelled to the South-West of England, through Cornwall and stayed at a quaint English Inn in a fishing village. The name of the Inn was the "Inn of the Rising Sun." The floors were so old that they were not level, but it didn't seem to matter. We had no plans to play marbles. To look out of our bedroom window and have a front row seat as it were watching the local fishermen coming and going and mending their nets was so interesting and exactly what one does on holiday with no pressure to be anywhere else.

Rob Burkham was my best man. Rob who met me at the door in Swiss L'abri and Rob who met me when I arrived at Covenant Seminary for my first ever six-week class of Greek.

Sheila's bridesmaid was Mandy, a member of Grace and Peace. One afternoon before the wedding I met Mandy in the Covenant Seminary bookshop. We were both looking at books and Mandy opened our conversation telling me that she was planning to get married. Still adapting to being in America, I asked her if she needed help looking for someone, or was that all taken care of? It was all taken care of.

Naturally, Sheila was expecting me to wear a suit on our wedding day. I went to "Famous Bar" and chose a three-piece suit in a pleasant navy-blue material. When I asked the salesclerk, how much I owed him I was shocked. He said, "that will be $180.00." I said, "For that price you can unwrap it and hang it up for sale again. That is too much for that suit!" At that moment I think I might have slipped into my bartering mode of doing business which I picked up on my travels. In Egypt, to learn how to work out an honest and fair worth for goods bought we learned that to be careful shoppers you had to take the price offered, divide by 5, half that figure and beat the man down finally saying words to the effect, "you are stealing from me with your price and then walk away."

Often then, the merchant would run after us and offer us his "final price" which was acceptably lower. We then would confirm or refuse the sale. We rarely paid the price in the shop. It was often on the street before he walked back to his shop. In a recent day in Istanbul, Turkey, Stephen and I were offered a price for a travel booklet for 37 Turkish lira. We enjoyed paying 5 Turkish lira for the well-produced booklet.

After telling Sheila that I would not pay $180 for a 3-piece suit she held her ground and told me that we needed to be married with me wearing a suit. It was the only one I wanted and some 10 days later I had to return to "Famous Bar." Imagine my joy when I saw the same suite, "my suit" on sale for $110.00. Part of my problem was that as a teenager my mother insisted that I wear a suit to church each week. However, in England even when I was 18 years old, I could choose my own cloth and have a 3-piece suit tailor-made and fitted for only 18 English pounds.

Though a bit out of place chronologically, an experience comes to mind that happened in Donegal, Ireland, during the 6 years we spent in England after graduating from seminary, being ordained, and ministering in Grand Cayman Island. Sheila and I, Andrew and Stephen were driving and camping in the south of Ireland. Early one morning I drove out of our campsite into the town of Donegal to find a chemist/pharmacy to get a prescription for Sheila's headache. Next to the pharmacy, in a shop window I saw a beautiful blue ladies Irish Tweed suit with a jacket and matching skirt displayed in the window. I went in and bought it for Sheila before I got her prescription. It certainly caught my eye. It was grand. It was beautiful. I must have owned a credit card at the time because I certainly could not afford to buy it with the money I had in my pocket.

After buying the light blue tweed outfit I looked around the shop to discover that not just the front window but the shop, on investigation covered the whole block. It was the main outlet for the world-famous Irish tweed, suits, and jackets. One front window displayed what was in stock on the inside. Before I left with Sheila's prescription, not only had I bought the suit for Sheila, but I also bought three well-fitting Irish Tweed jackets for myself! One was an almost matching light blue tweed jacket that matched the color of Sheila's new suite. Another was a light brown tweed jacket and the third was a tweed jacket with an earthy mix of matching browns, dark greens, and yellows. In fact, a beautiful Irish tweed jacket of autumn color threads.

I was able to wear all three Irish tweed jackets for years before I outgrew them. Sheila just recently gave her tweed jacket and skirt away!

As is often the case, one story in our journey reminds me of another story. This was also during the six years we spent in the UK before returning to America. We were camping on the Isle of Wight which is in the English Channel between England and France. This was the first time we consciously as a family decided to take a car trip in between jobs. When I had three or four days before my next known job, we would go to our bank and draw out cash for our trip. So, without any planning, we drove down the driveway of Whitehill Chase and before we reached the main Bordon Road, we stopped to pray asking God whether we would turn right or left. That kind of no plan! It was not long before we decided to head for the Isle of Wight.

We looked forward to the ferry ride from England to the Isle of Wight.

We arrived to learn that we would be on the island at the same time as some tall ships in all their glory with yards of sail that each ship was rigged for a race around the island. I was convinced I needed to buy a telescope. I tried to convince Sheila that I needed a telescope to fully appreciate the race. Eventually, I went into the shop to buy one. When I reached for the money envelope in my shirt pocket, it was not there!

We spent considerable time retracing our steps as it was a lot of money—70 English pounds. We prayed to God that he would help us find the money. We knew that the Bible states that God is omniscient, that means that he knows everything that goes on in His world. Finally, we were back where we started. We were leaning on the railing overlooking the ocean. Then we noticed a light brown object about 50 yards away, floating in the ocean. What was more interesting to us was that there were also two small boys swimming near the brown object.

I shouted out to the boys that I would give them a pound each if they could bring the envelope to me. It was a prayer answered, before our eyes!

Application being if you lose an earring while getting ready for church or an event, you may think you have lost it but remember God knows where it is. Ask Him to help you find it. "God, would you please show me where the earring is." Just remember, when you find it remember that you asked God to help you find it and He helped you find it. Do not forget to give thanks!

Back at the telescope shop I apologized that all my money was wet. "No problem" the lady said. She showed us a washing line of wet money drying in the back room! I also recall that we prayed for a "real campsite." We were asking God to guide us to a site that was not covered with painted lines dictating where we could camp. We wanted a location that did not remind us of organized suburbia. We wanted to be in the countryside and in a site that had running water and a public toilet facility. When we drove to the campsite that we found it had just that. We later found out that at that time, our campsite was the only campsite on the island that was literally not suburbanized. It was a field in a country area with running water and a toilet facility for the campers.

Later we found a fisherman who sold us a fresh lobster. We asked him to cook it for us.

To have lobster for a meal while camping was a real treat. The next morning, we got up early before the sun came up. Stephen had been suffering with a stomach upset and asked a question as we walked along the cliff which was, "Daddy, does God have a bottom?" The answer given was, "Since God doesn't have a body or a bottom, no. However, when God came down to earth as a man, Jesus had a body and a bottom." Andrew also had a question as we watched the sun rise, as we walked along the cliff and it was, "Daddy, did we get up before God this morning?" Answer given, "No we didn't. God neither slumbers nor sleeps.

Thanking God that he had helped us find our "non planned" trip money, we set off home and arrived safely to find the next job waiting for me. God was good to us as a family and led us, guided us, and provided for us, on our trip, as He has promised to do during our life. We had also prayed that God would direct us to a camp site like the old days. By that I mean that it was a real campsite in the country.

Some might ask why I tell such seemingly insignificant stories about prayers I have offered. That is a great question and the answer, in part, is because spiritual lessons are often derived from our daily circumstances and experiences. God cares about the "small things" in our lives as well as the "large things." We see that same concern in all of creation. It is evident whether we look at God's creation through a microscope or a telescope—God is a God of details. Remember the words of Jesus in Matthew 10:29–31 (ESV):

> "Are not two sparrows sold for a penny? And not one of them will fall to the ground apart from your Father. But even the hairs of your head are all numbered. Fear not, therefore; you are of more value than many sparrows."

God cares about the details of creation, and He cares about the details in our lives. In part, it is for that reason that we read in 1 Thessalonians 5:16–18 (ESV):

> Rejoice always, pray without ceasing, give thanks in all circumstances; for this is the will of God in Christ Jesus for you.

If we cultivate a life of "praying without ceasing" in a continuous conversation with God, we will pray for the "small things" in our lives as well as the "large things."

Soon after we were married Sheila was asked if she would cook and clean each weekday for a doctor, Dr. Shearer, whose wife tragically had left him. The doctor had adopted five biracial children and had one of his own. Sheila and I would go to his home after class driving our black Volkswagen "Beetle," Sheila would clean and do laundry and get the evening meal ready for the doctor and his family. Instead of a seminarian diet, Monday through Friday, we were catapulted into having roast beef, lamb, pork, or chicken each evening.

Providence, Not Luck

I don't believe in luck or fate. Those are ideas deeply rooted in Middle Ages for the former and ancient Greek mythology for the latter. I believe in providence—the providence of God (see Ephesians 1:11). Things don't "just happen" in our lives. Circumstances are not without cause. Often that cause is God.

One afternoon at seminary, Sheila and I were low in spirit and a choice presented itself to us. Either we would go to the Missions Conference, or we would go to a movie. We chose to 'flip a coin,' to determine between a movie or a missions' conference. We tossed the coin. I believe the Lord determined the result. Proverbs 16:33 states, "We toss the coin, but it is the Lord who controls its decision." We went to the mission's conference. After the meeting I met Earl Witmer who headed the Board of Home Missions. He mentioned that Randy Nabors was looking for an assistant. I began talking to ask Earl about the possibility of a job. Earl explained that the job opening was for a secretarial assistant, but he noticed my British accent. "Would you be interested in an opportunity in Grand Cayman Island?" "You mean a job straight out of seminary? Sure!" Grand Cayman Island south of Miami and Cuba was a British Crown colony.

Subsequently, I was accepted by the mission board, The Board of Home Missions, and our family of Sheila, Andrew (18 months), and me, were bound for Grand Cayman Island on Christmas Eve 1977. Earl arranged for me to "raise funds in three large churches." I did not raise a cent. The first question in one church was, "Do you like to do deep sea diving?" I knew that the "Wall" off Grand Cayman was a well-known attraction for deep sea divers. I explained to the questioner that I had sinusitis as a child, and I would not be doing any deep-sea diving. I thought that would be a church that might support us. As I said, "I didn't raise a cent!"

Earl took over the raising of funds and the Lord provided us with full support while we were there, and even after we left the island. The Mission funded us while we got situated in England. Earl was to become my boss and quickly became a wise and close friend. He was the Director of the Board of Home Ministries in the Reformed Presbyterian Church, Evangelical Synod (RPCES).

Preparing for Licensure

After graduating from seminary, I had to prepare for my Licensure exams which would qualify me to preach in the churches of the RPCES denomination. As I include this story I remember the phrase, "the Lord pulled me through" in preparation for ministry.

At the time, it was a terrifying ordeal that I faced. I needed to take six weeks off work and focus on pulling together all that I had been taught during my seminary education. Many of my classmates went home to be Licensed, I speculated, so that they would not have to be examined by their professors. I think I was the only one who was examined by the presbytery in St. Louis. My reason was my professors knew me.

An urgent prayer was sent to the Almighty to help me through this important and necessary hurdle. I was terrified about the whole ordeal, but I thought that since God had bought me this far somehow, he would again graciously and mercifully "pull me through." I received an interesting providence in answer to my prayers for my Licensure. How could I afford to stop working for six weeks and then produce the ability to pass my Licensure exams?

As well as being terrified I could not see an answer. When you have no idea, you pray to get an idea—an idea that is pleasing to God. That weekend Rick Smith and I were celebrating that we were half-way through re-roofing his folks' three-story house. It was the house of Ted and Gladys. Ted was an elder at Grace and Peace as well as a professor at Washington University in St. Louis. Ted was also the designer of the intriguing book cover of the L'Abri story. The book cover showed the collection of interesting people gathered after church in the Swiss Alps. It was the book cover that was partly used by God to cause me to want to go to Swiss L'Abri.

The fact that Rick Smith and I were half-way through putting a new roof on such an old and grand home was significant because the Monday morning after that I was unable to work because on Sunday at the church picnic, I sprained my ankle badly playing volleyball. Because of the height of the roof and the fact that we were working without scaffolding, there was no way I could "soldier on" and go back up on the roof. I was off work for six weeks. Obviously, God had other plans for me in those six weeks. My ankles had always been strong during my days of playing soccer and my travels. After my prayer I twisted my ankle on a beautifully kept lawn!

Amazingly, I was able with God's help to prepare for Licensure, such a task I had never tried to accomplish before, and God enabled me to pass and become licensed, to preach. Another amazing part to the prayer was that during those six weeks more money came in through the church in donations for me than I could have earned if I had continued working. Maybe you can see why I am so sure that praying to the only true and living God who created the heavens and the earth, is so necessary in life? And it was prayerfully that we embarked in our new ministry on Grand Cayman Island.

— 18 —

ISLAND MINISTRY

Associate Pastor, Grand Cayman Island, 1977–1979

If you are open to the leading of God, you will be taken to some remarkable places and have extraordinary experiences far beyond what you imagined to be possible in your life. That was certainly true of our time in the Cayman Islands. Many people in ministry might look back on their early years and consider them their "desert" or "wilderness" years, using the biblical themes of Moses, the Israelites, Jesus, or Paul and their experiences. I can't do that; mine were island years!

Most people would likely need a map to locate Grand Cayman Island that is part of the autonomous British Overseas Territory known as the Cayman Islands. The territory, comprised of three islands (Grand Cayman, Cayman Brac and Little Cayman), in the western Caribbean Sea and encompass 2264-square kilometers south of Cuba. There is one thing to know for certain—the weather is different than in St. Louis!

Sheila and I arrived on Grand Cayman Island in the afternoon on Christmas Eve 1977. Pastor Jonas Shepherd had arranged for me to attend a meeting that evening. I do not remember what the meeting was for. My ordination date would come later in our time there. It was March 18th, 1979, on Grand Cayman Island. Dr. William Barker and Dr. Paul Gilchrist officiated the ordination service in Boatswain Bay Presbyterian Church.

After being on the island of Grand Cayman for three weeks we had a delightful visit from Earl Witmer and another brother, a minister from the Florida presbytery, Rev. Graham. As we walked along the 7-mile beach, with its beautiful white sand, the question was asked, "Paddy, what do you think is going on here?" The question was framed in reference to the ministry. I had just completed my first three weeks of it.

My response was to say that I grew up in a biblical evangelical home, and my dad, the Rev. Alan J. N. Cook, M.A., was the Rector of St Peters-upon-Cornhill, London E.C.1. I mentioned that because I had some experience in the Church. My answer to Earl's question was, "I think the senior pastor ought to repent or be removed." During his time on the island Jonas had overseen an expansion of the church facility and the church was now debt free. No small accomplishment.

Our two years of ministry there were filled with memorable experiences, and it was a time of great learning for me. Shortly after our arrival in the Cayman Islands, in February 1978, the local *Norwester Magazine* published a brief article regarding our arrival and ministry under the heading "Sharing the Work at Bosun Bay." It read:

> A warm welcome to the Rev. Patrick Cook and his wife Sheila and their infant son Andrew McFarlane, who arrived in Grand Cayman to share the pastoral duties at Boatswain Bay Evangelical Presbyterian Church in West Bay. The young minister will be assisting the Rev. Jonas Shepherd, minister in charge, in the work there for the next two years with special emphasis on the training of elders and lay workers in the congregation, and the development of the youth ministry. Mr. Cook was born in Cambridge, England. Two other members of his family are also in the ministry. His father, an evangelical Anglican in the City of London, and his elder brother Peter, as a chaplain in Belfast, Northern Ireland. He is a graduate of Brighton College of Technology with a degree in building construction and has just recently gained his Master of Divinity degree from Covenant Theological Seminary in St. Louis, Missouri.

> His wife has taken up supervision of the Lighthouse School for Handicapped children, is from Montreal, Canada. She has had special training at Park College, Missouri, and the University of Minnesota. She holds a B.A. degree in French, having studied that language for five years in Switzerland, principally at the University of Neuchatel.

It was a nice article, and it introduced us to folks, but it didn't tell everything. One thing it left out was my challenge of how to claim my Buick Skylark that was sitting waiting for me on the Quay in full view! Moving anywhere overseas is always a challenge and especially so if there are vehicles involved—at least it was for me.

As I talked with the police in Georgetown, it was late in the afternoon. I had not had time to get a tag or secure insurance to drive the car home. I was clearly told that in this instance it would be alright. You can imagine that my first "run in" with the police on Grand Cayman was being stopped on the way home to Boatswain Bay as I drove from Georgetown the capital alongside the beautiful 7-mile sandy beach, taking in beachside restaurants like the Lobster Pot, with its natural island foliage covering the outside walls. The roof was a thatched pattern using local foliage, woven beautifully, and delightfully different.

I asked the policeman who had flagged me down what was the matter. He asked for my papers for the car. I finished our polite conversation with words like, "I will be more than upset when I go into town tomorrow to find out that I had been stopped for papers when I had been told by a uniformed police officer that he thought that in my situation it would be all right." The officer did not take kindly to me saying that so I added that if the advice that I was given was a lie I would be more than just upset. Thankfully, it all worked out smoothly.

After meeting the police in this way, I was flagged down again on my way to the other side of the island to meet a small group of worshipers meeting in a private home. This time I asked the policeman, what was the matter, and I was told that I did not have enough lights showing on the car. I did have a light that seemed sometimes to go out. As I walked around the car, I was able to see that all my lights were on. So, I asked how many lights I needed. It was decided that I had enough lights, so we parted in good spirits.

Another time, shortly after these incidents, I was flagged down again, so I pulled over outside Mr. Bertie's shop. He came out to see what was happening. I asked the policeman what the trouble was again. This time I was told I was not allowed to drive my car without a registration plate. That puzzled me as in the rear window my registration plate was clearly visible. This time was a few days after I arrived in Grand Cayman. I asked the policeman, if he would look at the back of my car and tell me if he saw my registration plate.

Imagine my surprise when he said he could not see it. So, I showed him my registration plate propped up in the rear window. Now he told me that it needed to be screwed onto the back of the car. I did not know that. I told him I had just arrived and had not had time to screw the plate on the area that was set aside for it. Mr. Bertie came out with a screwdriver, so I took the plate out of the back window and screwed it to where it was supposed to be and again all was well, and we all parted in good spirits.

Mr. Bertie was an elder in our church and a well-respected Justice of the Peace on Grand Cayman Island. After I had been on the island for well over a year when my father and stepmother were visiting, we were driving into Georgetown to introduce Dad to the Chief of Police as Dad had been invited to speak to the Island Rotary Club. We had more than six in the car. The policeman wanted to ticket us for having more than 6 in the car. I told him that we were going to visit the Chief of Police, and we would talk to him about the incident.

I told him that if he planned to give me a ticket for having more than six in the car, he had 48 hours to buy a bus and get it on the island. That would be by Monday morning as Sheila regularly had to drive with 13 small children to the school for handicapped children that operated out of the church as the government had not provided a bus for the children to get to school. Again, thankfully we were not given a ticket, and we parted in good spirits!

Many things were different on Grand Caymen. For example, we ate turtle meat on Grand Cayman, and I liked it. We also enjoyed turtle soup and that was good too. We lived next door to the turtle farm. There were four houses in our little cul-de-sac. Our house overlooked the road that went around the turtle farm in Boatswain Bay at the northwest end of the island.

We joined the Caymanians buzzed by the mosquito mist, sprayed from the planes that doused the island in season. Island living isn't all paradise! The other thing we relied on was the "sweet rain" as the Caymanians called it. Like many houses we had a tank under the house that collected all the rainwater that God sent to us. The trick was to be able to clean out the tank just before the rainy season. I do not know how people fared doing that.

To clean our floor, we opened the back door, turned on the hose and watched the water run onto the porch and into the sandy garden. Two or three times a year I would be able to leave the island and fly with Cayman Airways to Florida for our RPCES, Florida Presbytery meetings. I was told that when I arrived back on the island, if I had taken 'alcohol' on the plane from the flight attendant that the whole church would have found out about it. Probably so. That's how it is in a small community!

Sheila was not able to leave the island as she was the principal and only teacher in the little school for handicapped children that was founded and operated out of our Boatswain Bay Presbyterian church building. Miss Sheila was more susceptible to the phenomenon of dealing with becoming "island wacky."

Being on such a small island and only three main roads to explore it is easy to feel the experience of becoming Island-wacky. I remember that we left the third road to explore as something to look forward to. The trip was called a little adventure. As it happened, we had to try to conquer the route on a second attempt as the first attempt we ran out of gas. Yes, it was a little adventure, but it was also a little embarrassing.

One of the witnessing experiences that I remember after one presbytery meeting was at the airport in Florida. After the presbytery meeting, I was feeling low in spirit, and somewhat frustrated. As I thought about my frustrations after the presbytery, I came upon a member of Hari Krishna in the airport. He *Looked* "so peaceful."

I was the one that was supposed to demonstrate peacefulness as a Christian! He came up to me and asked me if I would like a book that he was offering me. Initially I said, "No thank you." But then it was beautifully produced, and it was in color so I changed my mind and told him that I would take it and thank you. Then he asked me if I would like to give a donation to the cause. I asked him which cause, he was asking about. "The Hari Krishna cause." I politely said, "No thank you." As soon as I said that he tried to grab the book back. I happened to be quicker than him and told him that was my book because he had just given it to me. He did not like that and spat in my face. I took the time to explain to him what had just happened. I also told him that whatever he believed he had just behaved as an awfully bad human being because he tried to steal my book and then spat in my face.

I explained to him that we were in a very public place and a lot of folks were watching us and though they could not hear our conversation they had seen him try to steal my book and had seen him spit in my face. I have to say, now the roles were reversed. I became the one at peace and he was the one who had become steamed in the situation. I then felt better now and more peaceful. I generously offered to give him my book. He took it and I walked away feeling great! The feeling of peacefulness was in line with the reality of what had just happened. By confronting a false religion, I was given a fresh perspective of God's peace love and mercy.

At the beginning of my ministry in Grand Cayman I started submitting weekly articles to the *Cayman Times*. I went to their offices and was politely and pleasantly received. Relying on the detailed material from Walter Martin's classic book, *The Kingdom of The Cults*, where his chapters were argued carefully and in detail. He carefully challenged the major cults by holding them accountable to the absolute truth of Holy Scripture, the Bible. The *Cayman Times* faithfully ran each article I submitted for which I was so thankful.

One of the men in the church in Boatswain Bay, was working on a construction site building a new hotel, so under God and through our brother, I was given permission to offer a short weekly homily and then be available to either pray or answer questions. If my memory serves me correctly, I do not recall any of the workers who rebelled and who did not listen with the others on site while they ate lunch. So, every other Wednesday I held an "open air" meeting on a local construction site while the workers ate their lunch.

The other Wednesday I was granted permission to go into Georgetown prison facility to talk with the prisoners. Following a few visits to the prison I began attending court hearings in the Georgetown courthouse. Judge Hercules from Jamaica was presiding at the time we were in Grand Cayman. The reason for attending his court hearings was to connect a crime with a prisoner's name to triangulate that when I asked a prisoner why he was in prison I had a handle on whether he was telling me the truth as to why he had been imprisoned.

The other ministry was to visit folks from the church who lived off the beaten track. It was a delight to have Joseph Ebanks, a deacon from the church who faithfully came each time to show me where the folks lived. I had to chuckle as often when Joseph and I walked up the path to the home, I heard hymn music playing. I like singing hymns, so it was never an issue.

On Saturday nights Sheila and I became leaders of the church Youth group. It was always a challenge to think of activities to do each week. We would go to the beach and play volleyball and have snacks and drinks. Sometimes we held Saturday meetings in our home. After 20 years we returned to the island and had a wonderful reunion with folks. One of the youth group members shocked us by saying a big thank you to us as she told us that it was the best part of her week."Who knew? We did not get much feedback from folks at that age so that was an interesting memory of our return visit. All four of our children returned to Grand Cayman and had an enjoyable visit.

Admittedly, Matthew was only 2 years old when we visited Grand Cayman as a family in 1996. We have continued to keep in touch with Roxma and her husband Peter. They pray for the ministry often. Roxma was a student at Covenant College. Our log home was six minutes away from the college off Scenic Highway.

One of my favorite memories from Grand Cayman was walking the famous Seven Mile Beach on our day off and ending up at a restaurant for breakfast. The beach is spectacular and renowned for its pure white sands and idyllic ocean scenery. It attracts swimmers, snorkelers, and beachcombers from near and far. It is frequently photographed and has appeared in publications around the globe. Apparently, because we were in our bathing costumes, we heard a rumor that we walked naked along the Seven Mile beach. Not true!

As an Englishman, I never thought that I would stay in America although I loved the freedoms that were afforded to us living in America. American's love and enjoy success and often encourage and help those reaching for it. Many "Brits" are basically jealous of success. Let me illustrate what I mean with a construction site illustration. In England I experienced practical jokers. After successfully impersonating the 4th son of King Saud of Arabia as a 19-year-old student, I am for practical jokes but not if the purpose is to put people down. On one occasion in England, I could not find my handsaw on a job. Not only was it hidden from view it was nailed up on a wall! Also, the handle was greased so that when I finally discovered it and reached to retrieve it, I got grease all over my hand.

In America, if I could not find my saw, it was not long before a co-worker offered me the use of his saw until I located my own saw. Being an Englishman I was looking forward to returning home to England with my wife and family—home to England from Grand Cayman Island in the fall of 1979.

19

"BACK TO BLIGHTY"

From G.C.I. to Ealing, London, 1979–1985

During the First World War, British troops often referred to England as "Blighty" and often referenced going "back to Blighty." Of course, the warfare I was engaged in was spiritual warfare and not physical combat; but it too took a toll, and I was glad to be able to return home and regroup spiritually and in the company of friends and family.

"Tentmaking" and Evangelism

Back in England, we were warmly welcomed home to the church in Ealing, which was the original church of English L'Abri. At the time, the current pastor of the church Max Harris was in America and was in the process of deciding to minister in the US. We were offered his apartment which we enjoyed and were thankful for. Sheila particularly enjoyed the freedom to go outside and walk to the local park with Andrew along with the freedom to walk to the local shops.

One Saturday night an elder from the church came to me and asked me if I could preach the next day. For whatever reason, his sermon was not coming together in time for the next day. I remember being at peace and saying. No, I am not that gifted that I could do that in the next 24 hours. But I was enabled with confidence to encourage him to pray that God would be faithful and give him the sermon that he needed for the service the next day. I remember that he was faithful in crying out to God and God was faithful and gave him a fine and finished message.

On another afternoon I had completely forgotten that I had committed to preach in the evening service and was reminded of my commitment late in the afternoon of the day I was due to preach. I do not recall the pain that throbbed in my heart and the ensuing anxiety that I must have gone through regarding the upcoming service. However, I am sure it was like that of our brother whose sermon was not coming together in time. What do you do when you are in such a frightening predicament? You recall the prayer of the prophet, Jonah chapter two. You pray to the only true and living God.

What happened for me was that I was enabled with confidence to settle on Psalm 119 for my text for the evening. When I asked someone to read the text for the evening sermon, they asked what passage I needed them to read. I said, "Psalm 119 please." When asked which verses, I said "all of the verses please, in Psalm 119." I was asked again about how many verses and again I asked that all should be read.

The person then asked me if there was time during the service to read all 176 verses. When I told him, it would only take about 15 minutes he nodded and started reading. Little did he know that by reading the whole psalm he was giving the congregation half of my sermon. As he read all the verses a few thoughts came to mind, for which I had to thank God because I had done no work on a sermon that I had forgotten I was responsible for preparing.

A couple of people even came up to me after the message and thanked me. They said that they had been blessed of God to receive it. Because half of the sermon came straight from God's Word, they should have received a blessing! Of course, I was not dragged before kings and given words to speak as the Scriptures promise in Matthew 10:18–19. I could not help but think of that verse afterwards that God had promised he would give us the words to speak on such occasions. The fact that I was a delinquent preacher who had forgotten that he was preaching that night made me very thankful that God had rescued me. You can imagine how thankful I was when God was so faithful when I had not been faithful. I think I learned more than anyone else that evening!

After four months in Ealing, we moved down to the area of English L'Abri in Greatham, Hampshire. We were offered a single room in Bramshott, Hampshire. A delightful English village. Stephen was born while we lived there. The room had a small kitchen and bathroom. Andrew slept in the shower and each night we removed the sack of potatoes from the shower for him since he was only 2 years old. Sheila looked for a larger apartment for us but did not find anything.

Eventually, we were offered accommodation at Whitehill Chase in Bordon. Unbelievably, it was a property of about 20 acres in a built-up area. We were offered an area in the main house that had been a hunting lodge. We had a kitchen on the ground floor opposite Terry Wright's office, the warden for the property. Upstairs we had a living room with a fireplace and two bedrooms and a bathroom with a separate toilet in the passageway. We were blessed with two beautiful lawns on which the boys could play. Once when Andrew and Stephen had a snow day, we took a one-gallon plastic carton that used to have ice cream in it and made bricks of snow. With pressed snow bricks we built a snow fortress. That year Sheila was given a strange Christmas present of a soccer ball, and a garden goal post and net. I tried to explain why it was to be her present. The boys and I would spend so much time outside playing soccer that she would have peace and quiet in our flat. Regrettably, I did not do a good job selling that idea!

One of the pleasantries of living in England is enjoying some of the many English pubs dotted throughout the English countryside. John Blake, one of my friends from church, and I would arrange to go to an English pub for fellowship and a drink. Part of the enjoyment was driving through the country lanes and finding an English pub with a cozy log fire burning in the hearth. One of my favorite pub snacks was a soft white bread sandwich with Irish butter, sharp cheddar cheese inside along with a hot crispy fried English sausage. One such pub is engrained in my mind. I discovered it during my time with the MG drivers' club. I do not recall any of the conversations, but I do remember a unique English pub somewhere close to the A 272. Part of its uniqueness was that there was only space for about 14 drinkers inside.

Driving from Haywards Heath, west along the A 272 to Winchester and beyond was one of my favorite roads to drive. When I returned to England from America there was a meeting of the International Presbyterian Church Synod that I attended. I was told it was the first time Frances Schaeffer was not present at such a synod meeting. At the meeting I was appointed as a Presbyterian Evangelist to the International Presbyterian Church (IPC) a church that grew out of the ministry of English L'Abri in Greatham, Hampshire. After my appointment a L'Abri worker slipped a twenty-pound note into my hand. That was the sum of any visible encouragement for the title I proudly accepted.

It turned out that it was a title with no apparent job description or oversight, so I needed to find a job. My first job was for an established English tradesman near Liphook, in Hampshire, a Mr. Moss. He worked in his carpenter's shop and employed one young man full-time as a painter. Interestingly his painter did a 7-year apprenticeship to become a painter. His apprenticeship included mixing his own paint and repairing various surfaces to receive an undercoat before adding another coat and finally a finish coat. In England there is a lot of rain and damp weather, so wood needs to be carefully prepared, dry, and properly painted in the correct temperature range to protect it for all the English dampness. My first assignment was to replace a complex wooden truss by making a new one for the local cricket pavilion. It was an idyllic location. I must have done something right because on completion of the large newly constructed truss I had exactly 6 inches of wood left over. No praise was given, but I was hired.

In England, I was working as a self-employed contractor. More properly as an odd job man in people's homes. In England "well to do folks" were not always able to know, trust and communicate with a tradesman. I had taken a job painting. Painting the outside of a rather nice house, in Hazelmere, Hampshire. A Stock-broker type of village in the heart of the English countryside. Since I was offered a range of jobs I usually arranged to work by the hour. I explained that to give a fixed price for painting a house, not knowing if some of the windows might be rotten and therefore unpaintable, without extra preparation and repair, I would have to add 25% profit to my estimated hours and materials. "I did not want to lose money working for you and I am sure you do not want to pay 25% more than you needed to" was my usual arrangement. Basically, if you do not like the quality of my work or how long I take you can fire me. No hard feelings. We almost always arranged to work for an hourly rate. A good estimator is usually the most experienced and knowledgeable person in a building company.

Because I always wanted to talk to my clients about Jesus, I could not talk to them and include that talk in my hourly rate for painting their house. So, after praying about it the idea came to me that whenever the lady of the house went out for an errand, I would work much harder. That way when she returned, I could honestly afford to spend some time talking to her. One of the consequences of doing that was also in Hazelmere. I knew that several ladies were watching behind their curtains to see how I worked, especially when the lady of the house went out. How else could I explain that in Hazelmere I painted 5 houses in the same road, all very profitable? One after the other. One client, along with my wages gave me a treasured Louis Vuitton leather travel case for the work I did for her.

Candidating in Churches

During the six years that we were in Greatham, England I was invited to preach twice. Both times were because, I was about to candidate in a church. I was anxious to be able to preach and be critiqued before candidating. The first time I candidated in a church in Ballyclare, Northern

Ireland. I remember meeting David Watson and I thoroughly enjoyed the fellowship and hospitality of this brother and his family. On the occasion I found myself at a youth meeting in his home. It was beautiful to be there and enjoy the robust and glorious singing from the group of young people.

Sitting in the church before the service I saw probably 8 large healthy-looking men, walk up the isle on the right-hand side of the sanctuary and enter a room. I was invited to join them. They were there to pray for the blessing of God on the worship service and the preacher of the morning. I have to say that it was the closest time in my life when I thought that I would levitate. The praying was sincere, uplifting to say the least, and so powerfully encouraging! I was thankful that the Lord was faithful and accepted my sermon as acceptable before such godly men. I was not accepted to minister in their midst as they determined rightly that I was not experienced enough, which I agreed with.

The second time I candidated at a church during my six years living in the UK, was in Canada, in Halifax Nova Scotia. Because I felt so "rusty," I arranged to spend 10 days in the church before the presbytery that would be examining me and bone up on what I thought I might be asked. It turned out that I had landed in a church in turmoil. For me it meant that I did not have much study time as I stayed with a different family each night. Consequently, I had to listen to how each one saw the turmoil. What had happened was that the American church planting arm of the denomination had "installed" an American pastor in the local Canadian church in between presbytery meetings, which were six months apart. The new pastor was ministering at the university and some of the students were converted under his ministry and the hyper Calvinist elders were incensed.

Bob Hamilton, the moderator of the Canadian Presbytery presided over a split presbytery. Previously he and his wife had been missionaries in Mafraq, Jordan. On three or four occasions during the meeting as moderator he cast the deciding vote. Each time I approached him to compliment him for his courage and biblical stance casting his deciding vote.

A group of the hyper Calvinistic Canadian elders walked out of the presbytery because they did not get their way, consequently the whole presbytery had to drive 200 miles to collect enough elders to make a quorum to complete the business of the presbytery. It was sad to see all that happen.

To resolve the problem every member of the church in question was allotted 2 minutes to stand and say what they thought the problem was in the church. They could speak, read an e-mail, or play a recording for the presbytery and say whatever they wished to the presbytery about how they understood the situation. The Presbytery appropriately went into an "Executive Session" The only restriction was that they had to realize that it was a court of the Lord Jesus Christ, and He was listening. They could say whatever they thought that they needed to say but it had to be appropriately delivered bearing in mind where they were and who was listening. The problem of the church came out into the open early and clearly and votes were taken and each time the moderator cast his deciding vote with courage and biblical clarity.

On Friday night at presbytery around 10:00 pm one of the elders refused to vote for me because he had not heard me preach. As a result, another pastor Rev. Tony Dallison, and I, had to preach the next morning. I was to preach at 8:00 am. I got home with my hosts at 11:00 pm and after visiting with them for the first time went to my room around midnight. I finished my sermon at 7:00 am and by 8:00 am I began to preach for the presbytery. There was not too much sleep that night!

The sermon I thought was as good as I could have delivered considering the tension of the previous days. After the sermon, I was examined and asked how and where I became a Christian. When I told them that I became a Christian in my father's Anglican church, some of the Canadian elders were beside themselves. They could not and would not believe that I had or could become a Christian in an Anglican church. "How is that possible?" they asked. "By grace through faith," I replied. They failed me on my Christian experience!" These were the same elders who did not get their way and rather than accept the biblical ruling of the local presbytery stormed out of the presbytery meeting hoping that their unbiblical action would not allow the ruling of the presbytery to stand. Unfortunately for them as mentioned above, the presbytery all drove some 200 miles, and collected enough members to form a quorum. By doing that the business of the presbytery was completed. The divisive elders were eventually disciplined and removed as elders from the church/presbytery.

In another church we were in there was an extremely delicate situation which was not handled biblically in my opinion. The pastor was heard but the people were frustrated that they were not given the appropriate opportunities to say what they thought the problem was before the presbytery. I, with counsel, wrote a ten-page letter, that apparently, was never read or answered. It turned out to be uncannily close to identifying what I thought was the problem that the pastor later eventually acknowledged in written form. After everything was decided some 3 or 4 years later, I was invited to a meeting to ask me if I had any questions that I wanted to ask.

Before I spoke, I was told the case would not be revisited or reopened or changed. I replied I had about 12 questions that I thought were significant enough to ask but bearing in mind what I was just told the opportunity given to me was 4 years too late. The other question I was asked floored me. "Why then did you come to the meeting?" I told them that since the meeting was around 1:00 pm I assumed that I might get a free lunch. I was wrong about that!

Instead of handling the situation like the one in Canada, we had a member of presbytery come and preach a 16-point message. We didn't benefit by hearing from him, because he didn't benefit by hearing from us. What it did accomplish was to again, leave no time for the congregation to voice what they thought was the problem as they understood it. The congregation was denied an opportunity to present what they thought the problem was, at the appropriate time consequently, the problem was not resolved. There was no conviction of sin, no repentance offered, and no solution gained. Eventually, soon after, most of us had left the church, the church died, and the presbytery closed the church. This situation did not end well. It is also likely to be repeated.

Some years later it was repeated in the church that the pastor went to. When I was told about this sad situation by the pastor who "founded that church" I asked what kind of discipline was applied this time. No effective discipline was administered. The same pastor was let go and told to move on. That situation was not handled in a presbyterian format either. I pray to God that because the situation was not resolved biblically a second time that it doesn't happen a third time. I think it might.

*** According to the brother who founded the second church later told me it did happen a 3rd time. Again, sadly not in a presbyterian format. In the book below "The Apostolic Church, which is it?" The Canadian situation above in my opinion was resolved in a presbyterian format. The three sequel failed situations mentioned above were not. Even though in all church discipline cases all the brothers are depraved, if they had been faithful to their calling, even as sinful participants, a Biblical format if used can resolve a messy situation and substantial healing can be achieved so that God's name can be glorified, publicly.

There is a classic book written on biblical church government written by Thomas Witherow, titled *The Apostolic Church; Which Is It?* We were introduced to it in our course work at Covenant Seminary by Dr. George Knight III. It presented the three forms of Church government: the hierarchical church, (The Anglican, Roman Catholic Church) the independent church (Baptist—Congregational church), and the shared leadership church (Presbyterian church).

I believe the third option is the only biblical form of church government. If a congregant has a theological disagreement, with his pastor, he is encouraged to appeal his case to the local presbytery of ministers. After that an appeal can be made to the synod of the denomination and the national ministers of the denomination. However, the problem with the Presbyterian form of government is that all the members of the denomination are depraved (as are members of any denomination); that means that sometimes the biblical system does not work or is just not adhered to as it should be.

On both occasions, that I was invited to preach in Greatham, a significant line of folks waited to thank me after church for the sermon that God had given me. I do not believe it was my scholarship that was being recognized. I do believe it was the power of the Holy Spirit that moved them to thank me.

For any person who wants to serve God there need only be a willingness to serve. When God calls us, we must respond and be willing to serve. He will do the rest. When we respond, then like the prophet Isaiah, we too will be able to say: "I heard the voice of the Lord, saying, whom shall I send, and who will go for us? Then said I, here am I; send me." (Isaiah 6:8).

— 20 —

GOD'S TIMING FOR GOD'S WORK

Final Return to America and Kansas City, 1985

I was so thankful and proud that while in America, God carried me through seminary and subsequently ordained me into the gospel ministry. As I noted earlier, my ordination service was on Grand Cayman Island. Being English it, never occurred to me that I would not settle with my wife and family in England. As I understood the situation the view of the Presbytery of the IPC was that I was welcomed home and if understood what they were saying to me, that if after 10 years or so the congregation may decide that I should be a full-time Evangelist in the denomination. I would know then. I was so convinced that God had placed a call on me as an Evangelist, as a minister of the gospel, we decided that we ought to return to America. So eventually, that is what we did. I knew that I could not work and become a minister at the same time. However, I had many things to learn. On that I was right. It was around 6 years before we were able to return to America. Throughout the centuries, patience has been considered a virtue. There is a reason for that. With time, and in God's providence, often there comes wisdom. In our world of instant gratification patience is not a common trait, and yet, we are told many times in the Psalms to wait for God, to "be still, and know that I am God" Psalm 46:10).

For me, finally, it was Sheila's father who told me that I now had two degrees. One in Building construction and an M.Div. allowing me to be an ordained minister of the gospel. It was his opinion that I should use one of them instead of doing odd jobs in people's houses. He made me a generous offer to work for him in his construction company in Kansas City. A salary of $40,000 a year and a company car. It was an amazing offer but there was one problem. He insisted that I give up the call to the ministry and focus all my energy on his construction company. That, I could not do! Of course, I prayed about what to do and I was given the idea to talk to Dr. Os Guinness. He was so wise and encouraging. He told me: "Take the job. And if God wants you back in the gospel ministry, he will arrange all that." He did.

I took the advice of Os and off we went—back to America. We were so convinced that this was the right thing to do that we packed up our household items and our belongings to be shipped, *before* we were given our visas to return to America. We had our appointment at the American Embassy in London, and as we made our way out of London through the slow-moving traffic, with our visas. I remember the stares we received as we were stuck in London traffic, as we made our way home. Passengers in buses and coaches looked down on us eating a picnic dinner on our laps using the numerous stops driving out of London to eat our picnic. What was different was that Sheila had prepared a picnic with plates, knives, forks, and spoons so that we could eat our dinner on our laps. At that stage in life, we did not eat out. At the time we did not think it strange to be using nice plates for our picnic. Judging by the number of stares we received; we were probably the only ones who thought like that!

After 6 months in Kansas City, we were able to buy our first house. I believe the interest rate for a mortgage was around 18%! When we first visited the local school around the corner in Prairie Village that Andrew and Stephen eventually attended, I read these words over the front entrance: "Everyone is a winner." As I murmured too loudly for Sheila's ears, "How is that even possible?" She reminded me why we were at the school—to introduce ourselves and our two young children to the neighborhood school.

Assistant Pastor of Evangelism in the Presbyterian Church in America (PCA)

After eight months back in the U.S. I was able to enter full-time ministry in a church. The initial offer was $16,000.00 a year. I had to turn the offer down as I could not go from $40,000 a year down to $16,000 a year, overnight. I explained that with a part time salary we would probably have to move back to St. Louis where all my contacts were located.

In the providence of God, a man in the congregation came up with a donation to provide the balance of the money to make the salary offer $30,000 a year. The elders of the church approved the sum. However, the deacons were only offering $25,000. I asked the elders if they would like me to remind the deacons that the elders "run" the church and not the deacons. Gratefully they said, "Would you?" "Thank you!" I told them I would take care of it.

Subsequently, I met with the chairman of the deacon's board along with another deacon. *(Interestingly, God chose the other deacon, Dale Vaughn, to become the first donor for my present ministry.) At the time of writing this page he has been able to faithfully send his check to Presbyterian Evangelistic Fellowship (PEF) now Reformed Evangelistic Fellowship (REF) for 35 years).* I was able to tell them that I had accepted the offer of the job for $30,000.00 and the elders had approved the arrangement. The response was, "Well when I do the hiring and firing ..." I stopped the other brother at that point to remind him that the elders govern the church, not the deacons. After a brief pause the question was asked of me, "What is your program?" "Program for what I asked?" "What are you going to do on Monday?"

"I don't know. It's only Friday." "Well, if we are going to pay you $30,000, we'll need to know what your program will be. After a brief time to process the question I responded, by saying, "I don't have a program in mind. It does not seem right to me to object to me before I have done anything. If you do not like what I have done at the end of my first week, that would be a better time to fire me rather than before I had done anything right or wrong." It was clear that they needed more information, and I was prompted to say, "Well what I can tell you is that I will read my Bible and pray." "And we are going to pay you all that money and you tell us that you are going to read your Bible and pray?" As I just mentioned, "If you don't like what I do by the end of the week that would be the time to fire me, but not before I begin!"

On Sunday before my first day at work the youth pastor, Steve, asked if I could help him out by visiting the mother of one of the youth in his youth group who was in hospital. The hospital was about a mile from my house. I dropped by on my way home from evening church. When it was time to leave, I was able to say, "I'll drop by again first thing in the morning on my way to work." On Monday, my second visit at the hospital, it struck me that I was at work, so I found a comfortable chair in the waiting room and sat down to read my Bible. Shortly, the husband came and sat down beside me and poured his heart out to me. During the day, 14 family members came and did the same. I do not remember any of the conversations but at the end of the day the husband, Jack, a JCB digger operator, dressed comfortably in jeans a check shirt and construction boots, asked if I could come back on Tuesday, the next day and talk to his two children and take them in to see their mother. He said, "I don't think I can handle it." I responded "Sure." On Tuesday, with two young children and two knees I was prompted to sit one of each knee while we visited with their mum.

The next day Wednesday, the mother died. During the day Jack came up to me and happily announced that he had become a Christian. Jack asked me if I would take the funeral on Saturday. I arranged to go to his home on Thursday evening to talk about the funeral, music etc. A newly trusted surgeon does not tell his patient that the operation is the first operation that he has ever done.

As a newly ordained minister I did not tell Jack that his wife's funeral would be my first. I asked Jack who was doing the music for his wife's funeral. He told me it was Dolly Parton. I did not know who Dolly Parton was. He pulled out a record with a picture of Dolly Parton. As gently as I was able to, I told Jack that there were two conditions I had for taking his wife's funeral. I realized that he probably would not be able to find someone else to take the funeral the next day, but I had two conditions for conducting the funeral. My two conditions were, no Dolly Parton and the coffin is closed. He agreed to both conditions. By the grace of God, the funeral for Jack's wife went well.

The senior pastor helped me put the service together for which I was grateful. On Saturday morning I rode along with the funeral director to the church and talked with him and offered my services by saying, "If you ever get a client who doesn't have a pastor, you can always call me if you would like to. Subsequently, he did call me several times until in one funeral the Holy Spirit convinced a lady about something during my sermon. I was never told what convicted her, but what she did at the time of being convicted, was to get out of her seat and storm up the aisle towards me, making a scene. A couple of men from the funeral home intercepted her and ministered to her. The funeral director told me the gig was over! He was so embarrassed he did not want another scene like that.

In the providence of God my first week at the church was a blessed week. I took it upon myself to give the chairman of the deacon's board and his friend Dale Vaughn a report on Sunday the day after the funeral. The funeral was well attended with Jack and his family and friends that numbered over 100. So, I was able to speak to the Chairman and Dale, who amongst other careers was a retired railway man and air traffic controller, by saying, "I wanted to let you know that in our first week the Lord opened Jack's heart and he became a Christian and we had over a 100 non-Christians in the church this week. I wanted to warn you that I can't promise that every week." How encouraging was their response, "Any way you want to do it is fine by us!" A few months later I was voted in as chaplain to the young married couples' group which the Lord chose to bless and even increased in number.

I was invited to sit on the church committee on evangelism. After, six months nobody had talked to anybody about Jesus. I offered to get a telephone directory and just call somebody. That was not going to happen. Instead, the session decided to invite Dr. Ben Wilkinson for a week of evangelistic meetings to be held in the church. That was my first meeting with Dr. Ben Wilkinson.

About the same time, a sad situation developed where an elder nominee was being considered to become a PCA elder in our church. A fine man nominated with a faithful family with a responsible management job. However, it became known that he had not read the WCF. the Westminster Confession of Faith (WCF). The time of the ordination service was a busy time for him at work, and he was not able to commit to reading through it, even just once before the proposed ordination service. I was allowed to attend the session meetings of the church but as an assistant pastor, but I was not invited to vote.

The question was raised to remind the session that one of the ordination questions in the service of ordination of a new elder was that he be required to "sincerely receive and adopt the WCF." As a young and inexperienced minister, it occurred to me that for me to take part in a service of ordination of an elder nominee who had not read the WCF once and would not be able to before his ordination that I could not take part in such a service. I could not lay hands on him in an ordination service.

How could such a man assure the congregation that he sincerely receives and adopts the WCF if he has not even read it at least once. Eventually I made it known that I could not take part in the service and that if I were asked why, I did not take part in the ordination service when anybody asked me, I would be duty bound to declare it would not be biblical for me to. That would then present the session with a problem as to why they went ahead. I suggested that since the office of elder is a life-long appointment that we ought to wait until the nominee had read the WCF through at least once for me to be able to lay hands on him at his ordination service.

At a subsequent session meeting I walked in and one of the elders, without praying to open the session meeting, which is required, addressed me to say, "There is no more money for you." I replied, "All right we'll have to pray for some more money then." The elder repeated what he had just said. I replied by repeating what I had just said. Then it dawned on me what might be happening. So, I said, "Are you trying to fire me, because if you are you will need to have a biblical reason for firing me. You will need to tell me what my sin is. I need to tell you that if you have a biblical reason for firing me you need to tell me what that reason is. Then if you have a biblical reason, I am planning to repent. After that I am planning to be reconciled to you so that this matter can be dealt with biblically." I confess that I have sanitized the exchange because this is in printed form.

It took the session five months to fire me. I was extruded into the position of having to file charges in the presbytery for denial of my due process. I was never allowed to have any witnesses at any of the meetings over that time. On one occasion in shear frustration over the proceedings I banged my fist on the table. During the trial that was the only evidence of complaint that I recall that was sited against me. I went home that night and for some reason known unto God I picked up a copy of R.C. Sproul's book, *The Holiness of God.* I flipped open the book to Chapter, 5 "The Insanity of Luther." The following week at the session meeting I said words to the effect that, "There is a precedent that Martin Luther also in a meeting in Marburg banged his fist on the table in frustration and he also was known to often break wind. I would like it recorded in the minutes that I did bang my fist on the table in frustration, but I did not break wind." Three charges were filed in the presbytery on my behalf. The presbytery awarded me a victory in the first charge. After that it was decided that the other two charges be dropped. During the whole period of the five months, we never missed a mortgage payment and were able to pay all our bills.

A Providential Meeting

Even when we think there is nothing happening in our lives, God is working His plan behind the scenes. Remember the story of Joseph (especially Genesis 50:19–21). While I would not fully realize the plan for another three years, God used a providential meeting with Dr. Ben Wilkinson, the Executive Director of Presbyterian Evangelistic Fellowship (PEF) to continue His working in my life.

The church had invited Dr. Ben to come for a week to speak on evangelism. Not understanding that often visiting speakers preferred to be in a hotel where they could prepare for the daily speaking engagements and enjoy the refreshment of time alone without phone calls and local church responsibilities, I went to his hotel and asked him if he would like to stay with a family. He said he would like that very much. I took him home and saved the church $75.00 a night for the week. Looking back, the invitation to stay with us was probably more for me than for him.

I was in a difficult ministry position. I was not a pastor, and I was not a church planter. I've often said that I was not nice enough to be a pastor and I was not organized enough to be a church planter. But I did eventually understand that I was an evangelist. It was thanks to my mentor Dr. Ben Wilkinson that my calling was clarified. He was in our home in Prairie Village, Kansas for less than an hour, when he said, "You will never be happy until you are a full-time evangelist." That was in 1987. Later, I moved on from the work in the church and became a full-time evangelist with PEF. However, before joining PEF I took a job as a limo driver, taking executives to and from Kansas City International Airport.

When I started with PEF from Prairie Village, Kansas I prayed a simple prayer: "Lord, please give me people to talk to who will pay me.

I had no idea how to raise support for a ministry. As mentioned before, previously we were sent to minister in Grand Cayman Island. It was arranged that I speak in 3 large churches. I did not generate a cent for my upcoming ministry on Grand Cayman Island. But God faithfully provided all the time we were on Grand Cayman and indeed for the first six months that we were in England until we were resituated. We gave thanks to God of course for all the work that Earl Witmer had done as he oversaw our first ministry after seminary. Earl wanted to make sure that we were even taken care of between ministries! He was a fine Christian gentleman and a good friend!

I have never had trouble talking to people, but they have never paid me to talk to them. The answer to my simple prayer was that I got a job as a limo driver taking executives from their homes in Kansas City to Kansas City International Airport. Then waiting at the airport to collect clients off incoming flights to take them home.

So, I began my PEF ministry by becoming a limo driver. I did that for three years at the beginning of my ministry with PEF. I never took a call to pick up clients *before* 2 pm. In the mornings I worked on a mailing list and writing a Workshop on Reformed Evangelism. It has subsequently been translated into Albanian, Romanian and Russian.

After a couple of months of driving I received a significant check from Dale Vaughn. I called him to ask what it was for. He told me that it was to help support the ministry that I had been called to with PEF. He told me, "I know that you have started your ministry, and you are talking to people."

Dale was the first to begin supporting the ministry. He has faithfully sent his check and never failed to send it each month for thirty-five years. God has blessed us with the best supporters. I am so thankful that God has raised up a group of supporters that are of such a fine caliber. Most of them begin supporting us and then have faithfully kept supporting us each month. Dale, unknown to others, set the first example. In one of his calls to me he asked, "When are you going to finish that book of yours?" I asked him why he was asking? "I want to be able to read it before I die!" I think I replied with words to the effect, "Dale, you keep drinking your orange juice and I'll keep working on the book." I do not recall asking anybody except God for money. Most of the support for the ministry over the years has been given without asking for it with a few exceptions.

21

DRIVING PEOPLE AND PROCLAIMING JESUS

Limo Driver—for Kansas City Business Folks 1986–1989

On a Monday morning, the first day that I was no longer ministering at the church, I was painting the side of my house in Prairie Village, Kansas and my neighbor Mike came over and asked me how it was going. I had tears in my eyes, and he asked me, "What's up?" Well in common language I replied, "I just got fired from the church for telling the truth." His brother-in-law had also been through a similar experience. He was a very loving neighbor, he kindly offered to help me get a job with a limo company that his brother-in-law was working for. He bought me a $1,000 car and I began!

I was able to write all my repairs and maintenance charges off against tax with lifetime guarantees on all the moving parts and brakes etc. I wasn't Jehu of 2 Kings 9 and it wasn't one of the famous chariots of the Old Testament, but it enabled me to do the Lord's work!

As I reflect on my limo days, a bevy of conversations flash before me. My conversation opener was often used of the Lord and then for 40 minutes I often plunged into fruitful conversations that often blessed my soul and gave me a sense that God Himself had chosen me to be a limo driver! Mary, our daughter, sold our van with around 300,000 miles on it to a passer bye while in our home in Prairie Village, Kansas.

To get the job I had a simple interview with the limo company, and they asked me if I had ever had a driving accident. Initially, I just said no. My definition of a road accident is hitting a moving target, be it body or vehicle. Then I recalled a couple of incidents that I thought I ought to mention. "Well, I probably should mention that I turned a 12-seater Land-Rover over in the Taurus Mountains in Turkey towing a 12-birth camping trailer. The two-inch towing hook snapped off and the trailer separated from its chassis and the Land-Rover was on its side in a snow-bank. Oh, and I probably ought to mention that I dropped a 12-seater Land-Rover through the ice in the Hindu Kush, in Afghanistan." I don't recall the expression on the man's face but finally he said, "I am glad you told me that! Is there anything else that you want to tell me?"

"Yes, I will only be able to drive from 2:00 pm onwards. During the morning, I will not ever be available. If you call me at 1:55 pm I will not be available." That meant that my first client to drive was around 3:00 pm.

By making that clear, I had the mornings to myself to work on my PEF material, my mailing list, and writing my Workshop on Reformed Evangelism titled "**Boldly Proclaiming: The Message and Methods of God-Centered Witnessing.**" That way, the morning was mine and not theirs to call me.

The Providence of God for a Limo Driver

As I write this section, in a hotel in Riga, Latvia (April 22, 2018), I look back on my life and recall numerous instances where God has shown His merciful providential care and protection. Let me list a few examples and attempt to show you how they fit into my story.

One day two van loads of 12 clients needed to be transported from the airport to a location in Kansas City. Twelve exceptionally large healthy-looking men piled into two waiting vehicles. The fact that they all had the same 'man bags' caught my eye. They were all carrying chromium-looking metal-briefcases. After everyone was settled and we got under way I asked them, "What do all you big boys do for a living?" "Well, that might be a secret" was the answer that I was given. Then it dawned on me that they were a presidential Secret Service detail. They were in fact an advanced group of secret service men detailed to protect Vice President Dan Quale who was about to arrive in Kansas City. As you can imagine not much information was given and not much was asked for. However, I did glean that there was much sacrifice involved in being on a Presidential Secret Service Detail. By listening to their conversation that married life and family life were placed in second place to the requirements of the job that they had signed up to perform faithfully.

Often, family arrangements were arranged only to be changed at the last minute with an apparent 'excuse' that instead of being home early for a long-planned family event they were flying out to South America on their next assignment. What appeared to be a very glamorous job was, in fact, one that required total dedication to doing and going at a moment's notice to wherever the president or vice president was going. It was clear that many marriages had become a casualty due in part to the patriotic calling of the agents. The next time that you see a Secret Service detail, you might pray for the families of these men and for their marriages.

When it came time to pay, I asked how they wanted to take care of the fare. Would it be a credit card or how would you like to pay? "Oh, it will be cash they insisted, and no receipt!" I wrote a receipt anyway which was left on the seat.

On a rare morning trip, I dashed out of the house and Sheila called out after me, "You haven't taken any lunch with you for today." I told her that I would get something and off I went. That day the first and only gentleman that I picked up at the airport gave me the address of where he wanted to go and as a conversation starter, for some reason, known to God I was prompted to open the conversation this way: "I was raised on bacon and eggs and somehow my wife has me eating granola and toast. I don't know how that happened." His response was just as surprising as that which I had just opened the conversation. "Well, you tell your wife from me a big hearty congratulation." So, I replied, "And you are who now?" His response was one that I probably will never forget. "I am the current President of the American Heart Association." We had a good laugh about that later. However, it got even better. He then asked to be picked up a couple of hours later.

I called in his request to dispatch and then because sometimes I need to travel a distance and put miles on my vehicle for the next client, I asked him if I could audit his lecture and wait to take him back to the airport. He appeared incredibly pleased and told me I was welcome to also stay for lunch. He was giving some lectures to fulfil the requirement of doctors who needed to keep current in their continuing education. The lectures were interesting and then lunch. Oh boy, you imagine Sheila's face when I got home. "Did you manage to get some lunch along the way?" "I did. I started with, well basically I ended up with a 6-course lunch and desert." "What are you talking about?" When I told her that the doctors had a beautiful buffet, we had to chuckle that God provided such a fine lunch and I did not have to run unpaid miles between trips. With a generous tip basically, it turned into a good day. I believe I even thanked God that I was able to eat more than I needed without any ill effect.

Remember that as an evangelist you cannot talk to someone about Jesus outside the church if you are not talking to them. As a result, I was always looking for an appropriate way to start a conversation with whoever I met. In fact, a well-known "church planter" once asked me, "Paddy, how do you have a good conversation about Jesus with a stranger, someone you don't know?" I was prompted to say, "Have you ever tried saying 'hallo' to someone?" He replied quickly, "No, I'm serious." I replied, "No, I am serious too!" I had never said what I was about to say. I was convinced it was God prompting me by His Holy Spirit to say, "My point is this, you can't talk to someone about Jesus if you are not talking to them." Put another way, to talk to someone about Jesus you must be talking to them. It sounds silly, but it is quite profound.

Remember also, when you are talking to someone, you can always choose to change the subject. That works too! I think that all Christians believe in preaching and evangelism. However, few of us are good preachers and many of us are uncomfortable or even 'uptight' witnessing to someone we meet, that we often make them uncomfortable or uptight as they listen to us. On another occasion I took a client to visit the owner of the Royals baseball team in Kansas City. My client was extremely well dressed, with finely matching clothes and shoes. As we talked, I was basically saying that he must be good at his job as this was the third time I had taken him to meet this client. "What is it that you actually do for him?" "I'm in human relations." "Do you mind if I ask you why you appear to be so stressed?" His answer shocked me: "People really tick me off!"

I asked him if he had ever heard about the concept of forgiveness. Again, his response shocked: "Sounds interesting. Talk to me." I explained that if two people are saying different things they cannot both be right. There were only a few possibilities. Either one of them was right and the other wrong or they are both wrong, but they cannot both be right. Because there is objective truth, it is possible to find out who was right and who was wrong. We had arrived, but as I was driving away, I was thinking here I am working for $6.00 an hour while he is likely on a six-figure salary, and I am talking to him about the concept of forgiveness!

Another client sitting in the front seat of my Chevy van was the last person to get out after the others had paid and left the van. It was a miserable wet and cold afternoon. We exchanged stories and we gave each other the chance to forget about the miserable day outside the van while the windscreen wipers worked hard to give us visibility. Eventually I asked my passenger why his wife, who he obviously loved paid her fare separately and got off earlier at a different address.

He explained he had been diagnosed with Lou Gehrig's Disease (ALS) and rather than spend the family inheritance he had divorced his wife so that the government would pay for his expensive medical costs. I changed the subject and started talking about the Lord. He gave the impression that he was interested so I continued. Then I asked him if he would like a copy of John Blanchard's booklet called "Ultimate Questions." When I explained that in my opinion it was the best explanation of true Christianity (published in 44 languages) outside the Bible, he interrupted me and said, "No thank you I'm Jewish."

I was sad for him being terminally ill and without Christ. As we were pulling up to his apartment, I was prompted to ask, "Could you do me a favor?" "Sure, I would be pleased to. I enjoyed the ride and our conversation, and you've encouraged me and brightened my day. "What is the favor I can do for you?" I replied, "Would you take a copy of the pamphlet anyway?" "Why would I do that if I am Jewish?" I have never figured out why I said what I said next. "Well, I get brownie points for giving them away." To my utter amazement he gladly took a copy.

As I drove off, I was faithful. I had given him enough information that if he knew nothing about God and chose to read the booklet, he would have sufficient information to pray to God in repentance for his sins and receive forgiveness and become a believer in Jesus Christ. The fact that the reason I gave to him was not true has of course bothered me. However, he did have a sufficient explanation of the gospel.

Many years later, another story came to mind. "Brownie points" and the words "Sunshine boy." What is the connection? While stopping in the street in Tver, Russia to take a picture of the railway station, I decided that I would like the picture to add to a picture of a ship and an airplane, for some future reason. A Russian soldier in full uniform, confused about his role approached me. We were not at war; I was not the enemy and yet, in my opinion, according to him I might as well have been. He demanded to know what I was doing and why was I doing it. "I'm taking a picture of the railway station." That is what I assumed he was asking about. Finally, I just told him, "It is O.K. I am "a sunshine boy," and took off up the street. Pastor Eugene, Rick and Bibles for Russia's Founder/Director Alfred McCroskey asked me what we were talking about. I could honestly say, "I'm not really sure!"

Full-Time Ministry with Presbyterian Evangelistic Fellowship (PEF)

During the three years that I drove for the Limo Co. I collected only three moving violations. Doing 70,000 miles a year that is not hard to do. Finally, the company told me that for $2,000 for a three month-special insurance, I could keep driving for them. Well, Sheila announced that she had $2,000 in her savings and she suggested instead, "Why don't you go full-time for three months with PEF?" and that is how we started a full-time ministry. Sheila was already providing home care for a bunch of children so that is what we did. Sometimes a mum would leave an extra child as she had to go to the dentist. That happened on a day that Sheila had to go to the dentist. The extra fee helped pay for Sheila's dentist bill! And thus began the greatest ministry I have known.

PART TWO

PROCLAMATION

PEF/REF YEARS to the Present: 1988–202?

The years of preparation for my ministry were many, ranging from childhood to adulthood to ordination and ministry in the local church. It was a time of learning—learning about the world, learning about myself, and learning more about the Scriptures. It was also a time of experiencing—experiencing the world and my place in it through failures and successes. It was also a time of experiencing the friendship and love of others, and especially, the friendship and love of God. The latter was a friendship I never thought possible in my youth.

As we come to Part Two of my memoir, I have been in full-time ministry with PEF, now Reformed Evangelistic Fellowship, for thirty-eight years. That is a long time. If nothing else, I can say that I have become a faithful plodder—or maybe more appropriately, a faithful Sower, in the fields of the Lord!

In these pages, rather than give a year-by-year account of my life and ministry as I did in Part One, I want to present an overview of my ministry by giving glimpses of the work around the world that I have evangelized in. Those countries around the world on many continents, and more than once in many of those countries. What is important is not "Where has Paddy been?" Rather, it is "How has God worked through Paddy in the places to which He has led Paddy?" It's about God's work, not Paddy's work!

Going Where the Lord Leads

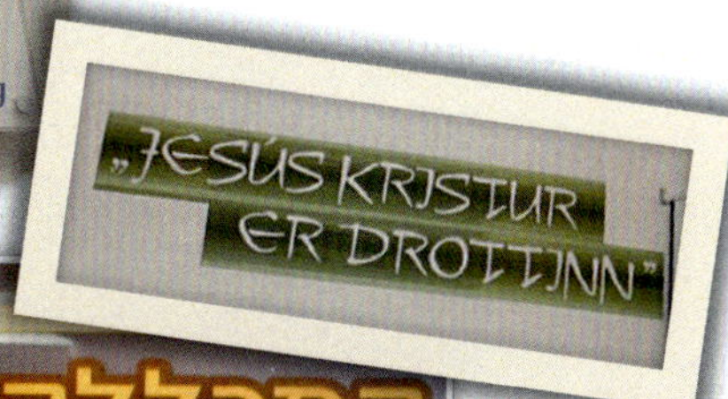

Vaduz Castle—Liechtenstein

Runway extension in Funchal,
Madeira Island
All the passengers pray—well, at least I did!

Ministry team in Auckland, New Zealand, 2011

Tools of the Trade

Books for the Baltic, 2016

Weighing Bags of Book Bound for Europe

Books for Oslo, Bergen, and Copenhagen

A Gift Graciously Given

Good Books for Good People,
Pastor Ismael, Azores, 2019

Spreading the Good Word in
Hungary, 2025

Aids to Remain Faithful
to the Word, Pastor Jose,
Canary Islands, 2019

Paddy and Slobodan, a Theological Student
in Serbia, 2025

Evangelism with Food!

The ministry continues, Israel, 2024!

Canary Islands, an interesting breakfast!

"And you Sir, fried egg, and sausage? Sorry, I don't speak English. I thought you said, "Baby eel and shrimp on your egg and chips."

An after church meal in Bulgaria!

Faith and Family

European Friends Enjoying Breakfast with Son Stephen and Daughter Mary at GPTS

Paddy the Stalwart Mariner! Albania to Corfu

Family Photo 2015

Beautiful through the years!

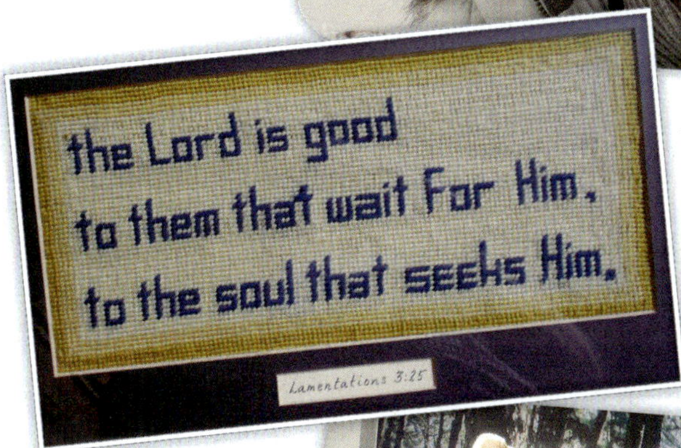

A reminder hanging in our home.

A handsome pair—I mean, bear!

Family Photo, 2025

Sea of Galilee

22

NEW BEGINNINGS

As I began my full-time ministry with PEF there was uncertainty and excitement—probably in equal parts. The uncertainty was a concern for financial support for the ministry, the details of the ministry yet to be worked out, and at times, the sensation of having jumped off a cliff and with both feet now planted firmly in mid-air and the inability to see anything else!

If there was uncertainty, and there was, there was also excitement. I was excited to see how God would use me and my few skills. I was excited to see God work in the lives of those He led me to as I sought to carry the Good News of Jesus Christ to thousands of people who I was yet to meet. I was also excited to where in the world God would lead me to, "in Jerusalem and in all Judea and Samaria, and to the end of the earth" (Acts 1:8, ESV).

I believe that everything that has happened in my ministry up to this point in my story was in clear preparation for the calling God has given me. Further, I believe that my calling is to bring glory to God in some small measure, that I may be an encouragement to others and show how the mercies of God took a young man who thought his way in life would be to ride a bicycle and deliver meat, to talking to people outside the church about Jesus.

The Focus of My Ministry

Today, PEF is known as REF (Reformed Evangelistic Fellowship), but the ministry and its vision has remained the same as it was in 1988. By

2004, I had been with PEF more than fifteen years. In the spring of 2004, I wrote a short article entitled "Come Follow" for the ministry magazine. Now, as I look back twenty years on that article, I believe that my ministry has remained true to what we were praying for as we began our journey with PEF. The vision, principles, and priorities of the first half have been continued and upheld in the second half.

The REF vision is simple and straightforward:

- **Reformed Dedicated** to the classic reformed doctrines of the Christian faith as put forth in the Westminster Standards and the 1689 Baptist Confession.
- **Evangelistic Sharing** the hope that is found within us with anyone, anytime, anywhere.
- **Fellowship**—Wherever a believer in Christ is found, the kingdom of God is there, and we share in that community all over the globe.

Based upon this vision, throughout the decades, the pattern of my work has fallen into three stages.

- **First,** I do "groundbreaking" work in a new country. I teach personal evangelism and do personal evangelism with nationals.
- **Second,** I disciple a leader in the Reformed faith with sound theological books and personal encouragement.
- **Third,** I do what I can to see that each person I disciple can be prepared formally with theological education so that he can serve in his country as an ordained Presbyterian pastor or evangelist.

One of my strongest desires and goals has been to help re-establish the Reformed faith in Europe. It has now been more than 500 years since the beginning of the Reformation in 1517 but in many places throughout Europe the truths of the Reformation are more of a legacy than a living faith.

Therefore, as I have the opportunity, I teach Reformed evangelism to churches in Europe, and I supply new theological books for discipleship authored by Reformed authors. I also encourage nationals who are interested in starting Presbyterian and reformed, confessional churches in their homeland. If those churches are going to be established, they need to have pastors and evangelists who not only have been ordained in the faith, but, who previously have received formal theological training.

Principles and Practices

The Christian faith is a personal faith—it is grounded in the belief of individuals. Ultimately, in the only Personal, true and living God. Therefore, I have been committed to talk with people about Jesus, inside and outside the church, across the street and across the sea.

I have attempted to obey the Great Commission—especially in Europe, Asia, and the Middle East. The purpose of my work is to have nationals start Presbyterian and Reformed churches where there are none. It is difficult to encourage nationals to start Presbyterian and Reformed churches when there are no examples around them. It is not an easy task, but God has raised up men to do just that!

Ministry is not a sprint—it is a marathon! I have run the race with the Lord's direction and the Lord's provision. It is a unique work. I am totally dependent on God to supply the money for the ministry and open doors of opportunity. To date God has taken me to 68 countries to minister—and the need continues. Unfortunately, there have been many needs and opportunities that I have not been enabled to meet. In each new country in which I have ministered, mostly, I have received an invitation from a minister before I traveled to that country.

As a REF Evangelist my philosophy of ministry has been and remains based on a complete trust in all of Holy Scripture, my understanding of who God is, and what it is that He requires of me. The ministry under PEF/REF continues to operate from a Reformed foundation. I don't co-operate with non-Reformed bodies overseas. I do personal evangelism with nationals and teach Reformed evangelism in their churches. I always travel with a national, who acts as my personal translator. I take that opportunity to disciple and encourage him along the way.

I provide nationals with new Reformed theological books. As noted above, I also seek nationals who are interested in pursuing formal theological training to equip them for the gospel ministry so that they can begin or continue to grow Presbyterian and Reformed churches in their home countries.

Much of my evangelism teaching ministry revolves around teaching a workshop I created titled "Boldly Proclaiming." This is a workshop on "The Message and Methods of God-Centered Witnessing." The workshop has been translated into languages such as Albanian, Russian, and Romanian. It is currently in the hands of nationals in countries such as Croatia, Turkey, Italy, Greece, China, Spain, Egypt, Czech Republic, and Bulgaria.

We have never had a large operating budget. However, God has always allowed us to finish each year, now for 38 years, "in the black," both as a family and as a ministry.

First Steps

The sixth-century BC Chinese philosopher and author Lao Tzu is credited with the often-heard words "A journey of a thousand miles begins with a single step." My journey has been hundreds of thousands of miles. It too began with a first step—a step of faith.

Several months after joining PEF, I was drawn to the idea of focusing on an international ministry under PEF. For many years Arnie Maves (d. 2016), worked behind what was then the Iron Curtain as an ordained PEF evangelist. He was returning to Romania after "the Wall came down" and I talked with him about going to Romania with him on his upcoming trip. After much thought and prayer, Arnie told me that if I were able to raise $2,500 in the two months before the trip, he would take that as a sign that I should go with him.

When the two months were up, my total for the trip was only $1,500.00. That figure amazed me as I do not recall ever having raised any money for missions. However, Sheila and I decided that because we had $1,000 in savings that we should tell Arnie that we had $1,500 raised and that we wanted to add $1,000 from our savings. Arnie did not accept that. He took it that we only raised $1,500 and not $2,500. "God is good all the time!" I did not go with Arnie on that trip to Romania. However, later in the ministry I invited him to come with us to Russia on a trip.

Some months later I met a man who came to PEF, I will not mention his name as it did not end well. He was all excited that I had a mailing list of folks. We had dinner at a restaurant in Atlanta. He had sword fish, and I do not remember what I ate but I know it was not swordfish!

The arrangement for our trip to Romania was that I should meet him under the clock at the Budapest railway station in Hungary on a certain day at a certain time. I was to dress to be as "unnoticed" as possible. I took that to mean I was to try not to stand out or even be noticed by what I would be wearing.

We were to meet under the clock at the train station in Budapest, Hungary, I had a little chuckle at the dress code for the trip as I always understood that the definition of a well-dressed Englishman was that he would pass unnoticed in a crowd. When I met my friend, I could not believe what he was wearing. A full-length water-proof leather over coat. This next statement is hard to believe, with thirteen pouches, bags and camera cases, computer paraphernalia hanging from his body. Red flag for Paddy!

The next red flag was demanding that I buy a bottle of water for myself from a shop we passed. He did not ever ask if I had done any travelling before. I think I had filled four British passports before the trip. A British passport had about 30 pages and an Arab visa could often take a whole page.

With bottled water, fresh bread, beans, and our private supply of toilet paper we boarded the overnight train that took us to the border and then across Romania to Bucharest. As we crossed the border in the dead of night, I was almost ashamed it was so easy. I thought of the many courageous brothers in Christ who had crossed the border for Christ before the revolution and tears came to my eyes in respect for the faith God had given them to believe verses like, "For me to live is Christ, and to die is gain." (Philippians 1:21). PEF's Arnie Maves was one of those people. On Sunday, I preached four sermons in different towns in the same shirt!

We received a request to visit a dying Romanian in his home as his family and friends wanted him to become a Christian as he did not appear to have long to live. My friend and I and two other pastors took off for the visit along with four translators. I was told to knock on his door. We were told he was expecting a visit. I certainly would not have done a visit like this back home, but this was Romania. So, I kept my thoughts to myself. We were invited in, and all took tea, no milk, no sugar.

After a short time on the visit, I could see that my friend was getting impatient. I had discerned correctly as he blurted out to his translator, "Ask him if he would like to become a Christian?" The man appeared to nod his head as if that might be exactly what he would like to do. I always value the prayer support that I travel with. Before my friend could say anything else I was prompted to ask through my translator, "Ask our friend if he knows anything about sin?" Apparently, he did not.

My friend was not happy that I took over the conversation. I was accompanying him on *his* trip. He made such a scene that I have completely forgotten what happened after that. However, as soon as we left and were walking home, I said to him, "How dare you speak the way you did. In my presence, don't you EVER do that again." The trip continued to go from bad to worse after that, and I do mean worse.

We had been invited to speak for a week at a Bible conference. Pastors brought folks from nearby churches; nobody had to walk more than 10 miles. I spoke at one of the morning sessions. I was told what to talk about in the session.

We arrived half an hour early, which allowed us to sense a little of the atmosphere in the room. I remember praying as I was about to speak that the Lord would take control of my thoughts. That I would only say what God wanted me to say and that I would not say what God had not purposed for me to say.

At lunchtime I received a tongue lashing from my traveling companion. "I told you to speak about evangelism and witnessing. Why didn't you talk about what I told you to talk about?" I responded by saying, "I went over your head. I spoke to the Almighty. Did you not hear my prayer before I spoke? We both sensed, I trust, that even though neither of us spoke Romanian, there was much disagreement and disunity in the group before the morning's lecture. The reason I talked about love, repentance and forgiveness was that I sensed, I believe rightly, that before we teach them about witnessing about the Lord Jesus Christ they ought to think about the state of their hearts and the state of the fellowship in the church before they invite others in to witness that part of their Christianity."

One of the last visits we made on the trip was to go to the seminary where Pastor George, was studying to say our goodbyes. I was told to stay in the car! George was one of four Romanian students who was allowed to enter seminary at that time. Because I had developed a relationship with George and his wife, Lydia, and received their hospitality, I got out of the car and entered the building to say goodbye to George. George came over to me and we agreed to keep in touch. Later, Lydia was to translate my workshop on Reformed Evangelism into Romanian. They were short of money so I asked Lydia if she would do the translation. She was delighted to help and do that. My traveling companion was cross with me when I got out of the car.

When we arrived home, I wrote a ten-page letter to Dr. Ben Wilkinson, the Executive Director of PEF, giving my reasons why I believed my colleague should not be accepted into PEF. My letter was received, and my suggestion adopted. It was a couple of years before I saw my traveling companion again. A group of PEF Evangelists were meeting in Pigeon Forge, Tennessee for a short retreat. During one of the sessions where we were all giving verbal reports my friend appeared and sat down at the back of the room. I was interested to hear an update from him. However, his update never came as when he was close to giving his update he stood and walked out of the building.

The trip was a rough beginning to my international ministry, but I learned many things that would ease future trips. Even if the first step is a stumble, it is still possible to continue the journey!

23

USING BUILDING SKILLS TO HELP BUILD THE CHURCH OF JESUS CHRIST

The fact that Jesus grew up working with his earthly father Joseph in Joseph's carpentry shop has always been an inspiration and encouragement to me. Jesus knew about wood, and how to craft it for the best results. He knew about sawdust, shavings, and splinters! He knew about sore thumbs and aching arms. He knew about callouses and cuts. He knew that anything done well takes time—that includes building the Church of Jesus Christ. Jesus knew patience and he knew people. It is interesting that so many of the stories, vocations, and images found in the Bible pertain to hard work, but also working with one's hands—herding, potter, fisherman, scribe, tanner, tentmaking, cooking, dyer of cloth, farming, vintner—the work of everyday people like you and me. The gospel is for everyone and is communicated in language any person can understand. But of course, I am partial to biblical imagery of building and construction!

Construction projects often lead to ministry opportunities. I should not have been surprised that this would be the case, but every time it happens, I smile and think back to my earlier days in the building and construction trade. God was preparing me even though I did not know it at the time. I thought I was doing what I wanted to do, but God knew otherwise!

Early in the ministry, to get into a new country for ministry we offered to do construction projects.

In small projects and in large projects, as with all my ministry, I have relied on prayer and God's guidance. We have all heard the adage "Rome wasn't built in a day." That saying comes from a French phrase that dates to 1190, and the English version goes back to about 1538, the era of the Reformation! What was true of Rome is even more true of the Church and Kingdom of God. Our duty as Christians is to be faithful builders in that endeavor in any role that God places us. And so, it has been for me—a carpenter for God's Kingdom!

Every day of my ministry has been filled with joy, surprises, and a desire to share the Good News with others. An analogy I use is that reviewing my evangelistic ministry is much like a builder or carpenter who looks back on forty or more years of building and repairing houses, structures, buildings, and businesses of many types. Rather than writing of every house in which carpenters have worked, they would likely speak of some of more memorable ones. Ones that are memorable for a variety of reasons. So too with my ministry. Let me share glimpses from the past.

England and Northern Ireland—1994

Every contractor knows that one job can lead to another through word-of-mouth. If you like the work someone is doing on your house, you may tell your friends or neighbors—or if you don't like the work! People-to-people is the key. A sign in your yard with the roofer's or painter's name and phone number may help, but more likely it is going to be your words that help the contractor get more neighborhood business. So too is it with evangelism and ministry opportunities. The key is people telling others the *good news* about what they have experienced. The gospel and the ministry are best spread personally and by word of mouth!

An evangelistic ministry is not only telling others about Jesus; it is also at times encouraging others who spread the gospel. So, it was in

England in 1994 when I had the opportunity to encourage Rev. David and Barbara Cross who were missionary church planters and were on an evangelism retreat with members of their congregation.

My opportunity to support and encourage them in their work in my native country was as much a spiritual boost for me as I hope my ministry was to them. Throughout Great Britain and Europe today Christianity is waning and the evangelistic need is as great as it was in decades past.

In Matthew 7:24–27, Jesus tells the parable of the man who built his house on sand rather than rock. The literal meaning is very clear—don't build your house on sand! However, even if you house or building has a firm foundation, over time the need for repairs will arise. That is exactly what happened to a large two-story Christian ministry center in Northern Ireland. There was a vibrant ministry in a large, beautiful home that had a slate roof that was leaking. Beware! When that happens, you probably have more than one simple repair that is needed. And so, it was in this case. It was the roof; it was what was under the roof; and it was the gutters—and that was only the outside!

Tom Cairns from Belfast N. Ireland, was a person I met on a mission trip to N. Ireland with Andrew, Stephen, and Paul a friend of Andrew's from high school. We spent 6 weeks in England, Scotland, and Wales and planned to spend 3 weeks ministering in N. Ireland. With a freezer full of delicious Irish steak and kidney pies and chips and pastries I worked fixing the slate roof of a ministry there. Working with slate is a challenge!

John Moxen and I had met at a missions' conference in Arkansas and John stayed in my home while I was in the process of re-roofing my own house. One thing leads to another! Sometimes we may ask ourselves "Why am I doing this?" or "Why is this happening now?" God has His reasons and plans!

When I arrived in Dun Drum, Northern Ireland, there were no ladders, scaffolding or tools to fix the roof of the ministry building. After praying, the gardener and janitor provided everything that we needed. We got tools and imitation black slates to use out of sight, as well as scaffolding and all new timber boards for the scaffolding tower. Where to start? The grass growing in the gutter was blown out after prayer for wisdom (and safety). The one-and-a-quarter inch fire hose was inserted, and the water turned on and all the grass blown out of the gutter in less than 5 minutes!

Tom subsequently took an interest in my ministry. Tom was a past chairman of the British Institute of Management Tom chose to get involved in the ministry in Romania, rather than Albania. He took the time and trouble to learn the Romanian language and faithfully raised the money over the years to allow the Romanians in Turnu Magarele to build a new church building. He also raised money for a camp site and buildings so that the church was able to hold youth camps locally.

Tom was an Irish prankster, as are many most of the Irish I know. He would often be driving through Belfast singing one of his favorite verses of, "Man. United." Short for his favorite English football team (soccer), Manchester United. Tom was the active secretary for the local soccer team in Belfast—Glentoran Football Club. Tom and I and his friend Keith went to watch Glentoran one Saturday. As we rounded a corner it looked like we had entered a war zone. There were a bunch of Land Rover's parked close to each other so that the crowds had to go through them in single file.

There was always a good-natured rivalry between local teams but apparently at the time with "The Troubles" (the ethno-nationalist controversy in Northern Ireland that lasted from 1968 to 1998 that also had deep religious overtones), extra arrangements to keep Protestants and Roman Catholic supporters separated was necessary. It was explained to me that at the end of a game alternately the Protestants or Catholics were let out of the ground first while the other supporters waited until they had all left the stadium.

One afternoon driving around Belfast Tom drove down a road lined with small, terraced houses; to look for a man, we will call Geordie. Outside his house there were two ladies, neighbors both with their hair in curlers with head scarves on deftly wielding brooms sweeping the sidewalk in front of their houses. Tom pulled up to the curb in a nice car and one of the ladies asked who he was and what he wanted. Tom immediately went into his gift of gab mode and told the ladies that as we passed their road I had said, "Gor she looks nice, I fancy her!" So, we came back to introduce ourselves! Well, thankfully after a short conversation the subject was changed, and Tom explained we were looking for Geordie. It sounded like Geordie was likely drunk and sleeping it off inside.

We didn't talk with Geordie that day. Later, Tom explained that Because I was an evangelist, he thought I should talk with Geordie about Jesus. "Sure," I said. Geordie apparently was in a lot of trouble as he had been sleeping with a Roman Catholic lady, fathered a child and changed sides by sleeping with a Protestant lady. He was a wanted man and a para-terrorist. It was arranged for safety reasons that I "Bump into him at the soccer match." That was the only way he was willing to meet with me. It was hard to track Geordie down. It was arranged that we have a meal in the European Continental hotel in Belfast. The IRA had bombed it several times and each time it was rebuilt.

There was a magnificent Christian bookshop in Belfast owned by a dear brother, John Greer. Because of its location, had been bombed a few times. Cheerfully John was able to rebuild his shop and even expand the size of it. That part he was happy about. I was in there looking for a commentary on the book of Jude. As soon as I asked for it, he called out and a customer responded, "Thomas Manton on Jude is what Paddy needs."

Geordie didn't show up for the meal at the Continental. Tom and his wife Sylvia and I did but Geordie did not. Later it was agreed that I would be dropped off at the house he was living at. I knocked on the door and I was shown in. I looked at his fish collection and I asked him if he wanted me to tell my stories first or wanted to tell his first.

The idea of telling stories arose because Geordie was in deep trouble and thought his situation was dire. It probably was but when it came down to it, he didn't have any stories he wanted to tell. I tried to copy

Edith Schaeffer's "Bird's Eye view of the Bible" lecture. It soon became apparent that Gordie was biblically illiterate. He had not even been to Sunday School to hear the basic biblical characters names. He didn't have much to say so at the end of my stories I left, and the next day went to John's bookshop. In the window was a book cover showing a terrorist in full battle fatigues. It was a book about the conversion of an Irish terrorist. I bought it and gave it to Tom to give to Geordie.

We were both hopeful that Geordie would pray and ask God for help. I don't know if he ever did. When I asked Tom why he asked me to talk to Gordie instead of him talking to him he said because I was leaving the country in a few days, and he wasn't!

Tom and Keith set up a charity as a café frying up Irish breakfasts and just charging a meager amount for a hearty meal of Eggs, Sausage, bacon beans toast, potato bread, tea etc. It was a chance for a family to eat out together, have a good meal at minimum cost. Tom started a conversation with an Irish Muslim ending up with Tom offering to go outside and settle matters. The man bowed out as he said he didn't have his back up 'wiv 'im.' He warned Tom to look out for him when he returned with his back up! This is an example of *how not* to do evangelism! I helped in the kitchen a few days and one man asked where Tom was. Keith told him that Tom had been temporarily let go as he didn't seem to know the difference between burnt toast and a sacrifice!

There have been many projects such as the repairs we made in Northern Ireland over the years and each of them re-enforced the fact that ministry is as much about "doing" as it is about "saying." We minster to people and we evangelize people where they are—not where they want to be.

Romania—1994

As I mentioned above, Tom Cairns, of Belfast Northern Ireland, was interested in Romania and Albania. He chose Romania. He learned the language and visited Romania often and under God Tom raised the money for the new church to be built along with local campground facilities. Pastor George wanted a glass church to help prove that Christianity was not a secret cult!

When I first met George and his fiancé, Lydia, George didn't have a passport. Because we were less than 100 miles as the crow flies from Craig Shepherd, in Sofia, Bulgaria we prayed about the three of us visiting Craig who had recently arrived in Sofia to head up the work there. Amazingly, in two days we managed to get George a passport. After we crossed the river into Bulgaria, we found a Customs shed, and about 40 taxi drivers who quoted $100 to take us to Sofia. It was supposed to cost $22.00. So, at 5 p.m. we set off walking to Sofia! After an hour a taxi driver arrived. We settled for $22.00. At a gas station I was surprised to be able to buy a telephone card. I called Craig asking if he could pick us up in Sofia, he didn't have a car yet. Our driver could not find the house. We stopped in Sofia half a dozen times asking for directions. We got lost and finally broke down. Craig's house had a #5, so did the house we broke down at. In faith, I shouted out and Craig appeared on his balcony! We went into town to buy hoses for his washing machine and Cables for his dryer. Had pizza, witnessed to the waitress with "Ultimate Questions" in Bulgarian and English.

At a camp with Pastor George and Lydia, I was able to be with a vibrant group of young people from the church in Turnu Magurele, Romania. When I saw 25 Romanian young people jumping on a donated trampoline, I assumed it didn't come with instructions that indicated only two people ought to jump together!

Earlier, literally an hour before I left my home in Prairie Village, Kansas, for a reason known only unto God, I went out and bought a soccer ball. I deflated it for packing and took it with me. I gave it to a boy in Romania. His mother had been praying for months for a soccer ball for him! She was so thankful! She could hardly believe it. I was taken aback myself!

When I arrived at Bucharest Airport, George would take the trouble to drive up from Turnu Magnarele to pick me up, which saved me having to catch a bus to his home way down south. We would have a meal and then drive home together enjoying catching up with each other's news. George and Lydia are extremely hard workers. George and another brother pastor 6 churches. He plays the organ, leads the worship, and preaches. Lydia is a very able translator for visiting speakers. She teaches English in several local schools and George teaches music in the local schools.

George graduated from seminary in Romania in the first class of 4 students in Romania after the Soviet Union collapsed and the wall came down. I am sure he is proud of graduating in the top four in his class! I know I would be!

Romania was and remains a country that is not wealthy. Living is basic and work is often nonexistent. Some folks walked to church to worship and walked 10 miles to get there. After making a day of it fellowshipping, they would walk another 10 miles to get home. They were so thankful to be able to worship freely! They would do it in all weathers and were happy to be able to do so. Before I met George and Lydia I worked with a Korean Pastor, Hong Key Chung. He had started a church, a seminary, and a fully robed choir. They also had a volleyball team. I met with the students and spoke in a few classes and then went out looking for people to talk to. One student was selling books by the side of the road and Hong Key just asked him if he would like to enroll in a Presbyterian seminary in Bucharest with a scholarship. He said yes and thank you!

In the early days of my ministry, working at my office meant working out of a briefcase. All I needed was a place to sit and I was in business. That worked out well at the time for me and pastor Hong Key. He was building the seminary in Romania (literally)—and I was able to carry a few buckets of concrete. In the times I spent working with Hong Key Chung the students would study in the morning and then in the afternoon we would go out in Bucharest to find folks to talk to. There was a seminary to be built so there was plenty to keep everybody busy.

Many of you know that I like to pray specific prayers. I have told many of you how I have prayed for bathrooms all over Europe. And how the Lord at the time of writing, has never failed me. Not only do the bathrooms have to be there, often, they must be vacant! It was well known that at the church each Sunday they *sing for an hour, pray for an hour,* and expect the preacher to *preach for an hour!* The problem was that I was going to the bathroom every 45 minutes. During one service, twice I took the lonely walk to the "slated" outhouse. I talked with George's father-in-law and I decided that I should place my trousers into my socks so that if the unthinkable happened I cold preach my whole sermon. God in His mercy, the God who held back the Red Sea, took care of the situation. Praise God! (It was a reminder to me that often God answers generally prayers generally, and specific prayers specifically!)

The story above is more than a funny story I tell on myself. It is a story that illustrates the very different conditions in which many Christians around the world worship from that which most of us are used to experiencing in our comfortable churches filled with modern conveniences and communications technology. My sincere encouragement is that the next time your church decides to spend $100,000 on a new gymnasium floor, spare a thought for your brothers and sisters in Christ around the world who worship each Lord's Day—often all day—and are unable to buy paint for the windows of their church or provide indoor plumbing for the basic necessities of life.

At one location, during a trip in Romania, two days were spent visiting house-to-house in a nearby Romani village. The poverty was apparent. Few families had any working member in the family. In Romania (and elsewhere), culturally, there is often shame when a person—and especially a man who is seen as the head of the household—has no work. In this village, few had work. Much of the time each day was spent foraging through garbage bins and dumps. For most of us, it was and is an inconceivable way of life. Due to passion and planning by God's people overseas, a ministry was started by a group of these people who were literally on the bottom of the social ladder. Their church is clearly a trophy of grace, with committed, faithful brothers and sisters, believing God can save and use anybody. They see the fruits of their labors in this impoverished community that is overlooked and ignored by most people, but not by God!

1990s Trips to Croatia, Corfu, and Albania

Construction complements the ministry of evangelism and it benefits missionaries, mission buildings, and Christians wherever and whenever it is done overseas. Such was certainly the case in Albania in 1995 and 1997 and 1998 working in Croatia. If you give people an unmarked map of Europe and ask them to pinpoint Croatia, you will probably get many answers, but few of them will be correct! Croatia, officially the Republic of Croatia, is a beautiful country in the Balkans.

Most of the week we were nailing "wet timber." Doing so is not preferred because the lumber will shrink once it dries. However, we often must work with what we have and when we have it. To help each other out, whenever we heard a team member hit his thumb, we all shouted out, "God, is good, ALL THE TIME!" Hopefully before he had time to cry out! On the trip to Croatia with my son, Stephen, I could not find out what tools to take. So, I prayed and took my own counsel. I was puzzled as I could not get a picture of my heavy construction skill-saw out of my mind! All week we carried and cut the wet timber 6" x 6" with my skill saw!

Every country in which I have ministered is unique. One of my early trips was to Albania—another often-overlooked country by Americans and Europeans. Yet it is a remarkable and beautiful country, and the gospel of Jesus Christ is spreading there and changing lives. One of the things that is the greatest blessing for me when I travel is to experience the love, kindness, and fellowship with Christian brothers and sisters in each country. As Christians, we are truly one people with one faith! "There is neither Jew nor Greek, there is neither slave nor free, there is no male and female, for you are all one in Christ Jesus" (Galatians 3:28 ESV). One such remarkable brother in Christ was Bertie.

Bertie was the first student from Europe who was accepted by Greenville Presbyterian Theological Seminary (GPTS). I was often advised never to bring international students to America because they might choose to stay in the United States rather than return home for ministry. I leave that to God. He will direct and lead according to His plan. Bertie never asked for anything. Not even a cup of coffee. In Albania, when we traveled to Elbason, Lezhe, or down south to Sarande, I took care of travel expenses, food, and accommodation. When it was time to talk about him studying in America the conversation went something like this: "Bertie, I don't need to have this conversation with you because I don't believe it is necessary. However, if you ever plan on staying in the US, I will shoot you. You will die and fall to the ground. The first thing I will do is ask God to forgive me. We are doing this so that you go home to your people." And, as we will see, he did just that!

Bertie truly and literally was a godsend for my ministry in Albania. Things got off to a slow start but that was just what God wanted! It is a reminder to me that I may be the willing builder of Christ's Church, but God is the architect!

I had planned to teach an evangelism workshop to Albanian Christians. A room was arranged in Tirana, for my lecture but nobody showed up! As Bertie and I were talking about what happened, we met this couple sitting at a wall of a water fountain in Tirana. We ended up giving them a 2 1/2-hour account of my workshop on Reformed evangelism, "Boldly Proclaiming." As a result, the very first lecture was given to the Norwegian couple.

I believe he was a Norwegian detective. Later, we did have our workshop and about 20 young people attended. It was exciting for me to see their enthusiasm for evangelism!

Bertie and I were walking down the main street in Durres, Albania and Bertie asked me how, he in a predominantly Muslim culture, could begin to get to know a young lady in preparation for engagement. In Albania it was not even possible to walk down the main street alone with such a young lady. It was at times like these I was so thankful for all the prayer support that we have as we travel in my evangelism ministry. What I said was, "Bertie, I would certainly start praying about such a situation. As a rule of thumb, I would look for a good 'looker,' a good 'cooker,' a hard worker and then I would disciple the devil out of her!"

All went well for some time and then I heard that Bertie had met Jenny, an American beauty. He had been praying! Imagine my concern changing to delight, when I heard that since Jenny was 14 years old, she wanted to be a missionary and marry a pastor! A close call!

During the same time that Bertie was praying for a Christian fiancée and wife, many people were praying about how Bertie could get to seminary in America. I called a seminary and finally gave up on their inactivity. I then called another two seminaries one of which after hearing their requirements I told them I was going to hang up on them and I wanted them to know why. They were requesting $24,000 in the bank and all my contacts. "I have never done this before. I am going to hang up and I want you to know why."

The first time I met Dr. Joseph "Joey" Pipa, Jr. was at General Assembly in Texas, I asked him, "What could you do for my friend Bertie in Albania?" Dr. Pipa was the president of GPTS. His answer went something like this. "Have him come in August, forget the TOEFL test [Test of English as a Foreign Language]. Come with $1,000 a month." Bertie was fully funded within 5 weeks of arriving in the US! Pastor Carl Robbins at Woodruff Road, PCA took Bertie in and provided a church home for Bertie while at seminary until he was licensed and ordained and commissioned as an Associate pastor of Woodruff Road, PCA. Bertie returned home and was sent to Albania with "Mission to Albania." It was a blessed time of the ministry while Bertie was at GPTS.

My trips to Albania also instilled in me a desire to have an evangelism ministry in Corfu, an island off the northwest coast of Greece and very close to Albania. However, Bertie and I both knew that he wouldn't be given a visa to travel with me to minister in Corfu. Still, each time I was in Albania we went to the consulate to ask. Each time our request was denied. Each time we asked if there was anybody else, we could ask. Each time we were unsuccessful and never did get a visa for Bertie, but we were introduced to folks in the consulate who we witnessed to and gave each one an Albanian Copy of *Ultimate Questions* written by John Blanchard. However, we did get to talk to folks who normally we would never have met or been able to witnessed to!

I asked PEF Evangelist, Arnie Maves for the name of the pastor on the island of Corfu who was a graduate of Westminster Seminary. Arnie told me to ask God. It was great advice. I prayed and 3 weeks later I was at a conference in St. Louis, at Covenant Seminary and met up with a Greek student I knew. Pastor Peter was a student at Covenant with me when I was there. Pastor Peter answered, "Miltiades." It was a great lesson to be taught to rely on God as if you were working behind the former Iron Curtain.

I asked Bertie who was the most influential person in Tirana, the capital of Albania. He replied, "The American ambassador." We took a leather-bound *New Geneva Study Bible* which, I believe, was presented to Ambassador Joseph Edward Lake, I believe. We were told that Senator John McCain was about to visit so we didn't meet with the ambassador.

From the time I met Bertie in Durres, Albania until the time he graduated from GPTS, where he was licensed to preach, and finally ordained into the gospel Ministry of the PCA, about 15 years had sped by. Woodruff Road PCA sent Bertie and his American wife Jenny to Albania under "Mission to Albania." As you can imagine during that time there were countless prayers answered and adventures along the way. It is not possible to go there now. We would often stop in a café to watch European soccer matches on TV and whenever we were enabled, we talked to people about Jesus that we met. We are so thankful to God for all that God is doing in Albania through Bertie and Jenny's ministry under, "Mission to Albania."

The last tribute here to that ministry is that after some 10 years of ministry, God raised up a Confessional Reformed Presbyterian church in Albania. Currently it is a particularized church with two ordained Albanian Elders. Out of the work God has enabled them to have translated, published, and paid for producing Calvin's *Institutes of the Christian Religion* in their Albanian language. Wow! What a God!

Building Christ's Church in Croatia

How Did I get to go to Croatia? I was handed a list of contacts in Croatia that Arnie Maves gave me. Two of the names had an asterisk beside them. It was suggested that I contact them first. Within 48 hours of being in the country I was preaching in Zagreb and worshipping with one of them and I was given the location of the second person. How? God did it!

On a trip to Croatia with my son Stephen in 1997, we teamed up with a construction boss who brought a team of his men—6 Christians and 3 non-believers from his construction company. We arrived on Thursday evening on site in Croatia and Stephen, being Stephen, asked me if we could go and see the Leaning Tower of Pisa. Because he thought the tower was in Venice and Venice was across the Adriatic Sea, I said it was unlikely. However, the men on the team all encouraged us to go as a "Father and Son, trip of a lifetime venture." (I should have recognized that a "Tower of Pisa" rather than a "Tower of Venice" might have been a geographic clue, but we didn't!) Of course, as one trained in the building and construction trade, I wanted to see it to maybe determine who signed off on the sloppy construction!

We did not start work until Monday morning. So off we went. There were no boats running from Croatia to Venice, across the Adriatic, so we rented a car, and headed north into Slovenia, before dropping down in a southwesterly direction to the city of Venice. When we had established that the Leaning Tower of Pisa was not in Venice, basically Stephen spent his time looking for a Juventus soccer shirt and I spent my time scurrying down alleyways looking for a place to sleep that we could afford. In the early days $80 a night for the two of us was out of the question. Eventually we left Venice around 10:30 pm. Stephen without his Juventus shirt and we were praying that we would find a nice place to sleep. Late in the evening we stopped to buy gas and decided to sleep in the car. It was fun and interesting. It was so cold that every half hour I started the engine to heat up the car. That was not the best plan for Stephan's desire for uninterrupted sleep. Travel plans don't always go as one expects!

In the morning when we saw where we were, it was a beautiful place to stop! We were surrounded by beautiful mountains on three sides. We headed off for Slovenia, Italy, Austria and finally Germany. By Friday we arrived in Austria, exhausted and sleep deprived. God directed us to a perfect guest house belonging to a delightful Austrian couple. It was picture perfect. The owner showed us our room with large white duvets on the beds. We watched a European soccer match on TV. We both fell asleep instantly, watching the game. We woke up around 6:00 p.m.

Stephen took over and we went to visit Hohensalzburg Fortress in Austria which is one of the largest medieval fortresses in Europe. Salzburg is the fourth largest city in Austria and one of my favorite cities. I agreed to visit the castle fortress in Salzburg provided we both agreed to find a good place to eat afterwards. Yes, it was traditionally Austrian, and we loved it!

Stephen wanted to go into Germany to add one more country to those he had visited. We set off for the famous Hofbräuhaus brewery in Munich. Unfortunately, it didn't serve breakfast that morning. The evening before we were to set off back to Croatia, we were driving around in Austria looking for and praying for a gas station. Traditionally at that time gas stations were not open on Sunday. It was getting late, and the pressure was on to find gas before we went to bed as we had to leave around 4 a.m. the following morning and the weather was turning for the worse. It was snowing hard and getting worse. We got lost but came upon an open gas station.

We got gas but as we drove off, a fearful red light appeared on the dashboard. Now we had to find out what that was all about before we continued our trip. We prayed again, fearing the worst. In sign language we beckoned the owner of the gas station to come over. We opened the window and helplessly pointed to our red light. He leaned in and took the hand brake off and all was well! Stephen pressured me with, "Don't you feel silly having to do that?" "Yes of course I do. But we will never see him again and we prayed for the light to go off and it went off! That is an answer to prayer!" The story is a reminder to me and to readers that we are told to "pray without ceasing" (1 Thessalonians 5:17). Beyond that, it is important to remember that God works in large ways and in small ways in each of our lives.

When reading about anything in the Balkans, we must never forget that the region was decimated by war during the 1990s. The destruction extended to churches and the homes of many Christians. There has been rebuilding, but it has been slow. Even so, God is rebuilding His Church! Throughout the war-torn Balkans, as elsewhere in eastern Europe, there is a great and an immediate need to offer and expand theological education. That is not to say that there is no Christian presence or witness. To be sure, there is such a presence, but it is small. In 2006, I conducted a "Boldly Proclaiming" seminar in Tordinci, Croatia. The Protestant Reformed parish of Tordinci, has been in existence since the Austrio-Hungarian Monarchy. This Reformed community in Tordinci has been a witness of the Reformation among Croats, since 1551! God is faithful!

24

THE BALKANS AND RUSSIA (2002–2008)

Balkans, not Baltic!

Unless a person lives in or near Serbia, Bulgaria, or Bosnia, it is unlikely that much is known about them. To the extent that anything is known, it is probably that both are in a region that was devastated by war in the 1990s. The church of Jesus Christ needs to be strengthened in every country and region around the globe, but as a builder might say—some countries need more "shoring up" than others (and no, that does not mean more beachfront property)!

Christianity has a long and historic presence in Serbia, yet during my travels there in the early 2000s, the religious demographic was stunning: 84% Eastern Orthodox, 6% Roman Catholic, 3% Muslim, *1% Protestant,* 1% Atheist and Agnostic, 5% Other. Clearly it is a country that the Reformation barely touched. Yet there are faithful builders of the Church in Serbia and beyond.

For any Christian seeking to fulfill the words of Jesus in Matthew 28:19–20 the task is simply this: Preach the simple truth to pierce hearts and change lives. We know that God will work in lives if we bring the "good news."

One such person doing that in Serbia was Pastor Petar, the faithful pastor of a small Reformed church, in Belgrade, Serbia. Even though the group is small, he has faithfully taught and discipled the congregation and encouraged them to remain faithful to the Scriptures. He translated Reformed theologian Louis Berkof's *Summary of Christian Doctrine* that I gave him on a previous trip. His efforts are a testimony to the need to provide sound theological resources to pastors and others working where there are few such resources available in any language.

The next time you pick up Christian book to read, I hope it will be a tangible reminder of the ministry of REF Global and need for Reformed books around the globe. Please also pray for Pastor Petar.

A similar ministry is occurring "next door" in Bulgaria. There, REF National Pastor Emmanuel Tinev, and his wife Svetlana, are faithfully ministering to build Christ's church. Emanuel is the pastor of the Reformed Church in Panagyurishte, Bulgaria. The church building in which they worship was stolen by the Communists and finally reclaimed after the collapse of the Soviet Union and the nations in its orbit. The church was remodeled and, rebuilt transforming it into a beautifully simple and classic church building.

The reclaiming and rebuilding of the church building is a beautiful story of God's provision for his people. The money for the project and all the donated labor came during a time of recession in Bulgaria. As you pray for the church in Bulgaria, pray that God will raise up Bulgarian men to be equipped to serve the church in Bulgaria. There is always a need for funds for much needed translation work for good theological books to be translated into Bulgarian.

Emmanuel and Svetlana live in Sofia, Bulgaria. Each Sunday they drive 70 miles over the mountains to Panagyurishte to feed their beloved flock in their beautifully reclaimed and re–modeled church building. We were blessed, being a part of the weekly Bible study fellowship in their home in Sofia.

Each week the group prays and eats together and studies the Bible. This is an extremely accomplished group of faithful believers in Bulgaria. Pray for them and their families and their church.

Whenever I travel and minister in the Balkans, I cannot help but be moved by a beautiful and historic part of Europe that repeatedly has been devastated by war and strife throughout the centuries. If it was not for faithful Christians who live there, the despair could become overwhelming (it's the same in many places around the globe). However, what I have repeatedly experienced over the decades is that I go to these places to minister to believers and witness to unbelievers, and knowing and unknowingly, the believers minister to me probably more than I to them! Every trip and every day are a poignant reminder of God's grace and His work in the lives of the faithful.

On every one of my evangelistic and missionary journeys, and in every country, I find that there are believers like Elijah—their "knees have not bowed" to other gods. They are building the Savior's church wherever God in His providence has placed them. One such person is Dr. Jasmin, who traveled with me to Bosnia.

While in Bosnia, Jasmin was able to visit many of his relatives who he had not seen for a while. They were proud of him with his new Doctor of Philosophy in Church History degree, and he was concerned for their souls. He gave many of them their first copy of Holy Scriptures. Today, years later, I pray that the Word of the only true and living God, will be read by them, and that the Holy Spirit will open the hearts of His chosen ones in Bosnia.

On the first trip that we drove into Bosnia, I had two concerns. One was I had the most awful tooth, ache with pain, a precursor to my Croatian root canal, with headaches and light nausea on less than well-maintained mountain roads. I did not want to stay behind and miss going into Bosnia—but it was a painful drive! After four hours we rolled into a compound which was a hospital. A couple of tablets arrived from somewhere and that gave some needed relief. Finally, for me, in the good providence of God I got my $68.00 Croatian root canal procedure. The $68.00 included 6 taxi rides.

My second concern was that our driver only had one eye. Admittedly it wasn't in the middle of his head. I asked someone if he was a good driver. "Oh yes he is a very good driver." When I followed up with, "How do you know?" The answer was so reassuring. "He's alive, isn't he?"

In this war-torn region where many people might ask "where is" or "where was God," there is evidence of God's presence and protection. In Bosnia, I met a dear lady was the founder of a Bosnian prayer ministry. Without too much thought I asked her what I initially thought was a significant question.

"I noticed that your home is the only house standing in your street. How did that happen?" With all peace and confidence, she looked me in the eye and said, "Well, I have a prayer ministry." How many of us would have such a perspective? Working with refugees in Bosnia who were slowly rebuilding their lives, it became clear, many of them owned nothing except their names and the borrowed clothes that they are wearing. It was very humbling. Again, I think they ministered to me more than I to them.

Russia

There is a Russian proverb that says, "Without effort, you won't even pull a fish out of a pond." And it's true, whether we are fishing for food or fishing for converts! Russia is an enormous country with so much history and so many majestic sites that one could spend a lifetime learning about it and still barely begin to understand it.

In Christian ministry, one never knows what the day will bring or who God will bring into your life. A memorable of example of this occurred during one of my journeys to Russia.

Arriving at Moscow's International airport, I was introduced to a Russian military officer who asked me if we would return to Russia to help train Russian military officers who wanted to be chaplains. David Dare and I spent a week in Russia beginning that process, working with the Russian Military Christian Union (RMCU). We did so and gave an in-person week-long seminary to 33 Russian officers who were serving in locations across 11 time zones. Remember, Russia is huge!

How did this come about? God did it! This was one of the most amazing opportunities that God gave to us ministering in Russian under the auspices of what was then, PEF now REF Global.

Planning the ministry to the Russian military officers, was another story. It was tolerated chaos. Dates changed, locations changed, numbers attending changed. The following became our theme song: "We the willing, led by the unknowing, (brother Oleg) are doing the impossible, for the ungrateful. (We didn't know how grateful Oleg was!) We have done so much, for so long, with so little, we are now qualified, to do anything, with nothing." Even so, we had an unforgettable trip.

As always, God was in charge in Russia and allowed David and me to be an encouragement and blessing to the men. Each morning, after a good breakfast, we were picked up from our hotel in Moscow, by Oleg's driver, for a 2 ½-hour drive through the city and out into the surrounding countryside. We began our lectures each morning at 10:30.

In the evening our translator drove us back to Moscow's city limits and we used the Russian Metro to get back to our hotel. Many of the stations were covered in marble with elegant chandeliers and magnificent stone statues. It was not an inconvenience at all, as we finally conquered the 3 levels of the Russian metro. No small accomplishment! Thirty-four New Geneva Study Bibles in Russian, were presented to our coordinator, Oleg, for the men along with some apologetics works that were presented. I was presented with a fine Russian windup watch by one of the officers. (When I want to know the time; the answer is "It's time to pray for Russian believers!)

David did a great job lecturing and used army videos to demonstrate Chaplains at work. A friend of 30 years, and a West Point graduate he was a great traveling companion. With respect to snoring, we both gave as good as we got! David led a "field communion service" which was the highlight of the week. During our lectures a visiting brother pastor was introduced who had recently been released from a long prison term for his faith. It was a humbling and blessed experience to offer him the lectern to have him bless us all with his courageous testimony.

After the conference we received many encouraging letters and notes of appreciation. It was another one of those instances in which we were equally enriched and blessed by what had transpired. A sampling of the translated notes received from the Russian officers is presented below as a testimony of God's faithfulness:

> *"I was glad to hear the Lord's truth from your mouths which built me up. I would very much hope that we meet again. May the Lord bless your labors in serving? And may He glorify Himself through your lives. May the peace of God be with you."*
>
> *"This is the first time at such a conference and am very glad, because I heard the Word of God and I am always glad to receive it, then apply it to my life and to tell other people. I thank God for you and this conference."*
>
> *"Thank you! I am fortunate that I have such brothers. I love you with the love of Jesus Christ."*
>
> *"Dear David and Paddy, I wish to bless the Lord and you for your love toward Russia and for your sacrifice. I thank God that I was able to come to Moscow and hear your lectures and was much enlightened for my benefit. I take advantage of the opportunity to invite you to be my guest in the Northern Caucasus in the city of Vladisavkaz. May God bless you and your families."*
>
> *"I was glad to hear the Lord's truth from your mouths which built me up."*
>
> *"Blessings to Paddy for his teaching which still more strengthened my heart and hope in the Lord. I have a still greater desire to witness about Christ. Thanks for the practical advice in the matter of witnessing."*

Ministering to these officers was unexpected opportunity and an amazing experience.

One evening in a Moscow hotel, while waiting to catch the train to St. Petersburg, we were able to witness to a young Russian from Vladivostok, who we "bumped into." We didn't have the time or the money to go to Vladivostok, but God took care of those details for us, with another divine appointment. Similarly, on one trip we travelled on the "Red Arrow"— the overnight train which runs for 8 hours between Moscow and St. Petersburg. It was there that we "bumped into" an international group of military specialists. I am thankful that I am still able to pass as an Englishman in faraway places. It is a reminder that there are no "accidents" or "coincidences," nor is there "fate" with God. In the providence of God, I have traveled in 68 countries, so it will be no surprise that God has caused me to meet many interesting people.

Gary Robinson was one of those people. Gary was a backup singer from Nashville when I met him. He came with me to Russia in 1966. He later developed a ministry with Russian orphanages. I have lost contact with Gary, but I cannot forget him! Gary used his "evangelistic set of teeth." He did that and caused folks to stop on the sidewalk while he made animal balloons for the children and gave a tract in Russian to the parents.

When I think of Gary, I think of his method of talking to people about Jesus outside the church. We would be walking through the streets of Moscow when suddenly Gary would produce his set of false teeth. I do not know who owned them originally but when Gary put them in his mouth they would stick out at an angle and be impossible not to notice.

A pattern developed that when he put these teeth in, children walking with their mothers would be so shocked that they would stop and stare at Gary. That caused the mother to also stop. Now that Gary had stopped them, he would take out a bunch of colored balloons and make a balloon animal for the child. While he had the child's attention, he would tell them Bible stories. As he said goodbye to the astonished Russians, he would be sure to give the mum a gospel track in Russian. As they went on their way they would turn around and wave with big smiles at the man with the very strange teeth.

God blessed Gary with an amazing voice. He was able to sing almost anything at the drop of a hat and of course without his large teeth. On one occasion, we heard a small group of university students playing and singing operatic music as we attempted to learn how to get around in the Russian underground. Gary knew the work and joined in before we even turned the corner in the Russian underground system. The Russian underground system is acoustically wonderful! The students kept playing and singing with Gary standing with them and singing along beautifully. Their eyes lit up with encouragement and thankfulness in their facial expressions. As we went on our way, they needed to keep playing so Gary was unable to talk to them about Jesus. The beauty of the harmony and the quality of the sound they all made was something I will never forget.

Gary was very insistent that we travel from Moscow to St. Petersburg for a special evening of classical Russian music and dancing. I was cold on the idea at first as I was not comfortable spending precious mission money on such an evening. Well, I am glad he persuaded us all to go for the never to be forgotten evening's experience. True to form and to my horror out came "Gary's evangelistic teeth" during the performance. I am laughing as I write this because the musicians were professional and not at all put out by Gary's "outreach!" However, one by one a group of them started to smile and laugh while still playing their beautiful music.

Folks were invited to join in with the performers and Gary went up during the performance to take part on stage, in their Cossack dance routine. He fit right in as a Cossack dancer. He did so well that if I had not travelled with him all the way from Nashville, I would have assumed he was planted by the performers.

You may be asking where was the evangelism for the evening? Little did I know that was where I came in. If you look at pictures of Governor Chris Patten, at a quick glance you could be forgiven in thinking that I was his double. What happened next may be hard for you to believe. Initially, I had no idea why what was taking place. During the intermission there was a group of Chinese tourists or students sitting near the front of the auditorium. About nine of them managed to clamber over the back of the seats and arrived in front of me having used the back of the seats as steppingstones. This was all a total surprise! The first Chinese person spoke to me, so I did not even have to figure out how to start a conversation with them, and asked, "How much to take a photograph of you?" I was prompted to say, "Nothing! Just read this!" In all, that sequence was repeated nine times with Chinese folks scrambling over the back of the seats even as the musicians came out after the intermission. This was all taking place down the front of this stately auditorium. Thankfully, they all made it back over the seats in time for the program to resume as the lights were being dimmed.

What had just happened?

The Chinese had assumed, wrongly, that I was the last Governor of Hong Kong (1992–1997), Lord Christopher Patten. If you compare our portraits, there is a strong facial resemblance! They wanted to know how much it would cost to take a picture of me. Imagine how they must have felt when I said, "It won't cost you anything to take my picture" and then I gave them each a gift! What was even more amazing was that for a reason known unto God I had nine copies of John Blanchard's *Ultimate Questions* in my Eddie Bower knapsack, and they were all in Chinese!

The story of the Chinese tourists in Russia is important for us because it reminds us that there are no boundaries for the gospel. In any country on any continent there are people from around the world and many of them will return to their home country. Any evangelistic effort may be fruit in more than one country! I was thrilled that I was given the opportunity to witness to 9 Chinese people for the first time in my life!

25

ITALY AND BEYOND

We all know the adage of medieval origin, "All roads lead to Rome." So, it is with my many travels. As I have crisscrossed the globe, the roads have indeed led to and through Rome and Italy on more than one occasion.

On a trip to the Czech Republic I met Chris Maclellan, who had an apartment in Rome, Italy. I was offered the use of the apartment if I would facilitate the different groups that would be arriving over the summer, wash the sheets, cut the grass, etc. It was a grand neighborhood, and I caused a "bit of a stir" when Chris discovered that rather than arrange for an expensive firm to come in to cut the lawn I did it myself. I discovered that an Irishman and his family were renting next door, so I called to ask if he had a lawn mower. I was offered the use of the lawn mower, bought some gas, and cut the lawn myself and enjoyed meeting the Irishman!

Outside Rome's main railway station, I was talking with an American lady who before she married, was Pattie Demps. "You need to meet Dr. Mario" she said. Later I discovered that she had only met him once. Well, Dr. Mario lived in Viterbo, Italy so I found a curbside telephone kiosk, put a few coins in the machine and dialed Sheila back home in Kansas City. Pattie and I needed to travel together to Viterbo by train. I explained that I really was interested in meeting Mario. I told Sheila that I was strangely comfortable with the idea and asked what she thought. No problem. So, Pattie and I took the train to Viterbo.

Arriving in Viterbo, we found that Dr. Mario was about to hold church under a chestnut tree on his property. I was impressed that as he didn't know me, I was not invited to speak during the worship time. However, after the service and before a fellowship meal he asked if I would like to speak for ten minutes. I accepted of course but before I said anything, I was prompted to offer him a suitcase of new theological books. I pulled out a book on the top. It was a commentary of the Book of Psalms by Dr. James Mongomery Boice. It was a three-volume set. It is great commentary on the Book of Psalms. Tears formed on Mario's face, and he said: "I have been praying for a good commentary on the Psalms." That was a divine appointment. God has demonstrated such things many times on trips. When we prayed for divine appointments on trips and what books to take, God was listening to our prayers. Imagine the King of Kings, the only ruler of princes including in his busy day my prayer request to take the books he wanted me to take to Italy!

I have also had occasion to meet with Greenville Presbyterian Theological Seminary alumni who are Presbyterian pastors ministering throughout Europe. One such trip and meeting was in Viterbo, Italy, along with Dr. Joesph Pipa, the seminary president. We traveled with the purpose of meeting with several pastors to encourage them in their work of bringing the gospel back to Europe. Such meetings are always a time of blessing and refreshment and a reminder to everyone present that they, like Elijah, are not alone in their endeavors.

It Starts with a Prayer

One Sunday at a fellowship lunch here at home, Sarah Hartman looked at me and asked, "Take me through a day for you."

"Well, it could start by looking in my diary and seeing nothing on the page. Say a few prayers, get an idea, make a few phone calls and a trip is born. It might be a trip to encourage local folks ministering in certain city, country, or region. Such was the case for a trip to Switzerland and Austria. Italy and Liechtenstein were added later. Out of such ideas, contacts, and prayers, a trip is born!"

A ship cannot be steered unless it is moving. In the same way, now we are "moving," and I seek to find what else would God purpose. We began to pray that God would *specifically* guide our plans, show us, reveal to us, what else He had purposed for us to do and accomplish.

That is exactly what we did on a trip in Europe. It was a trip that He had already planned out, and it was planned out long before we even thought of going on the trip! Books were prayed for, chosen, bought, and weighed. Dates were chosen. Tickets were purchased. A Prayer Calendar was made. Prayers were offered and the blanks were filled in. Prayer calendars were e-mailed. Prayer calendars were printed, and "snail mailed." Ruedi told me that a pastor in Zurich was looking for a preacher for the first Sunday in May. Ouch! I'd just booked a non-refundable ticket for May 11. I called the pastor in Zurich, and he invited me to preach, subject to me being able to change my flight.

I was able to change my non-refundable ticket without a penalty. It was $20.00 cheaper and on top of that, I was offered a generous fee for preaching. The final ticket, $762.00 round trip less $200.00 a grand sum of $562.00!

Ruedi met me at the airport in Zurich, offering door-to-door service, to my beautiful Swiss attic room. After church, I was asked, "Is someone looking after you?" I was about to answer, "The Father, Son, and Holy Spirit," when Guensoo a gracious lady from the congregation said, "No I mean for lunch?" I told her "I need to tell you a secret. I am 65 years old, and I have never refused an invitation for lunch ever!" Guensoo's husband was a Swiss Banker, but unfortunately, we did not meet him.

Ruedi and I had prayed for an invite to Sunday lunch so that Ruedi and Jane would meet new people. This is a simple illustration of a specific prayer being answered. I'm so glad that our God isn't deaf. More evidence of God's grace!

Later, we were able to meet with the pastor in Zurich, after his vacation. We had a delightful lunch with the pastor and his wife, when they returned home, again hosted by Guensoo. The pastor admitted that he was relieved that we had met, and that we had such an encouraging time together, because after the service in Zurich, there was a "coffee hour" at which that I finally arrived.

I tried to shake hands with everyone, around 300 people, as they left the sanctuary. I asked them how they were, and how they were "fixed" for the next life. So much so, that when I met the pastor at lunch, he said, "When I came back, I was told that you said everybody is going to hell, if they didn't love Jesus. Was that true?"

Yes, pretty much."

"Also, after the service you checked up on everybody as they left the church, how they were fixed for the next life? Was that also true?"

"Yes, pretty much."

After lunch, with 2–3 hours of good fellowship, we left the pastor some books.

With 50 nationalities in the church in Zurich, the pastor saw the need for the church to put together a confession of faith *and he was able to use some of the books we left him, such as Truths We Confess* by R. C. Sproul to assist in his effort. Similarly, Guensoo often sends emails and inserts entire Psalms in them to encourage her non-Christian friends. Guensoo now has the 3-volume set of Dr. James Montgomery Boice's commentary on the Psalms to help her.

When I say, "God had this trip planned out, long before I ever thought of going on the trip. He knew what books were needed and who they were for," it's true! Whether in Italy, Switzerland, or even beautiful Liechtenstein which is 25 km wide and 10 km long and has a population of only 38,000 people, God is working and using willing disciples to spread the gospel and encourage believers such as Dr. Jürgen-Burkhard Klautke, a Reformed German pastor and seminary professor. Elder Art Crouch came with me on a trip in 2016. Scan the QR code to follow link.

https://drive.google.com/file/d/1IqQqr5NtU7
EZ5fOvsNJzVFlh4XE0YTAV/view

The above link will reveal a typical Newsletter on Paddy's REF Ministry Web page.

Each trip has a Trip Prayer Calendar before the trip and a Trip Newsletter after the trip.

Paddy's REF Web page: paddycook.blogspot.com

I often ask, "Who will God raise up to tell the next generation about Jesus?" Then I remember faithful men such as these who consistently teach and preach the Word of God in places most of us will never go and to people most of us will never meet. What can we do to help? Pray fervently.

26

IRAQ AND MOROCCO

For years after 2001, events in Iraq and Afghanistan captured international headlines. If there were two places in the world that a person from the United States or England could not safely travel, it was to these ancient and historic countries. Christians inside the country were often persecuted and fleeing, and Christians outside the countries were certainly not welcome. But then, in Iraq, there were small shifts in the political and cultural dynamics that created some opportunity for ministry. As always, God was working.

God Opens a Door for Ministry in Iraq

In 2009, Ed Nipper, who became a close friend, was a gifted and passionate evangelist, who came to a PEF Conference to present a need to minister in Iraq. I queued up to talk to him and left my contact information. The next thing I knew, a massive envelope of information arrived just before a trip. After the trip, another similar envelope arrived. I rarely arranged for a back-to-back trip, but I hadn't had time to open the second package of information. Instead of reading it all I drove up to Nashville to have lunch and talk with Ed. After being with him for 3 hours, I signed up for a ministry trip to Iraq.

One of the first questions Ed asked me was, "Paddy, what is your blood type?"

"I have no idea. Nobody has ever asked me. Why do you need to know?"

"Well, you might lose some. We are going to Iraq!"

My next question was, "Are you taking a gun, because I don't have one." No, Ed wasn't taking a gun but the folks we worked with would be armed. I told Ed I would stand behind him! Though said in jest, my words were a reminder that for many Christians around the world, their daily prayers include the psalmist words: "Teach me your way O LORD and lead me on a level path because of my enemies" (Psalm 27:11, ESV).

I have had more than one trip to Iraq and each trip was a blessing. Ministry activities have included teaching, preaching, book distribution and discipleship, evangelism, and a summer "Camp of the Medes" for children. One of the sets of books I was able to take to Iraq was Dr. Joeseph Morecraft's then 5-volume (now 8-volume in the 2nd edition) *Authentic Christianity: An Exposition of the Theology and Ethics of the Westminster Larger Catechism.*

Dr. Morecraft's work culminates a lifetime of learning, preaching, and pastoral care. It incorporates and expounds on the most stalwart of Reformed theology from recent centuries as well from the history of Reformed thought. He presents the theologians, commentators, and exegetes the teachings of the Larger Catechism through powerful insight and consistent application—all solidly grounded on the firm foundation of God's Word.

Many of us might look at such a massive work and think, "No thanks, not for me." But that is not the case elsewhere. In the United States we have an abundance of books and almost instant access to them. Most Christians do not have such a blessing. Books, and especially ones on Christianity, theology, and biblical commentaries are scarce and expensive. To be sure, carrying three or four suitcases of books overseas is quite an endeavor, but as always with God, the blessing outweighs the burden!

For more than three decades, working with PEF/REF as a missionary evangelist to Europe and elsewhere, I have pursued my call, my prayer, and my goal of taking the gospel to every country in Europe. My strategy is to help build the libraries of young pastors in Europe. Just as a bricklayer needs a plumb line and trowel to build a straight wall, a pastor needs sound books as a foundation for his study. To introduce European pastors to the Reformed faith and encourage them in their walk, I give them new theological books, the tools of their trade.

One of the most significant works I have been able to bless pastors with is *Authentic Christianity*. In the providence of God, I have given the original edition of Dr. Morecraft's work to pastors in Malta, Israel, New Zealand, Estonia, Latvia, Lithuania, Germany, Portugal, the Azores, Madeira Island, Gibraltar, Tenerife, Spain, Serbia, Bulgaria, Norway, Denmark, Finland, Italy, Greece, Iceland, Iraq and Sweden. (In Sweden, I gave one set of *Authentic Christianity* to the king of Sweden's chaplain for his personal use, and another set to him as a gift to the king and queen.) My prayer is that *Authentic Christianity* will be read and studied by Europeans and others for generations.

One of the book recipients in Iraq, was Pastor Yusif, a godly and dedicated minister of the gospel. Pastor Yusif graciously accepted the books—but he also read every word in them! Without his assistance (and truck that provided us transportation), the ministry trip would not have been as great as we experienced. The Middle East is renowned for hospitality, and such was certainly the case in Iraq. Meals and frequent tea times were always a joy.

Often the pattern of the evening was that a national would come over to our table and introduce himself. When he asked to take a photograph I would say, "I have a hug for you." "What is hug?" When he was close, I would ask if he was a Muslim or Protestant. Several times I was able to arrange to give him a copy of *Ultimate Questions* by John Blanchard.

In Iraq, there was also training given to teachers who wanted to use outdoor fairs to further their work. There was discussion on how to teach all learning styles and how to set fair tests to include these learning styles. Ed's wife Jo and my son Stephen, a graduate of GPTS.edu creatively took care of that department. The teaching seminars were of a very high standard and very well received in all the cities that they were given. Some of the local Muslim public-school teachers asked if lectures could be available for them to "keep up!" Evening lectures were arranged for them so they could enhance their teaching skills, and there were wonderful times of instruction to remarkable and dedicated teachers.

Morocco

If you ask most people what they know about Morocco, the answer is either, "Nothing" or "Isn't that where the move Casablanca takes place?" To be sure, it is the country of the setting of the famous 1942-wartime romance film *Casablanca* starring Ingrid Bergman, Humphrey Bogart, and Paul Henreid—but it is much more than that! If you look at a globe or a map, it's just under 3,000 miles from Iraq to Morocco to the east on the coast of North Africa and 5,000 from the United States to Morocco "as the crow flies." We weren't crows, but we (Ed Nipper and I) were flying.

We had prayed about which cities to visit, which hotels to stay in, and how long we should stay in each place. In God's providence, it all worked out. The hotel was by the beach, a few miles out of town with quiet local life all around.

Coming out of our room and seeing a lounge full of Muslims with their comfortable long shirts reminded us that we were in a Muslim, French-speaking African country.

The roof-top swimming pool was just what we as tourists planned to swim in each day, because that is what tourists do! Upon arrival, we decided that the next day we would go to the beach. However, this first night we are going out to find a "warrior prayer meeting."

We didn't have an address, but we did have a location. I discovered its existence on the internet before leaving the US. We thought that we would go early and get to know the area. Hopefully then, at the time of the meeting, we might see a trickle of folks entering. That didn't happen at all, as the shops were closed. We were openly conspicuous no matter what we did, and we didn't see any folks trickling.

At the time that the meeting was due to begin, nobody had done any trickling, anywhere. Ed suggested that it was time to go home. I was prompted to wait a little longer. We were leaning against a grand wrought iron gate to a nice property. Then I saw two of the largest and whitest eyeballs that I have ever seen peering straight at me through the iron gate. The owner of the eyes, a Madagascan, spoke. "You are welcome to come in." I looked at Ed and somehow, we both decided to go in. We were escorted up a few stone steps while our guide knocked on the door. An attractive, middle-aged lady opened the door. As we began to speak, she quickly and gently repeated the phrase, "a moment," "a moment." Her husband came to the front door and greeted us in English and invited us inside his home.

Well in the providence of God he turned out to be a French reformed pastor and a graduate of the reformed seminary, in Aix-en-Provence, France. Not only had God guided us to the correct building we were on our first evening talking to probably the only reformed presbyterian in the whole country. Now it wasn't the venue for the "warrior prayer meeting," but it was an amazing providence that only our God could arrange. We talked freely about our vacation plans, and I offered to help arrange seminary training for any Moroccan student who was ready to apply to study for the gospel ministry. I was also able to offer to help disciple a student who needed to prepare to study at seminary.

I was surprised that the offer was declined. The reason given, politely to me, I thought was strange. I was told that because they couldn't afford to pay an ordained minister, they did not want to send young men to seminary. I asked if he would consider letting me help students to study for the ministry.

Amazingly on our first trip outside our hotel in a country and city where we didn't know anybody, we came back to the hotel in the highest of spirits in wonderment of what God had purposed for us on the first night of our vacation. It was a great introduction and comfort that God was already answering prayers. We asked our questions and were given answers. We slept well and woke up to a great breakfast. We then set out to enjoy being tourists in Morocco.

Yes, we went to the beach, but you probably really want to know "Did you go to Rick's Café, the setting for the infamous film?" That's like asking, "Did you go to Graceland when you were in Memphis?" Of course we did! We had dinner at Rick's Café where the film *Casablanca* is shown 24 hours a day—a tourist trap Moroccan style!

Our travels took us to the beautiful and historic capital city of Rabat as well as to Tangier. In Tangier, we stayed at the famous Continental Hotel, built in 1870. The hotel has served as host to many famous people such as Sir Winston Churchill and artist Edgar Degas. It too has a movie connection, being the location for part of the filming of Bernardo Bertoluccci's *The Sheltering Sky* (1990). We also visited the famous Gran Café de Paris, which has been an institution in Tangier for decades for locals and tourists—and the site of the filming of a scene from the 2002 film *The Bourne Identity*. It may sound like we were on a Hollywood film pilgrimage, but we weren't. It is simply a testimony to the beauty, history, and culture of a remarkable country.

Any person who has traveled a great deal has learned lessons that should be shared and listened to by the wise. One of mine is "Always negotiate the taxi price before you get in." I was reminded of that in Morocco on the way to the airport.

Question for our taxi driver—"How much do we owe you?"

Answer: "200 dirhams."

Response: "Since I like you, I am going to give you 20 dirhams. If you upset me, it will be less!"

Reply: "Thank you."

Our previous driver had dropped us at the wrong terminal. Both Ed and I have been taxi-drivers, so we know what it should have cost without asking.

There is a Moroccan proverb that states: "A man who doesn't read is like a dog without training." On this trip we learned from our trip that Moroccan's like to read. That is a good thing for the people of a country that has only a very small Christian population—God is already preparing the hearts and minds of many people, who, although they do not know it, are awaiting the Good News of the Word—Jesus, the Word of John 1!

Even with all our regular prayer support we travel with we did have a significant failure. We tried to 'disciple' a parrot to sing, "Jesus loves me this I know for the Bible tells me so." It didn't end well.

27

NEW ZEALAND—WORLD RUGBY CUP

The phrase "bread and circuses" or "bread and games" is attributed to Juvenal, the Roman poet of the first century in his work *Satires*. It referred to a political strategy of the state gaining public approval, not by service or results, but by entertainment of the population through things such as the gladiatorial context that would distract the population from other issues. In 2011, the World Rugby Cup final was held in Auckland, New Zealand between France and New Zealand. The Men's Rugby World Cup is held every four years, and it is truly an international sporting event. It was not a case of "bread and circuses" by the host country, but it was a time of great sporting enthusiasm. It was a perfect time to be part of a team of seven street preachers for twelve days, preaching eight hours a day to thousands of fans from around the world.

Some people on our team came to connect with churches, encourage believers, and encourage "Street Preachers" who came to preach! God allowed us to do all that in Auckland. Thousands of people came from all over the world to attend the games. The streets were packed. We often positioned ourselves at street corners. Knowing that the lights changed every two minutes, we encouraged the folks with short exhortations to constantly changing congregations!

It was a most difficult task for me to learn to make a clear comprehensive and substantive gospel presentation for the 2 minutes before the traffic lights changed. After 10 days I think I had learned how that is to be done. Of course, the best answer is that our prayers for God to raise up educated national pastors in Europe, the Middle East, Morocco, and New Zealand will be answered in God's timing.

During out time in New Zealand, we were also able to preach locally in a park. Walking around Auckland, we stumbled into the University of Auckland's Graduation Day with hundreds of students and their families. A divine opportunity!

God provided a portable microphone that we hung around our neck when we preached, so we were able to be heard by many people without being intrusive. We were able to use our normal speaking voices and be heard without having to shout. It was very effective as it allowed our witness to reach many people who otherwise would not have been able to hear. People like to hear what is being said, but don't always have the courage or desire to be part of the crowd. Outdoor evangelism can be effective, but not if it is obnoxious.

Encouraging tangible fruit was meeting New Zealander Steve Cliff and his wife Laura. Steve was able to explain the local laws of Street preaching to a few local officials with good success. Steve has a passion and a gift for Street preaching. Steve became a graduate of Greenville Presbyterian Theological Seminary in Taylors, S.C. He now lives in Greenville, S.C. with Laura and their family and ministers there.

The days were long, but they went by quickly. It is impossible to even recall and report all the divine appointments and talks we had with folks as we walked through the day. We were on the streets from 12 noon until 8.00 p.m. each day for 12 days and there were seven of us, as well as local pastors who joined us for the time that they could spare, along with local Christians. We were also able to connect with local Christians, some who were discouraged "Street Preachers." We encouraged them!

And the game? New Zealand won 8–7!

— 28 —

ICELAND, NORWAY, DENMARK, FINLAND, AND SWEDEN

There are no coincidences with God. We often say in conversation, "I happened to meet ... " or "I happened to be ... " or even, "I stumbled upon (sometimes literally). All such instances are in God's plan—they simply have not yet been revealed to us. Someone once said that "God is the hand in the glove of history." It's true—in the lives of nations as well as in your life and my life.

Iceland

In 2013, I was clearly reminded of the truth above as I prepared for a trip with my son, Matthew for points north on the compass in the lands of ice and snow. I met a person named Tom, who lives in Maine, at a funeral on Lookout Mountain, Georgia. Tom had a long friendship with a man in the Faroe Islands, an autonomous territory of Denmark consisting of 18 islands situated between Iceland and Norway in the North Atlantic Ocean. Tom's friend ministers in Greenland and often stops over in Reykjavik, Iceland. The week before we left on our trip, he sent us the telephone number of an Icelandic pastor named Jogvan. But that came *after* our earlier "incidents."

Matthew broke his ankle in a climbing accident and got mono, three weeks before the trip. Three weeks before that, I fell 7 feet over a wall in the dark at a PEF Prayer Retreat, ended up in the hospital, and got 14 stitches in my head.

With those traumas behind us, Matthew and I headed north to Iceland. The 23-mile taxi ride from the airport to our hotel cost $150.00 and that was not a mistake. I almost dropped into the depths of depression. We fell asleep in our hotel and woke up at 4 p.m. on Saturday afternoon, with nowhere to go to church the next day and knowing no one. For the first time ever, I prayed asking the Lord, "What are we doing here with two fifty-pound suitcases of books?"

We telephoned Jogvan and asked for a ride to his church. He asked if would like to speak at the church. A visiting Icelander, a Project Manager of a large company in Reykjavik, was presenting his ministry and became my translator. This visitor was to receive half of our books. Two visitors! You prayed for divine appointments! I focused on Philemon 5:6 and Thessalonians 5:17. Pray about everything and talk to people about Jesus outside the church. The Lord blessed wonderfully. The people responded, "God definitely sent you to us!"

The goal of the trip was to live and obey Holy Scripture over a short space of time, so that our steps could be measured, the Lord's leading could be recalled and documented, and His fruit observed and recorded.

The scripture passages chosen for the trip were,

> "Commit your way to the LORD;
> trust in him, and he will act." Psalm 37:5 (ESV)
>
> "You chart the path ahead of me and tell me where to stop and rest.
> Every morning you know where I am." Psalm 139:3 (TLB)
>
> "Show me the path where I should go, O Lord; point out the right road for me to walk, lead me, teach me, for you are the God who gives me salvation. I have no hope except in you."
> Psalm 25:4,5 (TLB)

Matthew later wrote of the trip:

> We set out for a foreign country where we had never been and did not know anyone. We had specific goals of people we hoped to meet and suitcases full of theological books to give away, but we had no specific plan on how to find the people we were hoping to meet other than to find a church to visit and go to the university. We asked God to guide each of our steps and show us what to do. We met Christians who welcomed us in faith and met men who were blessed by the gift of lots of sound theological books that would help them in their own lives and in their Christian discipling. This was an important lesson and an important experience for me in every new thing.

On Monday morning after a good breakfast, we ventured outside and stood in the bus shelter. Matt was looking at the timetable in Icelandic. We were planning to take the bus downtown.

"Dad there is a bus coming let's get on it!"

"Matt let me tell you something. Never in my life have I got on a bus before I know where it is going!"

"Dad how big is the whole country? We're not going to get lost. Anyway, it's here now."

We got on the bus! After the shock of paying our $150.00 taxi ride; just when I was thinking lunch here would be too expensive, Matthew noticed a cheap lunch offer by paying attention to the details on the lunch menu board. We had the lunch time to ourselves, so we talked to our waiter. Matthew had an adventurist spirit and for one meal ordered the whale steak. I ordered lamb, *it* was delicious!

In case you are wondering, yes, Iceland in February is cold. It is called Iceland for a reason! We took warm clothes. Most of the space was for books for the church and students in Reykjavik. Matthew was our chief bus navigator. We slept in our own bed each night. He has the gift! It was great to travel with Matt.

A set of *Authentic Christianity* was left for the Icelandic church with my translator, who we met on Sunday, our second day and another set was given to a young chaplain at the University of Reykjavik. That lightened the suitcases considerably!

Iceland has a rich and wonderful history, including the world's oldest parliament.

The first Parliament in the world was established in Iceland in AD 930. All available land in Iceland was settled by then. Regional chieftains found it necessary to form a national government. Rejecting the idea of a king, they opted for a commonwealth. Parliament was convened, laws were made and disputes settled.

If you ever have the chance to visit Iceland, go! God is working there, and you will have a wonderful experience—even if you don't have whale steak!

Norway

In 2013, my ministry also took me to Oslo and Bergen in Norway. If ever there was a country that looks exactly like the picture in *National Geographic,* it is Norway. It is stunningly beautiful! It is a country of tranquility and industry.

The purpose of the trip was to take books to encourage the Church. The suitcases were filled with books. There were some clothes, PEF/REF is not known for the fashion statement of its evangelists. It is known for bringing the Good News and books about the Good News! The books are to equip God's people as they proclaim the gospel and live the Christian life in testimony to the salvific work of Jesus Christ.

Beyond the books, why did we at PEF take a mission trip to Scandinavia? We did so to be faithful to the Great Commission; to bring honor and glory to the Lord Jesus Christ and His church; and to offer Norwegians an alternative to Islam and all the other "isms."

This was an unusual trip in that we went uninvited by Christians in Norway. We didn't know anybody, but we knew that God has elect in Norway who needed to be encouraged. We knew that God would lead us. God would guide us, and God would provide for us. He did!

One of the delights of global ministry is the opportunity to enjoy the cuisine of the many countries and cultures. Each one is different, and each one carries a history of cultural hospitality. Regardless of how much or how little the people have, it is always humbling to share coffee, tea, or a meal. In Hebrews 13:2, we are told: "**Do not neglect to show hospitality to strangers**, for thereby some have entertained angels unawares" (ESV). Many times, I have been reminded of that verse and how Christians around the globe have shown kindness and hospitality to me and to others. To be sure, we are not angels, but we accepted their hospitality and took it to practice for entertaining angels!

Breakfast in Scandinavia is a serious event—and probably not for those who are on a diet! The Scandinavian smorgasbord, a buffet-style meal of Swedish origin is a famous part of life. In Oslo, we were blessed with a wonderful hotel room at a great price due to low occupancy and the breakfast smorgasbord awaited us every morning. It would take a panoramic camera to photograph the full range of choices that we were confronted with each morning. There were breads, meats, cheeses, fruit and juices, cooked eggs, sausages, pastries, coffees, and teas. Then there were tables offering other breads and fresh rolls with butter, ham, roast-beef, salmon and other fish, along with Brie cheese (and others), beetroot, and all of that before one made the trip to the chef's frying pan! It was very easy to eat enough breakfast to avoid having to buy lunch!

We spent time in Oslo and then took the train to historic Bergen, the second largest city in Norway. The train ride from Oslo, Norway to Bergen, Norway is sold rightly as the most beautiful train ride in the world. It was certainly the most beautiful train ride I have ever experienced. The verse that came to mind repeatedly during the trip was the first half of Genesis 1:31:" And God saw everything that he had made, and behold, it was very good" (ESV).

Bergen is a beautiful city with many bronze statues. One that caught my attention near the town hall (Småstrangaten) is a sculpture of a man sitting on the sidewalk. The inscription near it says: "No one is only what you see. Bergen Church City Mission." How true that is! Every person is created in the image of God and has inherent dignity and worth. Too often, we look at the outer person; but God does not. He looks at the soul. Luke 19:10 reminds us: For the Son of Man came to seek and to save the lost" (ESV).

The statues in Bergen are powerful and moving. I think they do what is desired by their sculptors. This one especially is a reminder to me of the words of Dr. Francis Schaeffer in his small book *Art and the Bible,* in which he writes: "The lordship of Christ should include an interest in the arts." Sculptures, paintings, and other artistic endeavors can be silent but very public witnesses to the truths of the Bible.

When we arrived in Bergan the breakfast bar was the best we had ever sat down to. We prayed for a church to worship in on Sunday. On Saturday we decided that we would go to the church near our hotel. (My favorite hotel.) After church we stayed to talk and have a hot drink. I was approached by an English-speaking Norwegian. Always welcome. When I discovered he was a medical doctor I explained I was looking for a Norwegian who wanted to talk to people about Jesus outside the church. "Oh, oh, you want to talk to Haakon!" "Yes, that is who I need to talk to." After talking with Haakon for a few minutes we invited him back to our hotel as I had told him I have 75 copies of *Ultimate Questions* by John Blanchard in Norwegian for him.

Haakon arranged our time in Bergen and arranged for us to speak to a group of students from the University of Bergen. One cold and very wet evening, *we went with him and a group from his church into a park, where they regularly and beautifully take fresh sandwiches and hot drinks to the addicts.* After we left, they decided that in future ventures to feed the hungry they would offer the sandwiches and say, "This is a gift from Jesus!"

We arrived in Norway known by no one, but God answered our prayers and gave us ample opportunity to share the gospel. Later I contacted Haakon to discover he was now studying for the ministry in Norway.

Denmark

Denmark is a marvelous country and its most populous city and capital, Copenhagen, is as delightful as are stories of one of its most famous residents and authors, Han Christian Andersen (1805–1875). Andersen gave us wonderful stories such as "The Emperor's New Clothes," "The Little Mermaid," and "The Ugly Duckling." We were there to tell a different story—the story of God's love.

In Copenhagen, we had an Afghan, ex-Muslim taxi driver from Turkey. He told us that he had left Islam and was studying other religions. It was a perfect opportunity to share the good news of Jesus with him. He listened to our witness, took our literature, and said that he believed that we were the only people in Copenhagen, who believed as we did! We assured him that such was not the case. Biblical Christianity does not have an enormous presence in Denmark, but there are faithful believers, e.g. Professor Jens and Professor Torben faithfully teaching at the seminary in Copenhagen who need our encouragement and prayers. Keith and I so enjoyed our fellowship with them. We had a fruitful time talking with local Danes. We also met with their Pastor, pastor Claus on a different trip and gave him a suitcase of books which he appreciated so much. It was a joy to travel with Keith who is a faithful supporter of the ministry. We also enjoyed the Danish food. In one restaurant we asked the waiter for his recommendation. He replied, "I can offer you Reindeer or Octopus!" along with many other interesting options.

It was a blessing to meet with some of these brothers and sisters in Christ and to pray with them, encourage them, and leave them with books and literature strengthen them in heart and mind. The generosity and hospitality were overflowing. Something else that struck me was the hundreds of bicycles outside train stations. Scandinavians love their bicycles, and they are all the healthier for it.

The Danes have rich literary history. They love stories and Christians in Denmark are working to proclaim the greatest story ever told to those who listen. Pray for them.

Finland

If you love sailing and sailing vessels (and I do), then Scandinavia is the place to go. There is a long maritime heritage dating to at least to the Viking raids of the late eighth century and the first recorded attack on the monastery of Lindisfarne (known also as Holy Island), on the tidal island off the northeast coast of England. Although those raiders were likely Norwegians who came directly over the North Sea, Finland was on the edger of the Viking world. Today, the harbor at Helsinki is filled with historic sailing ships and fishing boats. It is beautiful. It was snowing and a harbor covered in ice during our visit, yet still remarkable— it was what should be expected in Scandinavia in the winter!

I was able to travel to Finland with Art Crouch, a Presbyterian elder and longtime friend and senior counselor to my ministry.

There is a traditional Nordic dish, especially in Finland, known as Lutefisk. Served at Christmastime. Made from dried whitefish, usually cod, that has been cured in lye and has a gelatinous taste, it is an acquired taste! My recommendation is "No thank you." However, it is not the only cuisine available. The choice of octopus and reindeer was also interesting (especially the "meatballs of smoked reindeer")!

Among others, in Finland we met a lady who, at that time, had for 23 years had a prayer ministry. We read in Luke 18:1: "And he told them a parable to the effect that they ought always to pray and not lose heart" (ESV). Marlene is a person who has taken the words to Jesus to heart. She persisted in her prayers for the unbelievers in Finland. For us, she was an answer to prayer herself. We met her in Helsinki, and she has been a delightful encouragement to the ministry with suggestions of who we might contact to further the call that God has given us. Her example is a strong reminder that we should never cease praying (1 Thessalonians 5:17) and we should never underestimate the power and influence of a single person. If we are willing, God will use each of us where we are every day. As Dr. Schaeffer would say, "There are no little people or little places."

How did we meet Marlene? Providentially!

On our first Sunday morning in Helsinki, Art and I had our devotions and prayer time openly by design, after a fine breakfast and I do mean fine. Because we were the last to leave, and for causing our waitress to wait on a Sunday morning, I apologized to her. She was a believer, and I was able to present her with a small pile of books that introduced her to the Reformed faith. She was also the wife of a youth pastor who knew a person—Pastor Markus.

We decided to go to the church she recommended.

Art and I sat behind Marlene in the Helsinki church. After the service we struck up a conversation with Marlene who began to tell us about a pastor Marcus who liked to read! In fact, he liked to read theology! As I looked at Art I was prompted to say, "This could be our guy!" It turned out that God had purposed for us to meet Marlene in this church, on that day, in Helsinki! He does that kind of thing! It was the first time that Marlene had visited that church. It was our first time too! God had arranged another divine appointment to help us carry out his work in Finland, in answer to prayers offered for our trip to Finland.

Pastor Markus never received formal seminary training. His father-in-law trained him to become the senior pastor of a 600-member congregation. God arranged for Marlene to go to a certain church in Helsinki on a certain day at a certain time and arranged for Art and I to choose to sit behind her, in the same church, at the same time on the same Sunday. We discovered that when He prompted us to start a conversation with her! In other words, God chose Marlene to introduce us to the person that we travelled to Helsinki to find, meet and encourage.

On a return visit to Helsinki, we met Juan and his Finish wife. Pastor Markus was sick, and we were sorry to miss him. Again, we brought books for Markus, and it was obvious that Juan was thankful to God to receive them for use in the church. He eagerly asked, "Which book should I read first?" Juan was a Spanish-speaking Columbian, working with Cuban refugees.

Sweden

We set off for Sweden and had a good witness with our Iraqi Muslim taxi-driver, not so difficult with such a captive audience! However, we were unable to re-connect with him to give him a few books as arranged. We walked around part of Stockholm, found the university, and then walked about and left a message with a contact provided by my daughter Mary's pastor. We discovered later that he was away lecturing in Iran!

On a train in Sweden, a woman Dr. Eva, provided our first observable encouragement for ministry in Sweden. The city of Gothenburg, like Stockholm, was not where God was directing us to minister. Dr. Eva, travelling from Gothenburg to Stockholm, sat opposite me and was on her way to Stockholm to specifically pray for Sweden at a conference the next day. A young lady, a Swedish student sat next to me. We were soon talking back and forth about the goofiness of believing in evolution. That is, I was. Helena's grandmother was a Christian. It turned out she was sitting in the wrong seat but remained when the owner arrived. I pulled out two books on creationism, one for each, *The Lie: Evolution* and *War of Worldviews* by Ken Ham.

Uppsala was the place that God had arranged for us to do ministry in Sweden! Art and I did not know that, so we had to keep asking God where he wanted us to be and what he wanted us to say. God was directing us to Uppsala. There, we were predestined to meet a brother who had come to Sweden with his wife all the way from Madagascar! We were directed to meet Harsha, a colorful and interesting brother, who has a large heart for refugees. At one time he himself was one and he understands their needs. We enjoyed our time meeting him and he invited us for a delicious buffet meal there in his restaurant, while he met with his 5:00 pm appointment.

That was the day when we met the chaplain to the King and Queen of Sweden! Art and I met with Harsha, who probably thought we would spend about half an hour together. Not so—we spent 5 hours together. Harsha had a 5 p.m. appointment, meeting his friend, a fellow Madagascan, who we discovered was chaplain to the King and Queen of Sweden. Harsha insisted we take his buffet lunch and help ourselves to whatever we wanted to eat. Some instructions are easier to obey than others! My mind goes back to my record breaking 24 ladies sized roast potatoes I ate in an Afghan's home next door to the British Embassy in Kabul, Afghanistan. They were great, Harsha's were better and the surroundings so comfortable and luxurious.

Part of Harsha's ministry is providing a Bible school for about 40 refugees. He also houses and feeds many of them. When you think of Sweden, pray that God will, lead, guide, and provide for Harsha and his ministry and his dear wife as she houses and feeds so many refugees.

Folks had told us that the Queen of Sweden is a devout Christian lady and employs Christians to work in the palace. Having given Harsha his 5-volume set of "*Authentic Christianity*," the next day I traveled back to Stockholm on the train to collect the other two sets that in God's good providence I had in our room. God already knew, when I was packing, that I would need 3 sets!

Often in my ministry, I am reminded of and encouraged by the words of St. Paul to his protégé, Timothy, when he writes: "When you come, bring the cloak that I left with Carpus at Troas, also the books, and above all the parchments" (2 Timothy 4:13, ESV). Whether in boxes or suitcases, books are heavy; however, books for ministry are never a burden!

29

LATVIA, LITHUANIA, AND ESTONIA

Latvia

Most people probably can't tell you the difference between Latvia and Lithuania—or find them on a map! The same is true for Estonia. Let me give you a clue—they are collectively known as the Baltics (they are adjacent to the Baltic Sea). That's Baltics, not Balkans! All of them are amazing countries!

Situated in northeastern Europe and graced with beautiful beaches and dense sprawling forests, Latvia is home to almost 2 million people. English is spoken widely and about a fourth of the population is Russian speaking. Long under Russian and then Soviet control, the Republic of Latvia gained full independence in 1991. About 75% of Latvians identify with Christianity in its many versions, but only about 7% regularly attend services. What does that mean? It means there is much work to be done to build and strengthen Christ's church in Latvia!

Riga is filled with great architecture and beautiful buildings and historic sites. In central Riga, there is what is known as "The Freedom Monument." It was built in 1935 to honor soldiers killed in the Latvian War of Independence (1918–1920) on a site previously occupied by a statute of Peter the Great. The 138 ft.-tall monument is a potent symbol of Latvian independence. During the Soviet era the authorities banned people from laying flowers at the base of the monument and placed a statue of Lenin a short distance away. Today is stands as a reminder of Latvia's past and a portent of its future.

In Lativa, PEF Evangelist, Martins Martinsons, a native of Riga, is working to see God raise Reformed churches in Riga. God has blessed the work of his hands and given him a godly team to be part of God's success story. Pray that God will enable him to see that! Martins and his wife, Anda, fluently speak Latvian (of course), English, and Russian. Riga, the capital of Latvia, already has two reformed churches and Martins was called to start a third—and did so! There is also a small and solid Baltic Reformed Theological Seminary. Michael "Hutch" Hutchinson and I were invited to sit in on a session meeting. It was encouraging and such a blessing to see the fruit of God's work in Riga, Latvia.

Please keep Pastor Martins and Anda in your prayers—and pray often for Riga!

Lithuania

Just to the south of Latvia is the Republic of Lithuania. It too, is a beautiful country with a long and rich history and heritage. Known for its beautiful landscapes, lakes, forests, and the Curonian Spit (a 60-mile-long curved sand dune), Lithuania is a county not to be missed. The Lithuanian language is the one of the oldest Indo-European languages but about a third of the population speaks English—always a plus for me! Roman Catholicism is the dominant religion (almost 75%) and less than 4% identify with any type of Protestantism. The latter is unfortunate because the Reformed faith and effects of the Reformation historically did reach into Lithuania, but it was not sustained. What does that mean today? It means that there is an old foundation and much work to be done to build Christ's church in Lithuania!

The capital of Lithuania is Vilnius and is home to Vilnius University, founded in 1579 by Jesuits, one of the oldest and most prominent universities in eastern and central Europe. It's home to an excellent Reformed ministry focused on translating reformed literature into Lithuanian and Russian. This jewel of a ministry is so professional and so meticulous in its work that it was a surprise and delight to experience it.

It was there that I met Julius. Julius is the director of "The Reformed Literature Center" in Vilnius. He was helped with the business by his dad who worked part-time with him. The focus of Julius's ministry is to translate Reformed Literature into Russian and Lithuanian. He is a person with a love of Reformed literature and a burning desire to have it spread throughout the Baltics and Russia.

Julius and I walked around Vilnius, the Royal Palace, and Vilnius University, the oldest university in Eastern Europe, founded as a Jesuit college in 1568 before becoming a school of higher learning in 1579 as noted above. We had a good lunch, and our sandwich was served on a roofing slate. A first for me! It made me think of my many lunches at building sites early in my life!

Now my tools of the trade are not hammers, levels, and saws, but theological books. It is with solid theological texts that I hope to help build the church of Jesus Christ wherever I am needed and sent. Through the years, supporters of PEF and my ministry have faithfully prayed that God would direct me to the people that He had already purposed for me to meet in the counties of Europe and elsewhere around the globe. I cannot afford to go looking for people to give theological books to. I must "bump into" them. My rational for this is that a bricklayer building a wall without a trowel is going to build a wall that doesn't look so good and is not so strong. A pastor needs good theological books to help him understand and teach the Bible. I need Gods help to find those men who need good tools!

Please tell others about the treasure (tools) of a Reformed literature ministry and contact Julius the Director of the Reformed Literature Centre in Vilnius, Lithuania. God in His providence has established this ministry in Vilnius.

Although I was able to spend time in Vilnius, I was also privileged to go to Kaunas, the second-largest city in Lithuania. In Kaunas there is a Reformed small congregation that uses the building of an older established church. It was an honor to be asked to preach from the pulpit there by the Reformed pastor, Pastor Jonas. Please pray for Lithuania and pray often for Pastor Jonas—the only Reformed pastor in Lithuania.

Estonia

North of Latvia, bordering the Baltic Sea and across the sea from Finland is the magnificent country of Estonia. A country of almost 1.5 million people, Estonia is known for its culture of dance, music, and choral events. Dominated by foreign powers for much of its history, Estonia gained independence in 1991. About two-thirds of the population speak Estonian as their first language. The majority of the remainder speak Russian. Tallin and Tartu and the two largest cities and most Estonians profess no religion.

The country is a compact and harmonious blend of medieval and modern architecture, a heady mix of medieval heritage and technological advancement, which has rebuilt itself in the post-Soviet era, adapting to the demands of the modern world while preserving a distinctly cultural identity. Estonia was and continues to be a prize strategic asset among the regional powers through the centuries. Religion does not play a particularly large part in Estonian life, although hundreds of years of foreign occupation led to many people converting to Christianity, including Lutheranism and Russian Orthodoxy. The most important aspects of Estonian culture are distinctly pagan in origin." I am told that "Skype" was invented in Estonia.

Who did we know in Estonia? Nobody, but God provided! Estonian Pastor Heldur was the answer to our prayers!

Eventually we met Heldur through Frank whose name was given to us by Dr. Eva. We took a 45-minute walk across town to his office. It was a little miracle that we arrived, because Art got directions from his cell phone that 'died' before we got there.

When we arrived, I was given the task to press the doorbell. There were six of them. I pressed #3.

Frank's secretary opened the door speaking excellent English. She invited us in. She knew that Frank was out of the country, so she gave us his Cell number.

I called Frank from our hotel. He asked were we met. I told him that we hadn't met, but we were looking forward to meeting him.

"How can I help you?"

"I'm looking for an Estonian who likes to read and wants to learn."

"Well, you have come such a long way! I'll get back to you."

And he did and could not have been more welcoming. We arrived in Estonia not knowing anyone. But that is fine—God knew them!

It was a privilege to bring greetings from the Reformed Presbyterian Church in America to the Estonian congregation in Tallinn. It was also a delight to have Martins and Anda come from Riga to meet Pastor Heldur and his wife, Varje and Art.

In addition to ministry in Tallinn, I was blessed to go to Tartu. There, we met a Christian brother, Dr. Tonu, who was serving as the interim Dean of the University of Tartu. We were able to leave him a suitcase of sound theological books. Previously, he was the first Chaplain to the University. Before that, he was head of the theology department and a friend of pastor Heldur!

We were privileged to be invited to address a group of young Russian-speaking professionals. Meeting with them for the first time made it a delightful evening. The Lord brought us together around a message that Hutch delivered on the topic that as Christians, we should, think Christianly and act Christianly and that means missions and evangelism. We were treated to their beautiful, enthusiastic singing in a worshipful offering to their Lord. Difficult apologetic concepts were translated as a team effort and a deep bond of love and respect was established. It was a beautiful evening in the Lord. As happens so many times, we went to minister to them, and they ministered to us!

Additionally, Hutch and I were interviewed by Pastor Heldur for an hour-long family radio program that was broadcasted throughout Estonia. The last time we met with Dr. Tonu he was saying goodbye to the American ambassador in Tallinn, who was leaving to go home to the US. Graciously, he offered Hutch and me a ride home back to Tartu in his limo by even coming to our hotel in Tallinn to pick us up. With all his responsibilities and probably a busy time at the embassy he still made time to talk with us on the way home even though I'm sure the idea of just falling asleep was very attractive to him. It poured with rain most of the time back to Tartu and as we got out of the car at the university, we had time to give him a large suitcase of books without getting too wet. We left him at his front door and had a short walk in the rain to get back to our hotel.

For the entire visit to Estonia, it was a wonderful and amazing divine appointment. God gave us all a great providence that among other consequences it allowed us to open ministries in Estonia that only God knew were going to happen just as He had planned years before!

You may be thinking, "This is a short chapter; why not longer?" Well, as noted above, the Baltic nations are long on history and culture but short on Reformed Christianity. There is much building yet to be done!

30

GREECE, MALTA, AND ISRAEL

My ministry has taken me from east to west to north and south. In every direction, the ministry and experience has been rewarding. However, the climate of the Mediterranean region has always been a joyful experience. I love the people, the cultures, and the weather! And always in the background there is the knowledge that this region was the world of the Bible and its people.

Greece

Before there was Rome, there was Greece. It is a mesmerizing country! In 1946, Greek philosopher, poet, and author Nikos Kazantzakis (1904–1957) wrote the novel that was translated into English as Zorba the Greek. A 1964 movie starring Anthony Quinn by the same title made Zorba a household word in the United States. At one point in the story, we find the words: "Happy is the man, I thought, who, before dying, has the good fortune to sail the Aegean Sea." As one who loves sailing (but suffers from *mal de mer*), the words from Zorba are true. Whether one arrives in Greece by sea, land, or air, every trip to Greece is a trip to a land of history and beauty. It is the land of Socrates, Plato, Aristotle, Hippocrates, Pythagoras, Euclid, and Homer (no, not Simpson, the real one)! It is also the birthplace of the Greek language, and the New Testament was written in Greek!

The religious demographics of Greece are easy to remember; 98% of the Greek people are identified as Greek Orthodox. I was told by Greeks that since they are not preached to and not discipled, that even if you wanted to have a conversation on the street about Jesus Christ, people wouldn't know what to talk about with me. That's fine—I always have a topic! Being in Greece, buoyed up by the prayers of those who support my ministry, I was surprised that so many people that I "bumped into" were not only willing to talk, but also eager to read the literature that was given to them.

That people were eager to receive books, and literature should not have been a surprise, given Greece's rich literary history—among which is Homer's epic poems of the Trojan War and its aftermath, Iliad and *Odyssey*. It was a strong reminder of the second half of Acts 17:1: "they received the word with all eagerness, examining the Scriptures daily to see if these things were so" (ESV).

There is in Berea, of which Acts 17 speaks of a Greek evangelical church in which I was privileged to preach many years ago. It was an experience I will never forget. Returning there to meet with Pastor Stavros, his family, and the elders of the church was an encouraging experience for me—and I pray for them.

People often ask me, "Paddy, what is the best method of evangelism?"

My answer, "After dinner evangelism."

"How does that work?"

"You invite me to dinner, and I'll show you!"

Nowhere is that done more easily and casually than in Greece. The people are wonderful, the food is delicious, and the conversations may have eternal consequences! As an aside, I encourage you to make sure that the missionaries you support financially have enough money to eat out frequently. People are comfortable eating, just as they were in Christ's day. It is a great time to mix with local folks and talk to them about Jesus outside of the walls of the church. (You can get people to go to dinner with you even though they might never consider going to church with you!)

I've been to and through Greece many times—it's an old country but visiting it and ministering in it never gets old. Western culture owes so much to the Greeks. Pray for the country and the people.

Malta

I have at least one thing in common with the Apostle Paul—we've both been to Malta. The difference is he was there because he was shipwrecked as he was being transported to Rome for trial (Acts 27–28) and I flew there intentionally! The shipwreck of Paul is considered one of the major events in the history of the island (a second being the Great Siege of Malta in 1565 by the Ottoman Empire). The siege of Malta was then repeated during the Second World War as Malta, then a British colony held out against the Axis powers from June 1940 until November 1942. The survival of Malta was a miracle in the Mediterranean!

There is a simple beauty about Malta. It is a place one might visit and never want to leave. In 2018, I had the privilege of ministering in Malta with Dr. Rick Light. I had a contact at a local church in Malta and called with a simple question: "Do you know anyone studying for the gospel ministry?" Andrea, a retired police officer, who was the pastor assistant (the pastor was out of town), answered my question. She did indeed, know someone! On our first full day in Malta, we met with John Paul a Maltese student studying for the gospel ministry, who was the answer to our prayers for a divine appointment in Malta. He received the first of our four 50 lb.-suitcases of new theological books, "the tools of the trade" for his library. What a blessing he was to us! He had already graduated from school with a degree in psychology, but he wanted more education, and he wanted to advance in his faith with the goal of becoming a minister. His ministry is desperately needed in Malta. Predominately Roman Catholic, there are only a few hundred evangelicals. However, there is a wonderful evangelical church on the island, Trinity Evangelical Church, with a faithful pastor who is a native Maltese—Pastor Paul—what a great name for a pastor in Malta! Malta also has a unique ministry started by Pastor Paul, the Malta Evangelical Library (see maltaevangelicallibrary.org). It is truly a ministry after my own heart and one that I encourage you to pray for and support.

Israel

Traveling east from Malta one eventually comes to the eastern shore of the Mediterranean Sea (average depth of 4900 ft.). Upon arriving in Tel Aviv, Israel, Eli, our "personal taxi driver" picked us up and drove us to Jerusalem. He later picked us up from Jerusalem and took us back to Tel Aviv via Netanya, where the Israeli College of the Bible is located. We always had lively and friendly conversations. He was convinced that Allah was the one true God. I explained he couldn't be as Mohamud, born in A.D. 550 or 571, came late to the "party!"

Eli, called the receptionist of the college from the road to let them know that we had come from America with two suitcases of new theological books to donate and asked if we could meet with the president for 5 minutes. Graciously, he met with us. He admired our heart but since he didn't know us or what books we were donating, appropriately he asked if we leave one suitcase, promising that his faculty would check them out. Because they taught all classes in Hebrew and Arabic, and sometimes Russian, if appropriate they would use them as reference books. Busy as he was, we didn't have time to go through the books with him but I was thankful that on the last day in Israel the Lord opened His door of opportunity to place a suitcase of books in a place that we believed would be blessed by having them and make good use of them as they were able.

As one walks the streets of Jerusalem, and especially the Old City, it is interesting to think about what the stones on which we tread could tell us. We wonder: "Who has come this way before us? What were the conversations? Might I be standing where Jesus stood?" Perhaps not as I believe that where Christ walked in Jerusalem was on a pathway lower than what is walked on today. There is so much history, so many stories, and so many prayers.

The Western Wall is the most holy place accessible to the Jewish people because of Muslim control of the Temple Mount. Known in recent centuries as the "Wailing Wall," it was built by Herod the Great as the retaining wall of the Temple Mount complex. The present plaza before it was created as an area for prayer when Israel captured the Old City in June 1967 during the Six-day War (also known as the 1967 Arab-Israeli War). At times, tens of thousands of people gather there for prayer. Today there is a line of water outlets with clean ice-cold water with toilets that are so clean that even on a hot day you could comfortably pray all day!

At this sacred site people pray, read scripture, leave prayers written on small pieces of paper and placed in the crevices of the wall. It is a place of great emotion—prayers, tears, remembrance, and hope.

My ministry has brought me to Jerusalem and the Holy Land many times and the stories are many. As I reflect on them against the backdrop of the biblical text and the regions witness to history, I must remember that the Holy Land is a geographic crossroads of history traversed by merchants, traders, armies, missionaries, refugees, pilgrims, disciples, wise men, and the King of Kings.

Israeli poet Yehuda Amichai has said "Jerusalem is a port city on the shore of eternity." I love that quote for many reasons, but primarily because I know its true—and it is my duty to tell anyone who will listen "Jesus paid the fare for you!"

Three thousand years ago the psalmist wrote a daily reminder for each of us:

"Pray for the peace of Jerusalem!
May they be secure who love you!"
(Psalm 122:6 ESV)

Remember Christians throughout the Holy Land who are working daily to build Christ's church.

— 31 —

DESTINATION: ALL THINGS PORTUGAL, SPAIN, CANARY ISLANDS–TENERIFE, AND GIBRALTAR

Portugal

In 2017 and 2019, I was invited to Portugal, the Azores, and Madeira. My son, Stephen, and I made the journey and, as always, I think it was as much a blessing to us as to those we met. One of our contacts was a wonderful person, Elder Antonio in Sines, Portugal.

Sines, the birthplace of Vasco da Gama (c. 1460–1524), is now a major industrial port and tanker terminal ringed with refinery pipelines. Sines has a museum dedicated to the great navigator, as well as an impressive castle. His voyages to India opened the sea route from western Europe to the East by way of the Cape of Good Hope. The city and the museum are tremendous. If you get a chance to go there, go!

Prayer for divine appointments allowed us to meet our new friend, Elder Antonio. It was such a delight and of course it was a reminder to take all our needs to the Lord Jesus Christ. We went to Portugal with the understanding that we need to work with a godly national. We do not seek to develop our own ministry. We desire to work with and under a national to encourage him in his ministry!

Elder Antonio told me that he had ordered a *Reformation Study Bible* from Ligonier Ministries, but he could not pay the customs fees and taxes. I was able to open one of my bags and say, "Antonio, brother, here is your leather-bound *Reformation Study Bible*." Being able to hold the Word God in our hands is a blessing we take for granted too often. Many of us have more Bibles than we ever use. Many people pray to have one. Remember Isaiah's words: "The grass withers, the flower fades, but the word of our God will stand forever" (Isaiah 40:8, ESV). When you hold a Bible in your hands, say a brief prayer of thanks and then open it and read it!

For those who have supported my ministry through the years, I must also write, "Thank you for your prayers for divine appointments." To witness situations like this gifting of a Bible with Antonio is so encouraging! If you are like me, perhaps you wonder at times if your efforts are worthwhile and accomplish anything. When you give someone a Bible, all doubt is gone!

In his book *No Little People*, Francis Schaeffer writes how we often misunderstand ourselves and how God works in our lives:

> It is wonderful to be a Christian, but I am such a small person, so limited in talents—energy or psychological strength or knowledge—that what I do is not really important." The Bible, however, has quite a different emphasis: with God there are no little people. One thing that has encouraged me, as I have wrestled with such questions in my own life, is the way that God used Moses's rod. A stick of wood. Many years ago, when I was a young pastor just out of seminary, this study of the use of Moses's rod, which I called, "God so Used a Stick of Wood, "was a crucial factor in giving me courage to press on. The story of Moses's rod began when God spoke to Moses from the burning bush, telling him to go and challenge Egypt, the greatest power of the day. Exodus 4:20 tells us the secret of all that followed: The rod of Moses had become the rod of God. (pp. 14–15).

How true that is for each of us!

We were able to go to Porto and Lisbon as well. Both are beautiful cities to walk in. The architecture is so pleasing to the eye. As one trained and educated in the world of building, seeing such beautiful structures is always a reminder to me that humans have creativity because we are created in the image of God—the *imago Dei*. God created and in a small but fallen way, we too can create and build and paint and compose. There is beauty in the world because of God the Creator and all that means for us and for all of Creation. (The Porto railway station interior is magnificent!)

In Lisbon, the maître d' (head waiter) in our hotel appeared to remember all the names of every guest. When we left, we thanked him and were surprised by the amazing witness and exchange of literature!

The sights are overwhelming. Places such as São Jorge Castle, a medieval castle and historical landmark located in Lisbon, offer much history and is a place where one could spend several days. As with so many cities and countries and historic sites, the desire to visit and revisit is high! And of course, in Portugal, don't forget the vineyards and the port wine. England and Portugal have a unique historical relationship—and much of it involves port. As an Englishman, I will vouch for it!

As we left Portugal, God had purposed for us to buy the last train ticket from Lisbon to Madrid. Instead of a morning trip, we had to lose ourselves in our hotel and take the night train. The extra cost for our sleeper cabin was covered and we were able to witness to our fellow bunk mates, one significantly. We still arrived in time for Sunday morning church.

The Azores

Look at a map, not of Europe, but of the Atlantic Ocean. See that archipelago in the middle of it—a thousand miles west of Portugal? That's the Azores, an autonomous region of Portugal. Transatlantic sailors know it well. The old nautical slogan "Any port in a storm" is certainly true of the Azores—for hundreds of miles, it is the *only* port. (Yes, I know the "drunken sailor" images, but I meant *port* as in harbor, not *port* as in the wine mentioned above.)

More seriously, in the Azores one can fully appreciate the words of Psalm 107: 22–33 (ESV):

> Some went down to the sea in ships,
> doing business on the great waters;
> they saw the deeds of the Lord,
> his wondrous works in the deep.
> For he commanded and raised the stormy wind,
> which lifted up the waves of the sea.
> They mounted up to heaven; they went down to the depths;
> their courage melted away in their evil plight;
> they reeled and staggered like drunken men
> and were at their wits' end.[b]
> Then they cried to the Lord in their trouble,
> and he delivered them from their distress.
> He made the storm be still,
> and the waves of the sea were hushed.
> Then they were glad that the water[c] were quiet,
> and he brought them to their desired haven.
> Let them thank the Lord for his steadfast love,
> for his wondrous works to the children of man!
> Let them extol him in the congregation of the people,
> and praise him in the assembly of the elders.

The church where we were privileged to minister in, faces the sea. At one of its major marinas, more than 1,400 yachts stop each year to replenish supplies and make repairs before finishing crossing the Atlantic Ocean.

The Azores were part of our "Every Country in Europe" ministry project in 2019. While there, two of our ministry partners were Pastor Ismael Couto and his wife, Liliana. After we left, he wrote a kind letter, saying in part:

> It's great to read that your trip went well! We are praying for your ministry, and we really hope that every day you keep blessing and encouraging people the way you have been doing. I started to translate into Portuguese "The Masculine Mandate" by Richard D. Phillips. What a good book for men! In January I will be reading and studying this book with them.
>
> I already used some of those booklets "Basics of Faith" to teach in the Church. It was a great treasure that you offered me! Thank you once again … I believe that all the material that you and Antonio offered us is giving the Church a new pleasure to evangelize. They are very happy!

That is what our ministry is about—evangelism and solid Christian literature! I am a co-laborer with Christians in their own countries desiring to build Christ's church. One goal of the ministry has always been to equip European pastors with sound theological books. More than data on a thumb drive, books are the "tools of the trade" for a faithful pastor. A bricklayer building a wall without a trowel or plumb line produces a wall that doesn't look so good or hold up well.

Madeira

Madeira is another autonomous Portuguese region that is a volcanic archipelago of four islands, two inhabited and two uninhabited. It also is "out there"—600 miles from Portugal. It is often called "The Pearl of the Atlantic" because of its beauty. (The Island of Port Santo is where Christopher Columbus once lived.)

The capital of Madeira is the historic city of Funchal—with one of the most treacherous airport runways in the world. At the time I was there, British Airways had posted a video showing the perspective from the cockpit of the approach to Funchal. At that time, there were only 20 captains with British Airways who are qualified to operate into Funchal,

Madeira's Airport. No instrument landing system (ILS) exists. The pilots must navigate the dangerous approach manually, against strong, variable Atlantic winds with mountains on one side and the Atlantic Ocean on the other. Approaches are often missed, and go-arounds are frequent." (Read about it online flying in and out of Madeira will *always* enhance your prayer life!)

It is there that we shared ministry with Pastor Roland Brown and his dear wife, Margaret. Roland pastors a church in Loughton, Essex, England for one month. The next month he pastors the English-speaking congregation in Funchal, Madeira Island. That's what you call a real commute!

Roland introduced me to Aurelio and Sietske, Madeirans, living in Porto da Cruz, and home from the mission field in Africa. They have a son named Joel. I didn't meet Joel, a gifted linguist who speaks 4 languages. He was studying in France, but I was able to provide a 5-year gift subscription of *Table Talk* to him. More good theological literature!

I was invited to preach to the English-speaking congregation in Funchal. My sermon text was Romans 1:1: "Paul, a servant of Christ Jesus, called to be an apostle, set apart for the gospel of God," (ESV). It was not your typical sermon text! I said that the Apostle Paul was a good role model for use because he was a person who was committed to a person, committed to a book, and committed to a task. Very simple!

I had to be careful to keep my sermon short, so I did not go over my time limit. In part, this was because the buses on Madeira do not run on Sundays and some of the congregation came to church by taxis and their taxis were waiting outside the church when services were finished. I didn't want to be the person who the congregation complained about and said: "That preacher went too long and made me miss my taxi. It was a long walk home!"

Would I return to Madeira? Absolutely! If for no other reason than the produce! Bananas, avocados, melons—all of them were wonderful!

Spain

Once you have left the Azores and Madeira, you look at the map (or chart) and ask, "What next?" Spain, of course! It was another father-son ministry adventure. Stephen and I were back together as a ministry team. We had worked together in N. Ireland, Italy, Germany, Austria, Switzerland, Lichtenstein, Iraq, Assyria, now on a trip to Spain, Tenerife, Gibraltar, and Portugal. Originally, we set off knowing nobody but knowing that God had his people he wanted us to encourage and bless with the tools of our trade, new, sound theological books. God faithfully answered prayers from many different countries, some praying every day, for the success of our mission. We were blessed that the Lord turned our travels into an epic trip! God introduced us to five Reformed pastors and one Reformed elder. We may not know where God's people are located, but that's ok, God knows, and it is He who directs our journeys.

Stephen had the first significant witness on our trip to Madrid. The man he sat next to leaving Atlanta, was an international DJ from Madrid. The DJ was tired and soon fell asleep. Stephen continued his witness, creatively turned to Google Translate to leave a message inside a Spanish copy of *Ultimate Questions* by John Blanchard. *Que Dios te descanso amigo mio*—"May God rest you my friend, Stephen." Probably not what Google had in mind, yet Christ will have dominion.

One of my favorite gifts I can give students or pastors that I work with in Europe, and I did so on this trip, is the set "Basics of the Reformed Faith," published by P&R Publishers. At present it has 32 booklets in the set. Each student I work with gets a set for his ministry in my first contact with him. Later they receive Louis Berkof's *Systematic Theology*. However, they are much more likely to take a pamphlet of the Reformed basics on the train or bus to work than their thick systematic theology under their arm! The set is also a wonderful resource for any serious-minded church to have on display at the back of their sanctuary. The people in your congregation need to be aware of this well-produced set. Each pamphlet that I have read has been a wonderful source of solid biblical information and clear-thinking theology that anyone can understand. In the United States, in the winter many people head to Florida; In the United Kingdom, and Ireland, in the winter many people head to Spain and Portugal. There are good and not so good aspects of that southward migration, but one of the good ones is the availability of English and Irish food. That is great for Paddy!

At an Irish bar in Madrid, eating a favorite dish from my proud English heritage—sausage, egg, and chips—there was a Cuban street protest was going on outside. I was so focused on the task at hand that I never did find out what the protest was about! Hopefully, not Englishmen!

We attended worship services at a Reformed church in Madrid and visited their church plant in Toledo. I never cease to be amazed at the hospitality and fellowship I find with other believers around the world. Hundreds of times I have experience the words of Paul in Galatians 3:28–29:

> There is neither Jew nor Greek, there is neither slave nor free, there is no male and female, for you are all one in Christ Jesus. And if you are Christ's, then you are Abraham's offspring, heirs according to promise. (ESV)

Language, culture, politics, and so much more all dissipates when you worship and fellowship with believers. It is the grace of God bestowed on those who are far from home. If you are in a city and lost or lonely—find a church where there is a common spirit of worship and the knowledge of God. We did, we found (God led us to) Pastor Juan and Pastor Markus.

Go to Madrid, go to Toledo and worship with believers there. You will be blessed beyond words. Toledo is an amazing and beautiful city picturesquely sited on a hill above Tagus River. Behind the old walls of the city lies much evidence of the city's rich history. The Romans built a fortress on the site of the present-day Alcazar. Later, the Visigoths (of "the barbarians" fame) made Toledo their capital in the 6th century and left behind several churches. In the Middle Ages, Toledo was a melting pot of Christian, Muslim, and Jewish cultures, and it was during this period that the city's most outstanding monument—its cathedral—was built. In the 16th century, the painter El Greco came to live in Toledo, and today the city is home to many of his works. But the greatest work in Toledo is the work that God is doing through evangelism and discipleship! Go to Toledo and pray for Toledo!

Stephen and I didn't have any trouble communicating and enjoying Pastor Juan in Madrid. He was an Irish man who had been in Madrid for 40 years as a Reformed pastor! In fact, we had a 'bit of a chuckle' when we met, as his brother, who was visiting from Ireland was standing beside him. I turned to him and asked, "Who are you, do you work in the church too?" "No, I'm Juan's brother from Ireland," he said. I need some dental work, and it is half the cost for me to have the work done here." Because we were outside a restaurant we went in and had a good meal and great fellowship!

You might ask, "Paddy, how do you meet people to evangelize?" To meet the locals, you eat in the restaurants they eat in, walk the streets they walk, travel on public transport as they do. You do what they do and go where they go. You mix with the folks. As you mix, you talk. You can't talk to people about Jesus unless you are talking to them! The next time you talk to someone, try it. See what God gives you to say. The first time you try it you might "mess up." The good news is that you have the rest of your life to get better at it, and you will. Until a week before our trip, we knew nobody in Tenerife where we were headed next. However, God did. Then Stephen remembered that he knew a man who had worked in Spain and returned to Clemson University. I arranged to visit him. We had a great time of fellowship. We both loved the Lord, and I left with pastor Juan's telephone number in Madrid! He was an Irishman who had been ministering in Spain for 40 years. What an encouraging way to set out on a trip!

Someone once said that an adventure is simply a picnic gone wrong—that was certainly the case with one of my meals! The food was brought to me, and the conversation was: "And you, sir, fried egg, and sausage? Sorry, I don't speak English. I thought you said, 'Baby eel and shrimp on the egg and chips.'"

Canary Islands–Tenerife

The Canary Islands to the west of Africa are a "must visit" for everyone—truly. The last attempt at conquering the Canary Islands was made in 1797 by Admiral Horatio Lord Nelson. He launched an attack on Santa Cruz de Tenerife. He not only failed to take the town but lost his arm in the battle.

Why did Stephen and I fly over the Atlantic Ocean to the Island of Tenerife? It was part of God's good providence. This is a ministry that will cross an ocean to meet one person! My ministry has always been grounded in the belief that to travel overseas just to meet one person makes the trip worthwhile. God knows who He is preparing for the meetings!

That was the rational when Jesus set out across the Sea of Galilee just to minister to the demoniac of Mark 5:1–20. After Jesus had ministered to him, a broken fragmented sinner, Jesus called the demon-possessed man to be a missionary to the 10 cities of the Decalogue. Then Jesus went back across the lake.

While we were in Madrid with Pastor Juan, we asked him if he knew anybody in Tenerife. We were thrilled to learn that he did. After a good breakfast in our hotel in Santa Cruz, we telephoned Pastor Jose only to find he did not speak any English. When you have no idea what to do you pray for an idea. We prayed and decided to call Pastor Juan back. We asked him if he could connect us to an English-speaking member of pastor Jose's congregation. He did that and did not know pastor Jose did not speak any English. It was then arranged that a lady in his congregation would arrange for us to get to church for their Sunday morning worship service.

Imagine our delight to meet Dr. José, his wife, and his family, including his son Micah. Micah is an accomplished electrical engineer and was not looking for a career change. We heard the fascinating story of Dr. Jose and how for 33 of his then 35 years in ministry he was Reformed in his theology. He had never had a day off and he had never had anyone fill his pulpit for him. He taught himself to be a seminary professor, the only one in the seminary that he started. He then trained a member of his congregation at the seminary. The first graduate was ordained and pastoring a mission church plant on Gran Canaria.

I asked Micah if he had ever thought of asking God if He wanted him to help his dad in the ministry. Dr. José was so thankful that God sent us. We tried to tell Micah to tell his dad that we were even more excited than his dad was! We were overjoyed that God had arranged our divine appointment to meet Pastor José.

I asked Micah if he had ever thought of helping his dad in the ministry. Interestingly Micah gave an understandably thoughtful but typical response to my question. Often ministers sons consider the ministry and then they realize who they are and what they need to become, and it can become an over whelming obstacle. "I have no money for seminary or books, etc."

We agreed that we would ask God to give Micah a call to the gospel ministry so that he could join his father in the ministry in Tenerife. A few months later Micah was confident that God had in fact given him a call to the gospel ministry. We were looking at the possibility of Micah coming to study at Greenville Presbyterian Theological Seminary in Greenville, South Carolina.

Then the world was hit with Covid. Please pray for Micah and the Reformed Presbyterian Church in Tenerife, Canary Islands!

While Micah was praying and waiting for his call and confirmation of that call to the gospel ministry, he had two eye operations off the Island and is now able to enjoy 20/20 vision in one eye and 40% vision in the other eye. Apparently, that is the best that he can now expect. When I asked him what that means as far as studying goes, he replied, "after 4 hours of studying, I get a headache." Without much knowledge or empathy, since I have good eyesight in both eyes, I told him I get a headache before he does!

Gibraltar

Here's the most important geography and historical fact you need to remember when you think of Spain and Gibraltar—Gibraltar is not Spanish, it's British! There is much history behind that, and it has been disputed, fought over, and negotiated about for centuries. It is fascinating history—but it's still British! It is a British Overseas Territory.

For many reasons, including its strategic location at the entry to the Mediterranean Sea, Gibraltar has been called the "Cradle of History." Tangiers and the North African coast can be seen on the horizon some 8.7 miles away from Gibraltar.

Historically, the 19th century was very prosperous for Gibraltar. During the Napoleonic Wars (1803–1815), Gibraltar became an important commercial center for the Royal Navy ships and for the corsairs taking the boats they captured from the enemy to sell as loot. As a result of the opening of the Suez Canal in 1869, Gibraltar acquired a considerable strategic importance as a mandatory pass for commerce between Great Britain and India. Today its government is a colony of the British Crown. Gibraltar is under the jurisdiction of the British Foreign Office and the Commonwealth.

Gibraltar covers 2.32 square miles which includes the land reclaimed from the sea. It is located at the most southerly tip of the Iberian Peninsula, (Spanish), next to the Bay of Algeciras with a commanding position looking over the Straits of Gibraltar. Its geographic location places it between Europe and Africa, between the Mediterranean Sea and the Atlantic Ocean. Its strategic position and its famous limestone rock features in most of its history. For the British and the Royal Navy, Gibraltar was a stronghold to be defended at all costs.

"The Rock of Gibraltar" has many secrets. It is a monolithic limestone mountain 1,398 ft. high dominating the western entrance to the Mediterranean Sea. It has 140 caves hidden in the rock. During the Second World War half the population were hidden in these caves for safety. The biggest cave, St. Michaels is currently an auditorium where concerts, dance performances, and theatre performances are celebrated. During the war the cave was also converted into an emergency hospital.

To enter Gibraltar from Spain, you walk along Winston Churchill Avenue and cross over the runway that the British enlarged during the Second World War. It is the only road in and out of the British territory. At the end of our time in Gibraltar, we used it and walked to Spain so that we can look for a travel agent to book a bus to take us to Seville and finally to Lisbon, Portugal. It is a unique border situation!

The population of Gibraltar is around 30,000, the majority of which are Spanish-speaking Roman Catholics who live alongside Anglicans, Protestants, Jews, Muslims, and Hindus. But it is still British and reminders are everywhere! One sure way of knowing you are in Gibraltar is when you see famous red Royal Mail pillar post boxes.

In Gibraltar, we had a divine appointment. We were delighted to meet a Scottish pastor ministering in Gibraltar—Pastor Ewen. We had never been to Gibraltar. We arrived knowing nobody. We left him with books and literature for his ministry. St. Andrews Church dating from 1854, now has a selection of Reformed theological books for the congregation to read and study.

We met the person who God had purposed for us to meet!

And the food? Yes, it was wonderful. Imagine God placing a genuine English fish and chip restaurant right next to our hotel on the Mediterranean coast!

Gibraltar is a strategic location in Europe with a strategic message of blood bought redemption and peace with God. Pray for Gibraltar!

As noted above, when we left Gibraltar, we walked into Spain. We took a Taxi from our Gibraltar hotel to the Spanish border. We then walked across into Spain. We went to a Spanish-speaking travel agency where we thought we understood them and who we thought understood us. We got that wrong! It caused us trouble, all day as we tried to get to Lisbon in time to check in to our non-refundable hotel.

We took a Spanish taxi to Algeciras Bus Station and waited for a bus that never came! Eventually, we took a bus to Seville, Spain and finally a train to Porto, waiting 2 hours in Seville for the air-conditioning on the bus to be repaired and Waiting 3 hours for the bus to take us to Lisbon, Portugal. Unfortunately, we were the only ones waiting for it! We arrived late in the evening thankfully, but at least we arrived!

32

THE MINISTRY CONTINUES: SWITZERLAND—ALBANIA—POLAND—UKRAINE

The years 2020 and 2021 will be remembered by many of us for the rest of our lives. The Covid-19 global pandemic was something few, if any, of us ever expected to experience. It was a tragedy and local, national, and international travel came to an abrupt halt. Our prayer ministry continued, and we benefited greatly from a new communications technology—Zoom. Although we could not physically be with our ministry partners around the globe, the work of the Lord continued, and it continues to the present!

By 2022, it was time to re-energize muscles that had diminished because they did not carry books for two years, break out the luggage to contain them, and resume our journeys of evangelism and the distribution of sound theological writings—have books, will travel and have gospel, will proclaim! It was time to go to Europe again.

On a trip to Albania, I had an overnight in Zurich. I walked from the train station across the river over the bridge to my hotel with suitcases of books and then back again in the evening to look for a restaurant with a Swiss steak on the menu. After dinner I walked about so I could find a conversation or two.

Zurich, on the River Limmat, is Switzerland's largest city, and the center of international and Swiss banking and trade in gold. The central landmark of the Old Town is the imposing twin-towered Grossmünster Church. According to legend, the church was founded by Charlemagne, the "father of Europe" and is constructed over the graves of the patron saints of Zurich—Regula and Felix.

It was from the pulpit in this church that Ulrich Zwingli (1484 –1531), the great Swiss Reformer, preached the Reformation. The city and the church are key sites of the Swiss Reformation and the Reformation at large. Like one also does in Geneva, to walk these Swiss streets is to walk in the footsteps of the Reformers.

Ulrich Zwingli's insistence that the Bible, not the Church, was the source of Christian truth made him a major force in the Protestant Reformation that swept Europe in the 16th century. He was born to a village bailiff and studied in Basel, Bern, and Vienna before becoming a Roman Catholic priest. He was appointed in 1519 to the Grossmünster Church in Zurich, where his growing Protestant conviction rapidly became clear.

In 1522, Zwingli proclaimed the Bible, not Roman Catholic hierarchy and tradition, to be the sole source of Christian authority, and he persuaded civic leaders and the churches of Zurich that things not prescribed in the Bible had no place in the church's life.

Zwingli, Luther, and Calvin had their agreements and disagreements regarding some theological points of the Reformed position, but they were unified in their desire to see the Reformation spread throughout Europe. Zwingli died in October 1531 in the Second Battle of Kappel, a conflict between Protestant and Catholic cantons of the Old Swiss Confederacy.

I understood recently that there was no Reformed, Confessional Presbyterian church in Zurich. So, Dr. Rick Light and I decided to make a trip to Zurich to see if God would use us to find a Swiss national to begin giving Reformed books to, with the prayer that eventually, Lord willing, God would raise up such a church as was the case in Albania some 30 years ago.

I was wonderfully mistaken! God had established a Reformed Presbyterian Church with a Swiss National as its Pastor. Imagine our delight in our God, who does all things well, when we discovered the Swiss Confessional Reformed Presbyterian Church was established 9 months before! Church planter, Pastor Florian is a graduate of Greenville, Theological Seminary, from their satellite campus in Newcastle, England.

We were able to leave the church many Reformed books to strengthen the saints and the church in Zurich. God was good!

Albania

Switzerland was our steppingstone to Albania. The Protestant Reformation had a significant influence in Albania, primarily through the translation of religious texts. But by the early nineteenth century, the flames of reform had burned out.

British missionaries sought to rekindle them but even today the numbers are small. In a recent poll, seventy percent of Albanians refused to identify a religious preference or heritage. The number of evangelical Protestants remains small—in the thousands, but there is a Reformed presence that has been growing in the past 30 years. There is a solid foundation and slowly the workers of the Lord have been rebuilding Christ's church in Albania.

Throughout Europe there are magnificent cathedrals that were constructed slowly by hand over hundreds of years. The design, the architecture, and the craftsmanship were all intentional. So too, is the ministry of aiding Christians around the globe for the past several decades to evangelize, strengthen, and build the body of Christ in countries where the Lord has been pleased to use my skills and desires. Centuries ago, skilled craftsmen-built cathedrals to the glory of God that would stand for centuries. Decades ago, I embarked on a ministry of evangelizing people for whom Christ died. Their decision would be one not to last for centuries, but for eternity.

From our hotel in Durrës, Albania, we could see the Grand Mosque of Durrës. Built in 1931 through Albanian Italian cooperation, it is a beautiful structure with an impressive minaret.

What one does not see in the city is an equally impressive church or cathedral. But God is faithful, and He is working in the lives of believers in Durrës and throughout Albania.

I have been blessed to minister in many countries around the world. Often, as I speak of my travels and ministry, I will hear words to the effect of "I don't know much about X, where is it again?" That's understandable. However, allow me to say—the less we know about a country, the more we need to pray for it. There is very likely a relationship between what we know about a country and the strength of Christianity in that country. The less we know, the more we need to pray!

Thirty years ago, there was no Presbyterian church in Albania. I asked Dr. Mike Milton if I could carry his bags on a trip to Albania. That trip did not happen. Later, I was able to take my first trip to Albania. God placed a desire in my heart to see Confessional Reformed Presbyterian Churches planted in Europe.

Everybody I met traveling, appeared to know what a Pentecostal, and what a Baptist was. However, nobody seemed to know what a Presbyterian was. I prayed to God, as a thankful "C" student offering with his help, to do something about that.

Years ago, I asked Arnie Maves, with PEF if he could tell me the name of the Westminster Seminary graduate ministering on the Greek island of Corfu. He told me he wouldn't. I probably said, "Oh come on Arnie, why not?" He told me that I needed to assume that all my ministry would be "behind enemy lines," and that I should learn to minister with that in mind. Pray about everything and ask God to reveal it to you. That may have been a reason why I prayed such an unlikely prayer to help start Reformed Presbyterian Churches in Europe.

Three weeks later I got my answer. Brother Miltiades. Art Crouch and I were traveling to a lecture at Covenant Seminary, in the good ole days. At the lecture I met a Covenant classmate, Peter Roukas. Peter was Greek and won the Homiletics prize one year. Miltiades is the man you need to meet.

On every trip with PEF/REF I always remembered Arnie's advice, "pray about everything." On every trip I have produced "a trip, Prayer Calendar." People don't pray every day for missionaries today as they did when I was growing up; but we have been thrilled to be told that, "as a family, we prayed every day for you for the length of the trip." I made sure that they tell their children who prayed that the devil trembles whenever they pray just like he does when Mummy and Daddy pray.

And so it was that after thirty years I was able to return to Albania. Upon leaving, my heart soared. Albania has strong Reformed believers. We need to pray for them and encourage them!

Poland and Ukraine

While I was in Zurich, an unexpected opportunity came up for a trip to Poland and Ukraine. A bacterial infection I picked up on the first trip flared up and as soon as I reached Poland I was incapacitated. I am grateful to Rev. Dr. George Gatgounis, for his care and management of the situation as well as for Clark McNutt who flew to Krakow to escort me home, where I spent a week in the hospital and several months recuperating. Even with the Russian invasion of Ukraine raging, Dr. Gatgounis was eventually able to move forward with his mission to Ukraine and deliver books for my REF Ministry.

On these trips, we were able to bless Reformed Presbyterian pastors with sets of Reformed theology books in Zurich, Switzerland; Durrës, Albania; and Kiev, Ukraine.

Retrospect

For thirty-five years, working with Presbyterian Evangelistic Fellowship as a missionary evangelist to Europe, I have pursued my call, my prayer, and my goal of taking the gospel to every country in Europe. My strategy is to help build the libraries of young pastors in Europe. Just as a bricklayer needs a plumb line and trowel to build a straight wall, a pastor needs sound books as a foundation for his study. To introduce European pastors to the Reformed faith and encourage them in their walk, I give them new theological books, the tools of their trade. Each student I meet with, receives a new suitcase, holding 50 lbs. of new theological books. I am thankful to everyone who has donated money for books through the years. It has made a difference!

Never underestimate the power of the printed word. Through the printed word in Bibles, theological treatises, and devotional writings, the Reformation swept across Europe 500 years ago. Through our prayers, may God be pleased to do it again in Europe and beyond.

"The grass withers, the flower fades,
but the word of our God will stand forever."

Isaiah 40:8 (ESV)

CONCLUSION

As I reflect upon this memoir and the decades of its stories, I am humbled—not by my experiences, but by the people God has brought into my life. Someone once said that in life we have many acquaintances and few friends. Perhaps that is so, and if true, then truly I have been blessed, for I have many friends as well as many acquaintances. My journeys have taken me around the world, to many countries, experiencing many cultures, and learning something every day.

I have seen the power and majesty of God's creation in the mountains, deserts, rivers, and snows on several continents and across the vast expanses of many nations. That too, has been awe inspiring and caused me to marvel at the goodness and greatness of our Creator.

God has placed in my heart a burden for people to know Him, to know of the life, death, and resurrection of the Risen Savior and His atoning sacrificial death, and to know the power of the Holy Spirit to encourage and enrich my steps—and their steps—wherever they go.

In Genesis 12:1–4 (and again in Hebrews 11:8) we read the story of Abraham who was called by God to leave his home in Ur of the Chaldees to travel to a destination that was unknown to him but known to God. In faith and in obedience, Abraham did so. If I was asked to give a title to that episode in biblical history, I'd probably title it "Going, Not Knowing."

Abraham went, following God's commission to him—and God blessed him for doing so. I'm certainly not a person of the stature of Abraham, I'm simply "Paddy the Englishman." However, I have sought for many years to be like Abraham and in faith, to be obedient to God and to God's calling.

As a disciple of Jesus Christ, I too have been given a commission as have all who claim His name as Savior and Lord. That commission was spoken by Christ after his death on a cross to forgive my sins and the sins of any who will ask for that forgiveness. It was spoken after his bodily resurrection from the grave and before his ascension into heaven. To his disciples who were in his presences, to all who followed him from the first century until the twenty-first century, and to me, "Paddy the Englishman" our Lord commanded: "Go into all the world and proclaim the gospel to the whole creation" (Mark 16:15, ESV).

I have obeyed, "going, not knowing." May my steps have been pleasing to the Lord.

ABOUT THE AUTHOR

Paddy and his brother Peter were born in England during World War II and both were educated in England and the United States. Their parents had great faith to look with hope to the future and start their family at such a dark time. They translated their faith to their sons through a lifetime of parish ministry, the weekly services, annual camps, and church programs. Especially formative for Paddy were the interesting and influential speakers and visitors who he was regularly exposed to through his mother's hospitality at home, including hosting international students pursuing their studies in England.

This exposure to so many temperaments and nationalities trained him to become an intuitive judge of character. The opportunity to travel presented itself to him in his late teens. His desire to "know" was ignited by his desire to "go." And so he went—first for adventure and then to evangelize—and he has been fulfilling that mission around the globe for decades. These are the seeds of the rest of the story.

Brothers Paddy and Peter in the late 1970s